The Reminiscences of
Rear Admiral Roy S. Benson
U.S. Navy (Retired)

Volume I

U.S. Naval Institute
Annapolis, Maryland
1984

Preface

For the benefit of those who will use and benefit from this volume of recorded oral recollections, it is worthy of note that Admiral Benson is a most conscientious interviewee. As is evident from reading the text of the transcript which follows, the admirl has done his homework. In preparing for each interview, he went through his papers and other records in order to refresh his memory; make notes on subjects he intended to discuss; and verify names, dates, and places. As a result of his thorough preparation, the transcript is rich in detail on his various tours of duty and thus quite valuable for individuals seeking a knowledge of events that Admiral Benson was involved in during his quite active naval career.

Fundamentally, Roy Benson is a submariner, and that comes through on page after page of his recollections. He had outstanding service in the submarines NAUTILUS and TRIGGER during World War II; both boats won the Presidential Unit Citation for the time he was on board. The admiral also describes the route by which submarines developed in the prewar years in order to bring them to the high state of technical and operational readiness which enabled them to excel in the war against Japan. Admiral Benson traces the modernization of submarines even further in describing his efforts as Commander Submarine Development Group Two in the years right after World War II. It was during this time that he was searching for ways in which submarines could be used in an antisubmarine role. Also during that period of the late 1940s, he had a firsthand view of the hazards that face submarines even in peacetime. As the embarked force commander, he was in the USS TUSK as she rescued survivors from the submarine COCHINO when the latter boat experienced a battery explosion and fire during operations in the Barents Sea. His description of the tragedy is a vivid one.

The memoir also covers his early years--growing up in New England, attending the Naval Academy, serving in a battleship and destroyers as a junior officer, and teaching navigation at the Naval Academy. His recollections of service on the China Station in the early 1930s well capture the atmosphere of that time and place. This first of two volumes concludes with Admiral Benson's service in the early 1950s as the Navy's Director of Public Information. The assignment was a particularly demanding one, because it occurred during the Korean War and because Benson had had no previous tours of duty in the public information field.

The interviews which resulted in this oral history were conducted by my very able predecessor, Dr. John T. Mason, Jr. His wide knowledge of the subject matter and skillful questioning were useful in eliciting information, even in a case when the interviewee was as well prepared as Admiral Benson. The concluding volume of this memoir, also based on interviews by Dr. Mason, will trace the admiral's career from 1952 until his retirement in January 1969.

                                              Paul Stillwell
                                              Director of Oral History
                                              U.S. Naval Institute
                                              June 1984

REAR ADMIRAL ROY STANLEY BENSON
UNITED STATES NAVY (RETIRED)

Roy Stanley Benson was born in Concord, New Hampshire, on 7 December 1906. He was graduated from high school in that city. He joined the Navy by entering the U.S. Naval Academy, Annapolis, Maryland, in 1925. Graduated and commissioned Ensign in June 1929, he subsequently was promoted as follows: Lieutenant (junior grade), 1932; Lieutenant, 1937; Lieutenant Commander, 1942; Commander, 1943; Captain, 1945; Rear Admiral, 1956.

After graduation from the Naval Academy in June 1929, he joined the USS NEW YORK, and served as a junior officer of that battleship until December 1930. Following three years' duty in the destroyer SMITH THOMPSON, operating on the Asiatic Station, he reported in June 1934 for submarine instruction at the Submarine Base, New London, Connecticut. Upon completing the course in December 1934, he had successive duty in the submarines R-14, S-42, and S-27. He then returned to the Naval Academy where from June 1937 until May 1939 he had duty as an instructor in Navigation.

In June 1939 he joined the destroyer HOVEY as executive officer, and served in like duty in the submarine NAUTILUS from February 1941 until August 1942. For meritorious services in the NAUTILUS, after the entry of the United States into World War II, he received a Letter of Commendation, with authorization to wear the Commendation Ribbon, from the Commander in Chief, Pacific Fleet. He also received a facsimile of, and ribbon for, the Presidential Unit Citation awarded the NAUTILUS for action during its first war patrol. The citations follows:

Letter of Commendation -- Commander in Chief, Pacific: "For material assistance during the successful attack on a screened Japanese aircraft carrier during the engagement off Midway Island in June 1942. The attack delivered despite repeated enemy anti-submarine measures consisting of gunfire barrage by surface ships and aircraft, depth charging and bombing, resulted in three torpedo hits being made on the 10,000 ton carrier, which sank the carrier."

Presidential Unit Citation -- USS NAUTILUS: "For outstanding performance in combat during three aggressive war patrols in enemy-controlled waters. Operating far from the home base, the NAUTILUS sought out the enemy and boldly struck inflicting severe damage on enemy shipping. Her fine fighting spirit implemented by the expert seamanship and skill of her officers and men reflect great credit upon the United States Naval Service."

After brief duty on the staff of the Commander, Submarine Squadron 10, he assumed command of the submarine TRIGGER on 29 August 1942. For distinguished service in command of the TRIGGER, he was awarded the Navy Cross, a Gold Star in lieu of a second

Rear Admiral R. S. Benson, USN (Ret.)   Page 2

Navy Cross, a Silver Star Medal and a Gold Star in lieu of a second Silver Star Medal. He also received a facsimile of, and ribbon for, the Presidential Unit Citation awarded the USS TRIGGER. The citations follow in part:

Navy Cross: "For extraordinary heroism and exceptional achievement as Commanding Officer of the USS TRIGGER during action against enemy Japanese forces in the Pacific Area while carrying out an assigned task. Skillfully maneuvering his submarine...[he] accomplished a difficult minelaying operation and personally observed the destruction of an 8,400 ton vessel resulting from contact with one of his mines. Later...he executed aggressive and daring attacks on hostile ships, sinking 15,271 tons of enemy shipping, and...brought his ship safely to port..."

Gold Star in lieu of second Navy Cross: "For extraordinary heroism...patrolling in dangerous, enemy-controlled waters [he] directed the operations and torpedo fire of his vessel with splendid initiative and expert tactical skill. On one occasion...his ship was responsible for the severe damaging of an enemy aircraft carrier...[he] contributed greatly to the success of his command in sinking an important amount of Japanese shipping."

Silver Star Medal: "For conspicuous gallantry and intrepidity...as Commanding Officer of the USS TRIGGER during a submarine patrol in enemy-controlled waters...spent close to the Japanese homeland. With great courage and daring, [he] pressed home the attacks against enemy forces and, as a result, the TRIGGER sank one freighter of 5,000 tons and damaged 24,100 tons of enemy shipping...bringing his vessel back to port with no material damage and with his crew in excellent fighting spirit."

Gold Star in lieu of second Silver Star Medal: "For gallantry and intrepidity in action...as Commanding Officer of a United States Submarine during a war patrol of that vessel. Despite adverse weather conditions, his determination and tenacity enabled him to deliver successful attacks which damaged or sank more than 21,000 tons of enemy shipping. His conduct throughout was an inspiration to his officers and men and in keeping with the highest traditions of the United States Naval Service."

Presidential Unit Citation -- USS TRIGGER: "For outstanding performance in combat during her Fifth, Sixth and Seventh War Patrols against the enemy. Employing highly daring and hazardous tactics, the USS TRIGGER struck at the enemy with consistent aggressiveness, seeking out and pursuing her targets with dogged determination regardless of unfavorable attack conditions. Her exceptionally notable record of severe damage inflicted on hostile shipping and the gallant fighting spirit of her officers and men reflect great credit upon the United States Naval Service."

Rear Admiral R. S. Benson, USN (Ret.)

Relieved of command of the TRIGGER in July 1943, he was placed in command of the Prospective Submarine Commanding Officer's School, Submarine Base, New London, Connecticut. From June until October 1944 he commanded the submarine RAZORBACK, and later commanded Submarine Division 43. For outstanding services he was awarded the Legion of Merit, citation stating in part:

"...He made many material contributions to the training, overhaul and general readiness of submarines in his division. During this time, submarines under his command completed many war patrols which resulted in the sinking and damaging of many thousands of tons of enemy shipping. Much of the credit for the many successful war patrols and the severe damage inflicted upon the enemy was due to his efficient administration, excellent judgment and inspiring leadership..."

Detached from sea duty in July 1945, he reported for duty in the Operational Readiness Section, Headquarters, Commander in Chief, U.S. Fleet, Navy Department, Washington, D.C. In March 1947, he was ordered to duty on the Staff of the Commander, Submarine Force, Atlantic Fleet, as readiness and new developments officer, and in 1948 became war plans and intelligence officer on that staff. In March 1949 he became the first Commander of Submarine Development Group Two, when that unit was commissioned, remaining in command until August 1950.

After serving for two years as the Navy's Director of Public Information, Office of Information in the Pentagon, he was a student at the National War College, Washington, D.C., from August 1952 until June 1953. He commanded the attack transport BAYFIELD of the Amphibious Force, Pacific Fleet during the period July 1953 until June 1954, serving most of the time with the Seventh Fleet in the Far East. From August 1954 until August 1955 he was Commander Amphibious Squadron Six, Amphibious Force, Atlantic Fleet, and spent most of that time with the Sixth Fleet in the Mediterranean.

In September 1955 he was assigned to the Bureau of Naval Personnel, Navy Department, and on 8 August 1956 became Assistant Chief of Naval Personnel (Education and Training). On 2 May 1957 he assumed command of Cruiser Division One in Yokosuka, Japan. In June 1958 he became Deputy Commander and Chief of Staff, Military Sea Transportation Service, with headquarters in Washington, D.C.

In March 1960 he assumed command of the Submarine Force, Pacific Fleet, with headquarters at Pearl Harbor, Hawaii, and from September 1962 until June 1966 was Assistant Vice Chief of Naval Operations and Director of Naval Administration, Navy Department, after which he served as director of a special task force until February 1969. "For exceptionally meritorious service...from August 1962 until February 1967..." he was awarded a Gold Star in lieu of the Second Legion of Merit. The citation continues in part:

"As Assistant Vice Chief of Naval Operations/Director of Naval Administration, Rear Admiral Benson consistently demonstrated outstanding leadership, resourcefulness and managerial ability in planning, organizing and coordinating the many diverse activities of his office. He was deeply involved in the planning for, and implementation of, the reorganization of the Navy Department and, in March 1966, directed the preliminary work leading to the preparation of studies and analyses which became part of the data input to the Task Force which he was designated to direct. As Director of a Task Force to study the structure of the Department of the Navy incident to the unilinear organization effected in May 1966, Rear Admiral Benson inspired confidence and created an atmosphere of objective and rational approach to the many problems of a complex organization and its related intricate tasks and responsibilities, contributing in large measure toward the implementation of many of the recommendations of the Task Force even before its final plan and recommendation had been promulgated. His tact, diplomacy and adroitness in gaining the acceptance of officials involved in these recommendations was a major achievement in itself..."

In April 1967 he reported as Commandant of the First Naval District, with additional duty as Commander of the Naval Base, Boston, Massachusetts, and "for exceptionally meritorious service...[in that capacity]..." he was awarded a Gold Star in lieu of the Third Legion of Merit. The citation further states in part:

"...Rear Admiral Benson displayed skilled diplomacy, sound judgment, and outstanding leadership in coordinating the activities of the many Naval commands in his area, thereby greatly enhancing the support provided to the operating forces of the Navy. His relationship with the civilian community was particularly exemplary and was characterized by mutual respect and vigorous action in solving mutual problems. [His] thorough knowledge of the organization and management of the Navy, coupled with his ability to communicate with conviction and expertise, made him an invaluable asset in enhancing the position of the Navy. Through his personal attention and constant support of recruitment in the Regular Navy and the Naval Reserve, he contributed greatly to the success of the Navy recruiting program in the First Naval District. Largely due to [his] skillful guidance, the First Naval District was commended by the Department of Defense for the excellent summer recreation program offered to disadvantaged youths of the area..."

On 1 January 1969 he was transferred to the Retired List of the U.S. Navy.

In addition to the Navy Cross with Gold Star, the Silver Star Medal with Gold Star, Legion of Merit with two Gold Stars, Commendation Ribbon and the Presidential Unit Citation Ribbon with two stars, Rear Admiral Benson has the Yangtze Service Medal; American Defense Service Medal, Fleet Clasp; American Campaign Medal; Asiatic-Pacific Campaign Medal with three stars; World War II Victory Medal; National Defense Service Medal with bronze star; Korean Service Medal; United Nations Service Medal; and the Philippine Liberation Ribbon. He has also been awarded the Royal Order of the Sword, Commander, First Class, from the Government of Sweden; Grand Star of Military Merit by the Government of Chile; and Peruvian Cross for Naval Merit (Grand Officer) Distintivo Blanco by the Government of Peru.

Rear Admiral Benson is well qualified in the Scandinavian languages. He is married to the former Vida Wimbrow Connole of Annapolis, Maryland. They have one son, Rickart Alan Connole.

DECLARATION OF TRUST

The undersigned does hereby appoint and designate as his (her) Trustee herein, the Secretary-Treasurer and Publisher of the United States Naval Institute to perform and discharge the following duties, powers, and privileges in connection with the possession and use of a certain taped interview between the undersigned and the Oral History Department of the United States Naval Institute.

1. Classification of Transcript.

   ( )a. If classified OPEN, the transcript(s) may be read or the recording(s) audited by the qualified personnel upon presentation of proper credentials, as determined by the Secretary-Treasurer of the U.S. Naval Institute.

   (✓)b. If classified PERMISSION REQUIRED TO CITE OR QUOTE, the user will be required to obtain permission in writing from the interviewee prior to quoting or citing from either the transcript(s) or the recording(s).

   ( )c. If classified PERMISSION REQUIRED, permission must be obtained in writing from the interviewee before the transcribed interview(s) can be examined or the tape recording(s) audited.

   ( )d. If classified CLOSED, the transcribed interview(s) and the tape recording(s) will be sealed until a time specified by the interviewee. This may be until the death of the interviewee or for any specified number of years.

2. It is expressly understood that in giving this authorization, I am in no way precluded from placing such restrictions as I may desire upon use of the interview at any time during my lifetime, nor does this authorization in any way affect my rights to the copyright of my literary expressions that may be contained in the interview.

Witness my hand and seal this 17th day of March 1981.

I hereby accept and consent to the foregoing Declaration of Trust and the powers therein conferred upon me as Trustee:

Interview No. 1 with Rear Admiral Roy S. Benson, U.S. Navy (Retired)

Place: Arnold, Maryland

Date: Wednesday, 5 March 1980

Subject: Biography

By: John T. Mason, Jr.

Q: Admiral Benson, I'm delighted that you have consented to do this series covering your very interesting naval career. Now, I wonder if you would begin this talking biography, because that is what it is, in a proper way by telling me where you were born and the date of your birth. Then something about your family background.

Adm. B.: Fine, thank you. I was born in Concord, New Hampshire, on the 7th of December 1906. I was the youngest of one girl and four boys. Both of my parents were Swedish immigrants.

Q: Were all of the children born in this country?

Adm. B.: All born in this country. My father came to the United States when he was fourteen and my mother when she was eighteen. They met in the United States. We always spoke Swedish at home; a rarity. Most immigrants in those days tried to forget the old mother tongue. They were going to be Americans. I never noticed that my parents had any foreign accent. They didn't have any difficulty in that respect at all. We were definitely bi-lingual. Except you mix them up every now and then.

Q: Oh, I expect so, and sometimes it's convenient to add a Swedish word rather than the American when you're talking.

Adm. B.: Well, it goes the other way, too. It's very easy. For example, if we were going to say: "Who has my razor blades?" the "Who has my" would come out Swedish and the "razor blades" would come out English. They do that in Quebec, I understand, a few English words in a French sentence. Anyhow, to come back to Concord, New Hampshire, I graduated from high school there in 1924.

Q: Well, first tell me something about your father and what was his business?

Adm. B.: Before he came to the United States he finished a painter apprenticeship in the old country at the age of fourteen. He had learned to do fancy lettering and the painting of the sides of carriages and things like that. He went into that type of business when he came to the United States. Actually, the Boston-Maine Railroad opened up a repair shop in Concord, New Hampshire, and they were looking for people to populate the repair shop.

My father applied for a job, and that's how it was we were in Concord, New Hampshire, rather than being down around Boston. I say Boston because both my parents arrived in the United States at Boston. It's a day shorter and a little cheaper to go from Gothenberg, Sweden, to Boston than it is to New York.

Q: Yes, and much more convenient too I suppose?

Adm. B.: Yes. So a lot of immigrants ended up around Boston.

Q: Were there many Swedish people up in the Concord area?

Adm. B.: Oh, yes. Lots of them. Many attracted by the granite quarries. When I was a child my father became a member of the New Hampshire legislature. Let's see, I think it was around 1912 when he was elected for one term to the New Hampshire legislature. A little bit before that, before his 40th birthday, he was the national president of a Swedish-American organization called Vasa Orden. It was the biggest Swedish-American organization in the country.

Q: Would you spell it for me?

Adm. B.: V-A-S-A, and O-R-D-E-N

Adm. B.: Yes, that is the way it is spelled. It seems to me quite remarkable. How does one get to be nationally known when you're painting things in Concord, New Hampshire?

Q: Did he travel a lot?

Adm. B.: Yes; he traveled a lot. I imagine a railroad pass didn't hurt any.

Q: I'm sure it helped, yes. And he was interested in politics and became a member of the legislature?

Adm. B.: Became a member of the legislature for one term. That bears on the subject of how and why did I go to the Naval Academy.

Q: The family had some political clout at that point?

Adm. B.: Not really, but my father had some know-how. It might be interesting to hear why and how I went to the Naval Academy.

Q: Tell me more about the family.

Adm. B.: Well, we had many, many relatives. During the period, about 1870 and 1900, four of the southern provinces of Sweden lost one-fourth of their population to immigration to the United States. I suppose that was true of almost all European countries. That was the land of liberty; that was the land where money grew on trees and so forth. They looked upon this as paradise. Why they wanted to get away from Europe I don't know, but away from Europe they wanted to go.

My Mother came here, arrived in Boston on her 18th birthday; she was alone. My father, when he came over, came with his parents. My Mother came here alone. And why? Because her older sister had run away from home and left a note saying, "I have gone to America." She had an aunt living in Andover, Massachusetts.

So my Mother's father said to her, the oldest sister at home, "Here is some money. Go to the United States and bring back your sister."

So, my Mother proceeded, she was then seventeen, all alone with a shipping tag on her, telling what her name was and where she was going. She proceeded to the United States. She did find her sister alright, but her sister's boyfriend had a good pal by the name of Charles Benson (actually "Carl Bengtsson"). He brought him around next time and that's how my mother met her husband-to-be. She never did get home. She never brought her older sister back to the old country.

Q: That was almost inevitable.

Adm. B.: Oh yes. But all of them came over. All her brothers and sisters came over. Her father did not come but her mother did. The Swedish Lutheran Church and the Vasa Orden were important. They were where they had friends who had the same background as they did. Vasa Orden was also a sickness and death benefit organization.

Q: It was fraternal in that sense then?

Adm. B.: Yes. If a member took sick, he or she got $5.00 a week. If one of them died they got $100.00. Something we look at as extremely modest. But in those days that wasn't modest. And the difference between five dollars and nothing is tremendous. This organization was very important, as was the church.

Q: It was a kind of Swedish social security, wasn't it?

Adm. B.: That's right. And all of the countries had it. The Sons of Norway, and the Sons of Italy, and the Greeks (AHEPA); they all had it. Oh yes, it's a holding together. Those organizations still run in this country. Probably have some other motives.

Benson #1 -7-

Q: What was the ambition that your family had for you?

Adm. B.: I don't believe there were any ambitions. In those days it wasn't usual for parents to be particularly interested in kids continuing to go to school forever. My father considered that going through high school was just about enough if not too much. College was a waste of time. My three older brothers did not get to college. My father, however, took a great interest when I talked to him about going to this college that didn't cost anything. He thought that was a pretty bright idea. Matter of fact, when I told him that not only did you not have to pay anything to go to this very fine college down in Maryland, but they would pay you to go. Well, his eyes glistened then. He thought that was pretty good.

Q: You went through the grade schools there?

Adm. B.: I went through the grade schools and the high schools in Concord, New Hampshire.

We were a musical family. All of us including my parents played musical instruments. We four boys had our own band; we hired out to play for dances and so forth. I originally was a

Benson #1 -8-

drummer. I took music lessons on the drums. A lot of people think,"How in the world can you take music lessons on the drums?" But, you do. Not only ordinary drums but xylophones and kettle drums. I took lessons on all of them.

Around 1922 or so I had heard a saxophone and I had seen a picture of one. But, I hadn't actually been in the presence of a saxophone. No one in my hometown had one. I finally saw one and listened to it. I went to the music store and placed an order for one saxophone. And the man said, "Well now, do you know how to play this?"

And I said, "No."

And he said, "We'd better get you an instruction book also."

And so we got a saxophone and an instruction book and I proceeded to teach myself to play it. But it wasn't difficult, because I could already read music. No problem at all.

Q: Where did your band play? What kind of music did you play? What kind of dancing did you play for?

Adm. B.: Well, in those days, up around that part of the country, if you were going to play for a dance, you played about forty-five minutes of concert music first. Then you had a little bit of intermission, and then the dance started.

Q: You mean there was a widespread appreciation for classical music?

Adm. B.: Yes. You'd play overtures and end up with "Stars and Stripes Forever". Usually when we went out to play for a dance at least one of us would play a solo.

Q: What did the dance music consist of? Foxtrots and waltzes?

Adm. B.: Yes, yes and square dances. There was no strictly professional orchestra in my home town. Everything was on a pickup. Someone would get a job to play for a dance. He would get on the telephone and call up people you knew played various instruments and hire them. So it wouldn't be at all unusual for you to arrive to play for a dance somewhere and there were a couple of guys in the band you had never seen before. That didn't make any difference. When I got to the Naval Academy I got into the musical business.

Q: Yes. What would a foursome get for playing at a dance in those days?

Adm. B.: Well, this was very easy. If you started at eight o'clock and played concert music for forty-five minutes, then an intermission, then if you played until eleven each one of you got four dollars. If you played till twelve you got five dollars. These are the union rates.

Q: Union rates: You had to belong to a union?

Adm. B.: Well, when we first started playing for dances we didn't belong--there was a musicians' union but we did not belong to it. Well, I was only fourteen. Finally my parents and some of the union members talked to my older brothers. We'd go play for a dance and they'd give us a couple of dollars. The union people would rather have us come up to their rates than to be undercutting them.

Anyhow, we all joined the union. You had to be eighteen to join the union. My oldest brother, I think was twenty and the next one was eighteen, so they were alright. But my brother, Charlie, was sixteen, he became eighteen and I was fourteen and became eighteen. We all became eighteen. That was pro forma.

All they were trying to do was get rid of this competition. Also, it made it easier for us. If we got a job and they wanted a seven piece orchestra, we could call up some of those people who were members of the union. It opened up a wider field.

This was a real ball to go and play for dances. Go all over the place, all the little towns and cities around. That was great! Great fun!

Q: What transportation did you have?

Adm. B.: Well, there was a guy by the name Jed La Flemme who had a great Pierce-Arrow. Tremendous great big thing. When we were going to more than just around town, especially if we had more than just a little four piece orchestra, if we had more people than that, we'd hire Jed La Flemme with his Pierce-Arrow. I think we used to call it a "Fierce Sparrow." That would be the transportation.

Of course, in the middle of the winter--it was tough playing for dances out in the countryside--you know in my hometown in Concord, New Hampshire, when I was a kid they didn't plow the streets when it snowed. They compacted the snow. Had these great big rollers and they'd roll 'em up and down the streets to compact the snow.

Q: There was extensive use of sleds, bobsleds?

Adm. B.: Yes. I remember very well the first automobile I saw. A man by the name Schoolcraft had this automobile. It really looked like a horseless carriage and it actually had a tiller rather than a wheel. I remember that very well. See, I happened to be growing up during the time of transition.

Also the airplane business. The Wright brothers' first flights were about a year after I was born.

Q: How did you do in school there? How did you take to it?

Adm. B.: I didn't have any difficulty in school at all. I didn't have a transcript of my marks, but you could take one of four courses. You could take the college preparatory, or you could take -- I don't know what they called the second one, the third one was commercial, and the fourth one was mechanical arts. I started out taking the commercial one. I thought there was hardly any chance of ever going to college so I started off on the commercial course. Shorthand, bookkeeping, typing and all that sort of thing.

Then around my junior year I got off a little bit. I still had the commercial course, but not quite, not quite sure what in the world it was I took, not quite commercial and not quite something else. But, I never had any difficulty with academics in high school. I graduated with forty people in my high school class. We still have reunions. I didn't have any difficulty in high school, but when I went to the Naval Academy I found that that wasn't very good. I became shipmates with many much better scholars.

Q: Yes, can you now tell me how you became interested in the Navy as such?

Adm. B.: Well, when I was a kid up in New Hampshire everybody knew all about West Point. But, who had ever heard of Annapolis or the Naval Academy? Not much. But you'd hear about West Point.

I had a brother Charlie, two years older than me. One evening we had an argument and he said to me, "You're so smart, why don't you go to West Point?"

I don't know if he was kidding me or what, but anyhow that's what he said. I remember the words vividly and I thought about it later in the evening. I didn't say anything to anyone but I said to myself, "You know, that's not a bad idea."

So, I wrote to the two congressmen and the two senators and asked them to give me an appointment to West Point. This was in, I'd say this was in the--around Labor Day, of 1924.

I hadn't gotten a job of any kind except the kind of jobs high school kids get in the summer. I had graduated. I hadn't settled down in any job, but I'd played for a lot of dances and that was good income.

So, I wrote to these two congressmen and senators. I don't know if I heard from the congressmen at all, but I did hear from the senators. One of the senators by the name of Keyes wrote to me and said, "I can offer you a second alternate appointment to West Point." Note that I asked for West Point. The other senator, George Higgins Moses--

Q: Oh yes, famous Moses.

Adm. B.: Famous! Yes, he was one of the country's leaders. He wrote and said, "No, I'm filled up on West Point, but you can compete for my Naval Academy appointment."

And so I said to myself, "Second alternate, huh, no chance of getting in there. I'm going to take a chance of getting into Annapolis."

So I wrote to one senator and turned down the West Point one and wrote to the other senator and told him that I accept the Annapolis one; competitive.

The very next day I ran into a classmate of mine in high school and he was wondering what I was going to do. I said, "I'm going to go to the Naval Academy."

He said, "Nah! I wouldn't want to go there. I'd like to go to West Point."

I said, "Write to them." And told him of my turndown.

So he wrote and got the second alternate's appointment, got to West Point and graduated from the West Point the same time I graduated from the Naval Academy. And so I would have gone to West Point if I had decided to get the second alternate's appointment.

Anyhow, now what am I going to do? Now for the first time I told my parents about this endeavor of mine. My father said, "Now what you have to do is become messenger boy up in the New Hampshire legislature when they open up just after New Year's. That's where you're going to meet your politicians." He said, "So you better start writing to all the people around this area who are going to be members of this legislature."

We did not know who to write to until the election day in November. But he said, "As soon as you know who is going to be from here in that legislature you must write to every one of them; because you have to get their interest in you." He also said, "Senator Moses will certainly visit the State House several times. Every time he comes to Concord, you know very well he goes to the State House if they are in session. You

Benson #1 -16-

must get a job up there so you can meet him.

I did go up to the high school and talk to the principal of the school. "What should I do?"

"Well," he said, "one of the things you should not do is come back here and take some refresher course. No, you have got to point directly at whatever it is that you're supposed to know at the Naval Academy and then we'll try to figure out what to do."

Q: How much time did you have?

Adm. B.: Well, this was in the fall of 1924 and the exams weren't going to be until the--oh--around March. Something like that in 1925.

About that time I heard that a graduate of the Naval Academy, then a JG, was home on leave and in the neighborhood. So I went over to see him.

He said, "You know in the Navy Department they have pamphlet which give questions which have been asked for the past ten years. You must write and get that and then you learn all the answers." He said, "Don't go and just take some courses or sit there with a book and flounder around. You get that pamphlet and you learn how to work every problem in there and learn the answers to every question they have asked in the last ten years. They may not ask the same questions, but generally the format is going to be roughly the same."

And so I did exactly that. When I took it up to the principal of the high school, he said, "Sure." He said, "Now you do this and then I want you to come up here once a week and we will check over what you're doing." He said, "But you've got to, if you're interested, you've got to bear down and learn answers to all of the questions that have been asked and learn how to work all of those problems in geometry and algebra and everything that has been done. You've got to work at it if you want to get in there."

And so I worked at them. I don't know how well I did, but many of the questions were very familiar.

Q: And the exams were held in the local post office, I take it?

Adm. B.: That's right. And I don't believe the exams were until about the first of April. By the way, instead of becoming one of the six messenger boys for the House of Representatives I became the special messenger boy for the Speaker of the House.

Q: Was that the year your father was in the legislature?

Adm. B.: No, he had been in about ten years before. Where he fitted in was in knowing what to do.

Q: He knew the procedures.

Adm. B.: Yes, and I met Senator Moses, at least half a dozen times. It happened that the Speaker of the House was the same party as Senator Moses and he indeed was in there every time he came to Concord, New Hampshire, of course.

Q: Did you make yourself known to Moses?

Adm. B.: The Speaker of the House introduced me. We met every time he was in Concord.

Q: But, what I mean, and he realized you were one of the applicants?

Adm. B.: Yes, yes. The Speaker of the House told him that. And the Speaker of the House was one of the people who wrote a recommendation to him with regard to me. And several of the other politicians in the State House wrote to him. I doubt if I did the best academically, but I suspect that his having met me--well

Benson #1 -19-

of course, I had to have made a favorable impression also. But I was on my best behavior at that time.

Q: But, you also had to do well enough scholastically.

Adm. B.: Yeah, you certainly had to pass. And, for instance, ancient history was one of the six subjects. I don't recall having had any ancient history course. But I learned it in a hurry. I guess I probably learned more in about those few months than I did in any academic year in high school.

Q: Well, you had a real incentive at that point.

Adm. B.: Oh yes. I really bore down on it and it was interesting. When a question came up in the exam in the post office I could almost see what part of the page the answer was. It was almost as if I had a gouge there.

Q: So you came out with the appointment from Senator Moses?

Adm. B.: Yes. And, imagine as naive as we were, I arrived in Annapolis without ever having had a physical exam. We apparently had not detected anywhere that there was going to be a physical exam. Apparently we had not run into that bit of fine print. So I came down here. I could very well have failed it for color blindness or almost anything else.

Q: Yes, and they were very strict in those days about eyes.

Adm. B.: Yes. So I arrived down here and never had a physical exam in my life. Okay, very fortunate. It could have fallen apart anywhere in several places.

Q: So, your parents were delighted with this development, I take it?

Adm. B.: Gee, they thought that was great.

In those days certainly in most European countries anyone who became an officer of the armed forces was almost nobility. Certainly they were well heeled. I think this was true throughout Europe.

Q: So it was a giant step forward; now tell me about your plebe summer.

Adm. B.: Well, I'm one of those who enjoyed my time as a midshipman. All the time. Of course, naturally, I was a little unhappy sometimes during our plebe year. Plebe summer was easy compared to plebe year from the point of view of upper classman. See, we did not have any upper classmen bothering us during plebe summer. It must have been a shock to my system to have left New Hampshire and come down here in the middle of June and start off plebe summer with a temperature about the same as the middle of the sun, and double time and run and jump and all kinds of things continually. But, you're so busy that you didn't have time to think about that. Also misery loves company and I guess we were all miserable, but we didn't know it. Cause we had a good time and we had a busy time; simply great.

Q: You took to the regimentation with great ease?

Adm. B.: No problem at all, I said that was easy.

I was the youngest of four boys. My sister had died when she was six. But I had three older brothers. My parents did not have to keep me in line cause I had three older brothers to keep me in line. And so, I'd been in line alright.

Entering the Naval Academy with the bell ringing and jumping and running, no problem at all. Easy.

Academic year, you know plebe academic year was much tougher in certain respects than it is today. That is, psychologically and physically because you could misbehave in the eyes of an upper classman and get yourself beat up a little bit.

Q: That was what we called hazing.

Adm. B.: Oh yes, and very seldom was it really bad. It was, in many cases, just as funny as the upper classmen. Nothing serious. Occasionally there was some person who was very sadistic. But generally very good.

Academically I had a little bit of difficulty in the beginning of my plebe year. They assumed that every plebe had had a better background than I had. Thirty or forty years later, when I was in our Bureau of Naval Personnel, I was curious. I asked the Naval Academy section, "Do you have any old records?"

I found some records with regard to my class and I found just over one-half my class had either had a year of college or a year of special preparatory school.

Benson #1 -23-

Q: How many were there in the class?

Adm. B.: We entered just under four hundred. Just a few over fifty percent had had a special schooling.

Q: Many of them came down to Annapolis and went to one of the schools here.

Adm. B.: That's right. There were several schools that prepared them for that. So I had a little difficulty early plebe year academically.

Q: In what particular subject?

Adm. B.: Ha! Well, let's see, beginning plebe year we had five subjects. We had English, which was mostly English literature with a little larding of naval history. But, than we had to take a language, you could take French or Spanish. And which one you took depended upon where you were in the line. In other words, "You take French, you take Spanish, you take French, you take Spanish." I was assigned French. I had not had a language in high school. I did not have a mental block because I knew another language. Most Americans have a mental block.

They think they cannot learn anything in a foreign language. But I did not have a mental block. I found that taking French was not difficult.

Q: It's not related to Swedish, but you were bi-lingual.

Adm. B.: I could get a 4.0 in French class simply because of pronouncing a French "U". Americans can't do it. Swedes can because we have two letters of the alphabet that either one will give you a 4.0 for French "U". There are some words that have been borrowed. The word for umbrella is almost identical. Many of them are almost identical.

Q: After all you had the Bernadottes on the throne.

Adm. B.: That's right. We had three other subjects. We had chemistry, mathematics, and mechanical drawing. Well, I wasn't very good in these. I guess these are probably sort of refresher. Most of my classmates had probably already had chemistry. I hadn't had high school math and mechanical drawing. Well, I didn't do very well in those either.

Matter of fact, I went home Christmas leave, my first Christmas leave, and I was on the fence in all three of these subjects. It could have gone either way, but I brought all my books home with me. I knew how to study and so from there on academically I never had any difficulty.

Q: That was the watershed, was it? The Christmas vacation?

Adm. B.: Yes, once I got over that first term I was all set. We had four months in a semester and whether you were sat or unsat for that term was the thing that counted. In other words, when the marks came out in the end of January if you were unsatisfactory in one or more subjects your case was discussed by the academic board. You could be dismissed right then or they could say, "Do better." And then at the end of the next term, maybe you'd be gone, or maybe you would have made out all right. But I never had any difficulty from then on.

Q: Did you get any assistance from upperclassmen or from your roommate?

Adm. B.: Well, probably the smartest thing I did academically was to change roommates after plebe year. My plebe year roommate was a real good guy, Joe d'Avi, but he and I just loved to shoot the breeze. He was a dancer and I was a saxophone player so we used to have a great time. We'd talk about the show business all the time. I did a little better than he did academically plebe year. We were both just sort of squeaking through. Well, I decided to change roommates and I asked a classmate, Warner Rodiman, who had been an honor student plebe year, to room with him. He was a very serious student. That helped me, I think, a great deal. For the next three years I roomed with him. He had a better foundation, he was a little smarter, and more serious. It was easier to get your school work done than it was with Joe d'Avi. Although Joe got a roommate who did very poorly, both of them graduated. How they did it, I don't know. But, they did squeak through. So, it probably didn't make much difference.

Q: So from that time on you had no problems?

Adm. B.: No problems with academics. Didn't do as well as I should have. Rickover always asks his candidates, "Did you do at the Naval Academy your best all the time?"

The honest ones will say, "Of course not."

Well, no one does his best all the time, I don't think.

Q: That's his standard isn't it?

Adm. B.: That's his standard, all right. I suppose he has done his best all the time. I don't know.

Q: He was a perfectionist from the beginning. Tell me about the summer cruises and what they added to your knowledge.

Adm. B.: Yes, in those days all of the midshipmen, but not the plebes, but all the midshipmen went on battleships, on the midshipmen's cruise. The summer of 1926 I was then a brand new youngster, brand new sophomore, and I went on the battleship UTAH. We had the NEW YORK, WYOMING, and UTAH. UTAH, by the way, was sunk at Pearl Harbor and is up to the north side of Pearl Harbor, instead of the ARIZONA side. She was no longer a battleship but was a remote control target, I believe. Anyhow, we went on these three battleships and we didn't go to very many exotic places. We went to Newport, Rhode Island, and we went to New York City, and we went to Philadelphia, and we went to Charleston, South Carolina.

Q: It was a coastal cruise?

Adm. B.: Coastal cruise. And then, these ships were coal burners. It was the last coal burning cruise of the midshipmen.

Q: That added to your knowledge considerably, didn't it?

Adm. B.: That's right. My class, 1929 plus the class of 1928, the total of the two together was smaller than the class of 1927. 1927 was always bigger than the class of 1928 and 1929 together. All through the years, even when they chose admirals 1927 had more flag officers than 1928 and 1929 put together. Matter of fact, 1927 was the biggest class that graduated until the class of 1939 graduated. 1939 broke the records. Anyhow, what does that have to do with the cruise?

Well, of all the midshipmen on board only a fourth were my classmates. So, you can be sure that we got our share of shoveling coal and other occupations on board the ship. We coaled ship at Newport, Rhode Island. Then we coaled at Philadelphia, and then in Guantanamo, Cuba.

The reason we went to Guantanamo was that we would fire gunnery practices down there in the West Indies.

Now, we went on to these various cities and in almost every one of the cities we would have a parade. We wore our ordinary white works uniform regularly, but when we went ashore on the midshipmen cruise, even on liberty, we went ashore in our stand-up collar whites. We didn't have shoulder marks, we had anchors on the collar. But, that's the way we went on liberty and the way we marched in parades in all these cities that we visited.

Coaling ship and shoveling coal was certainly something to keep you busy. I remember in Newport we had been coaling ship all day and there was a party over at one of the great big mansions there in Newport. We had barely gotten a chance to finish coaling ship and get a bath and get into our starched whites and to get over there. Regardless of how much you bathed you'd have some coal dust in your ears. And, you'd have coal dust around your eyes and so forth. Naturally we were in a hurry and here we came in our whites with coal dust here and there. They must have been very delighted.

I remember we had barely gotten there and they said the refreshments were served. Well, the refreshments disappeared because all the midshipmen consumed all the refreshments before you could even say "hello." Because we had been up at six a.m. and started coaling ship; the coaling of ship did not stop for the noon meal. We had great big things full of coffee, urns full of coffee. And, we had great big platters full of sandwiches. That's what we did when there was a lull, a very short lull, in the proceedings.

This is the way they coaled ship in those days. They had a great big piece of canvas, heavy canvas with a grommet at each corner. Down in the coal barge midshipmen would shovel the coal into this big thing of canvas. That canvas thing would almost be square as this room is long. It must have been, oh, twenty feet by twenty feet, something like that. We midshipmen would be down in the coal barge shoveling the coal into the canvas thing and then the hoist would grab the four corners and hoist away. When it got up on deck there was a great big hole. It looked like one of these covers they have in the street, except that it was bigger.

Q: A manhole you mean?

Adm. B.: Manhole is the name. They'd lift that out and then we would shovel the coal from the canvas into that hole. That hole went all the way down and as the coal bunkers got filled, as soon as the bottom one was filled they'd put the manhole on top of there and then they'd fill the other spaces. But you can imagine the coal dust was flying around like mad.

Q: How often did you have to go through this process?

Adm. B.: Well, we did it three times in three months. Of course, when the ship was going to get underway, who do you suppose shoveled the coal to make the ship run? You can guess it. Matter of fact, not only did we youngsters shovel the coal all the time, but we had to be augmented by people in the 1927 and 1928 cause there weren' enough of us to shovel all this stuff.

Well, the boilers looked like, well, a fire in a locomotive, except there were five of them side by side with five different openings that you'd open the door. This coal would be shoveled from a bunker out onto the floor of the boiler room. Then you'd shovel it into the fire. They called the coal shovels "scoops". A great big heavy thing, you could hardly lift it. You'd get this thing full of coal and then you're going to swing it because you don't want it to just empty it at the door and then push it. What you want to do is open the door of the fire and swing this scoop and miss the sides and spread it over the fire. Well, the chances you're hitting one side or the other and spilling the coal down on the floor is great. So, that used to be quite a mess.

Q: How many hours duty would you have on a job like this?

Adm. B.: We would have four hours on and eight hours off. Many times they would measure the coal. They would get what they called a bucket. The bucket stood about 2 feet high and about 1 foot diameter. And you'd shovel into the bucket and then move the bucket over near the fire and then get your coal out of the bucket and throw it in there. But that was even worse, seemed to me.

Then, of course, with any kind of a coal fired furnace every so often you had to clean the fire cause it's so full of clinkers and stuff. The first thing you had to do when you came on watch was to pull one of the five fires.

Q: Shut it down, so to speak?

Adm. B.: Yes. Pull the fire out on the floor and shovel into an ash hopper. The ash hopper looked like a large toilet. So you'd shovel all these ashes into this thing and then you'd clamp the top on it and pneumatically blow it up topside and it would be blown over the side.

Q: Was that for the clinkers as well?

Adm. B.: Yes, they would go in there too.

Q: They went in there too and they were pulverized and blown out?

Adm. B.: Well, they were blown out anyhow. Must have had a big pipe, somehow or other. But the thing to avoid, and of course we didn't have anything to do with this, the thing to avoid was to blow the ashes up there just about the time the liberty boat was along side and spread the ashes all over the liberty boat with all the guys in their whites. It occurred once in a while I understand. This was a great sport, hard work. We used to also holystone the decks. You know holystoning?

Q: Yes.

Adm. B.: They stopped doing that around, oh, I should say in the late 1930's. They found it was wearing the decks out too much. Of course, there were all kinds of brasswork to polish. They kept us busy. This was a great experience.

Q: Did you have any time for organized classes on board?

Adm. B.: No, we didn't have classes on board at that time.

My second class cruise was the first oil burner. I claim to be the last person on active duty to shovel coal on a battleship.

Q: You were also the last person on active duty among your classmen?

Adm. B.: That's correct.

Anyhow, the second cruise was made on the OKLAHOMA and NEVADA and they were oil burners. I want to tell you this was heaven on earth. That cruise we went around by the west coast. We went down through the Panama Canal and got up to San Diego, and we went Long Beach and we went to San Francisco. Then back down again and through the canal. That was a more delightful cruise. We still had people on watch on the bridge; engine rooms, etc., but they didn't have anywhere near the amount of physical labor that has to be done all the time.

Then our first class cruise we went up and down the Atlantic coast very much like our youngster cruise except we didn't have the coal.

Q: You were deprived of the European cruise?

Adm. B.: Yes, we didn't have one. They were reinstituted later because in 1938 I was teaching school at the Naval Academy and they went on a European cruise. But those cruises were real good. We'd go out for three months, but they all went on cruises. We didn't go to New London, Connecticut, and we didn't go to Pensacola, Florida. We did the flight training after graduation.

Benson #1 -35-

Q: Yes, I see. It was advantageous in a sense to have the whole body of midshipmen on one or two ships?

Adm. B.: Oh, yes. There is a great advantage to it.

Q: Did you do anything musical when you were a midshipman?

Adm. B.: I was a self-taught saxophonist and clarinetist. There was a midshipmen's dance orchestra that I aspired to join. It was called "The N A Ten". I didn't become a permanent member plebe year, but I played with The N A Ten quite often. Someone would take sick or someone get on the pap and go to the REINA or something and I'd find myself in there with my saxophone.

At the end of my plebe year the midshipman in Class of '27 who'd been elected the leader got hold of me and said, "I want you to be one of my saxophone players." And he said, "If you'll bring your instrument over to my room we'll transfer all the instruments over to the battleship NEVADA; we're all going to go on that one ship together."

He had arranged this. So, on this particular day during June week or before graduation I started off with my instruments to deliver them to his room. Well, as I came out of the room here stood this second classman, about to become a first classman, who I had never seen before. He said, "Continue to march, mister."

He wanted to know who in the world I was and what I was doing there and all that sort of thing. He said, "I've got something here that may interest you, and it never has had any use."

And he showed me a cricket bat. I said to myself, "I bet he's going to beat me up with the cricket bat." But he didn't. I thought sure I was going to get a good licking for bringing my saxophone over there. But he let me go.

On the midshipmen's cruise we had this N A Ten all on the same ship. Every so often we'd go over and play on one of the other ships, but we'd practice on this ship. Really we got more practice on midshipmen's cruise than we did during the academic year. I then played in the N A Ten for the next two years and then I was the leader the last year.

Q: And this group played for hops and things?

Adm. B.: No, we didn't play for the hops. What we primarily did was every Friday night after supper, down in Smoke Hall, we would move furniture around so that we would have two of the great big tables and the orchestra would be up on the table. We even put a piano up there so that the midshipmen could see us. Set them up like a stage. As soon as evening meal, Friday night, was over they announced, "The N A Ten will now play in Smoke Hall."

We would have left early and got all squared away and as soon as we heard the thundering herd we'd go into <u>Anchors Aweigh</u> or something; we did that for four years. But one of the differences we made during my first class year was we tried harder to keep up on the latest hits. Whenever a song came out and was instantly popular on the radio I would write to the publisher and he would send us a free orchestration. I knew from my Concord, New Hampshire experience, that you could get these orchestrations free. Cause they wanted to sell their autographed records, I guess. So, as a consequence of this, whenever a tune had become or was looking like it was going to be a hit, we could play it. These musicians, not only at the Naval Academy in this dance orchestra, but in my home town when I was a kid, could sight read with no trouble.

You know, it's surprising, we could take the orchestration of a new tune that we hadn't heard yet. You'd bump twice on the bass drum and away you'd play. We would play this thing right off at sight. Naturally, you could play them better as you played them, but we indeed could play them right off at sight. When I first was a first classman in charge of The N A Ten and got this bundle of orchestrations, I would turn them over to the piano player and have him see if he thought they were pretty good. If we detected one in the pile which was a real hit, we'd play it right away.

Our practice time was practically nonexistent. We used to practice from nine until five minutes of ten one night a week. That was all we practiced. But, what we did then was we would go over, we'd play the things we were going to play the next evening in Smoke Hall. Several of those would have been played on Thursday evening, at sight. Then we'd play them publicly the very next evening--no problem.

But, this was quite an experience too. I probably put more effort on that musical business than I did on my academics once I was out of trouble. It was a leader job.

When I was a midshipman, there were two things we had in the entertainment business that we don't really now have. One of them was, in around February, we had something called the gymkhana. It was the, sort of a circus. It was over in Macdonough Hall, the athletic place. It was a big open space like Dahlgren is. We'd have a circus and one of the specialities was they would have some midshipmen who were gymnasts dressed in the uniform of gorillas. They would climb up in the overhead of the place like monkeys. They were great! That circus was a lot of fun. An awful lot of work, I suppose, but a lot of fun.

Q: Was it a benefit of any sort?

Adm. B.: No, just good entertainment. They stopped them in the thirties. Apparently they decided it took too much of the midshipmen's time. You have to limit something somewhere.

Q: But it wasn't a money raiser?

Adm. B.: No, no. You know in those days, but while we're in Macdonough Hall, you know intercollegiate boxing was going on at that time. The fights at the Naval Academy, boxing Yale or Notre Dame or somebody, would be Saturday evening over in Macdonough Hall, and the uniform was full dress.

The midshipmen wore the standup collar full dress, and all the officers wore their white tie and tails. The women all wore their ball gowns. That was quite an event.

Q: For the boxing?

Adm. B.: For the boxing Saturday evening, now that was fun.

The other thing they had which we really don't have now was we had the musical club show. It was in the spring. It looked something like _Damn Yankee_ but not quite. Because _Damn Yankee_ music is down on the floor, in the pit, and the people are having a stage play

We had the masqueraders and we had the faculty around here put on the Navy relief show which was dramatics. We also had the Music Club show in which every musical activity at the Naval Academy appeared on the stage, in addition to tap dancers and a little bit of minstrel show and all that stuff--that was fun. But, that N A Ten of mine would actually appear on the stage and play a half a dozen pieces.

Q: And you say the N A Ten still exists?

Adm. B.: I understand that title still exists, but just what it does I'm not quite sure.

Q: Well, that certainly added to the picture of the Naval Academy in those days.

Adm. B.: We--on my first midshipman cruise, when we were down in Charleston, South Carolina, this event will make you laugh I'm sure. We were going to have a parade. Of course we were going to be in our starched whites because that was the only uniform we had to go ashore with in the summertime.

We were all set and it looked like it was going to rain, so they had us carry our rain coats. So we got over there and we started the parade and it also started to rain. But, no one had the authority to tell us to put on the rain clothes. So we marched in our starched whites carrying our rain clothes with the skies having opened up and pouring down on us. We marched in the rain anyhow.

Q: An example of excessive regulation.

Adm. B.: Yes, somebody should have been able to say, "Put on your rain clothes." It didn't hurt us any.

I hadn't been able to find my whites so I had borrowed a set of whites from a classmate of mine on board the ship. So he got my dirty whites along with his own.

Q: Were you involved at all in athletics?

Adm. B.: Not good enough to be varsity athletics. I had not been out for athletics when I was a high school kid.

Well, what did kids do when school was out when I was a kid? They had jobs. After school and Saturday was a routine. Nearly every kid had a job somewhere after school and on Saturdays. So I had never been out for athletics in high school.

I came to the Naval Academy and I went out for intramural sports. I never was good enough for varsity. Even in those days you were always out for something. If you weren't out for something, especially during your plebe year, you were out for something right now.

I found out early in my plebe year. I had not gone out for any athletics, I was planning on keeping up with my studies. This first classman said, "Now, Mr. Benson, what sport are you out for?"

I said, "Well, I've been thinking about going out for soccer, but I haven't started yet."

"Well," he said, "that's very fine because I need you in my company cross-country team."

So every afternoon I had to go out and run. We started running over where the field house is now; Thompson Field, it was called then. We'd start from there and we'd run down in front of the chapel and out over the bridge to the hospital and around the whole hospital grounds and back into where the field house is now. Now, for a runner that's very easy but there were no runners on those teams.

On Sundays, we always had to run against some other team. They weren't any better than we were. Let me tell you, that was terrible.

I never was interested in cross-country after that experience. But then it wasn't at all unusual on a Sunday right after lunch to have some upperclassman say, "What are you doing this afternoon, sir?"

"Well, I'm going to do"--so and so.

"Well fine, you're a good man."

And so he would collect you because he's been told by the company officer that he has got to have a boxing team or a wrestling or almost any kind of team; water polo or something to play against such-and-such a company. So you'd find yourself over in the gym and you and about a half a dozen other guys are about to have some athletic contest with one of the other companies. They're not any better than you are, but you'd better go out for one of the company teams; otherwise they're going to grab you and get you over to wrestle or something Sunday afternoon.

So even if you tried, you couldn't keep from being in the athletic business. Almost everybody signed up and actually belonged to an intramural team. If you didn't belong to one you'd find yourself a member of one you didn't want to belong to. This was all a good thing because participation was important.

Q: Athletics are terribly important to the development of a naval officer and that is why they stressed it. What about leave in those days? How much freedom did you have?

Adm. B.: Let's see. At the end of the midshipman cruise, June, July and August, we had what's called Sept. leave because it was in the month of September. I believe it amounted to about three and a half weeks.

Q: Did you go home in that period?

Adm. B.: Oh yes, I went up to Concord, New Hampshire, each one of those times. Then at Christmas we got from the twenty-third of December until the second of January. You had to be back sometime during the second of January.

During your first class year you had the class supper. All of the first classmen went to Baltimore; left in the middle of the afternoon and came back that night. They had all had dinner together in some restaurant in Baltimore. That was the limit of where we could go.

Q: There was no program in connection with the dinner?

Adm. B.: I don't remember one.

During your plebe year you could get out Saturday afternoon and Sunday afternoon. You'be be at noon meal and you'd be at supper.

Q: But the hours in between were free?

Adm. B.: Yes. During your youngster year, I believe you could also be out for about an hour the latter part of Wednesday. Of course a plebe couldn't go out to a hop, that is a dance. Youngsters and second classmen could also go out Wednesday afternoon in addition to Saturday afternoon and Sunday afternoon. First classmen could go out any afternoon in the week for about an hour. You could be outside from, say, about four-thirty until formation around six.

Where could you go? I don't think you could get out as far as Parole is now. But I know you could get out on part of West Street. I expect you could go across the Eastport bridge. But just how far you could go--of course you were limited just how far you could go anyhow because you weren't permitted to ride in a vehicle.

If your parents came down to visit you and they had an automobile, you could not get in that automobile to go anywhere. You were not permitted to get in that automobile to go from anywhere to anywhere. So that limited you to how far you were going to get away from the gate.

Now, on dance nights, if you're going to the dance, you had to check out and then you had to go to the dance. You had to check in at the dance. You couldn't get out of the dance early. When the dance was over you had forty-five minutes to check in at the main office. So you could get your girl friend back to her house and get to Bancroft Hall all in forty-five minutes. First classmen, I believe, could have an hour.

Q: Fifteen minutes more with the girl.

Adm. B.: That was it. So we didn't have very many liberties and there was nothing we could do. Nowhere we could go. Cause you couldn't ride anything. But there was no problem. Certain people used to go over the gate, go over the fence now and then. "Go over the wall," the expression was. But I don't know what there would be the reason for it--for kicks I guess.

Q: Just to beat the system, I suppose. Did you have any demerits during your career there?

Adm. B.: A few but not serious.

Benson #1 -47-

Q: You never attempted to go over the wall then?

Adm. B.: No. Some of my classmates did. I think they talked about it more than they did it.

Q: Did you have any friends in town?

Adm. B.: No I didn't. I understand now though in those days the way to have friends in town was to go to one in-town churches. If you went to one of them, in-town people would invite you home with them.

Q: Rather than go to the chapel.

Adm. B.: Yes, I went to the chapel and the reason I went to the chapel, the primary reason was, that they had the tryouts for the choir plebe summer and I'd been a choirboy in Concord, New Hampshire, and so I got in the choir. Beginning academic year I also got in the choir. I sang in the chapel choir for three years. But then I didn't sing in it first class year because, lo and behold, I found myself in charge of the Drum and Bugle Corps. We marched the midshipmen to chapel on Sundays. When it came time for chapel all the midshipmen who were not going out in town, were going to the Naval Academy Chapel and we were the music that would march them off to chapel.

I hadn't been in the Drum and Bugle Corps during the three previous years. It was always sort of a mystery to me that I found myself having directorship of Drum and Bugle Corps.

There was a classmate of mine who was the boss of the Drum and Bugle Corps but most of my first class year he was in the hospital or something and so I found myself running the Drum and Bugle Corps though I had never been in it before. Very strange. I was told by one of the officers in Bancroft Hall that they thought they would get a musician in to be the boss and maybe they could get the bugles in tune.

Q: When you were approaching graduation in June of 1929 did you know where you were to be assigned after that?

Adm. B.: Yes. You filled in a form in the spring of your senior year of, say, three choices or something. I had been in some slight demerit difficulty and the Commandant of Midshipmen, Captain Sinclair Gannon, talked things over and gave me guidance. I had learned already that he was a hard man to shave. Anyhow, I knew that when he left the Naval Academy at the end of my second class year, my junior year, he went to command the battleshi

NEW YORK on the east coast of the United States. So I said to myself, "When I'm going to put down my choices I do not want anything in the Atlantic Fleet because Captain Gannon is over there." If I remember correctly we could go to battleships or cruisers. I believe that's all we went to, battleships or cruisers. So, I didn't put down anything in the Atlantic Fleet. I put my first choice as a cruiser in the Pacific. I thought to myself, "I'd like to get that battleship business but, if I can keep from going to a battleship and could keep from going to the Atlantic Fleet maybe I'm home free."

I put in these choices and everything is fine except I was ordered to the battleship NEW YORK in the Atlantic Fleet.

Q: Inevitable that was.

Adm. B.: Yes. So about a dozen of us brand-new graduates reported to this battleship. The second morning we were on board we got all dressed in our full dress. The full dress had a coat that in the civilian world had been called the Prince Albert. It was a coat that looked very much like your regular blue uniform coat except that it reached to the knees. It had straps here such that you could put the epaulettes on. I'm not referring to shoulder marks, I'm talking about the actual "swabs". You've seen them I'm sure. You had a gold strip down the side of the trousers and you wore a sword belt outside of the coat. You had your fore and aft hat and your white gloves.

So we all got dressed in our full dress and marched up to call on the captain of the ship. So here are about a dozen of us all lined up all very fancy.

Q: Had an appointment been made with him?

Adm. B.: Yes, an appointment had been made with him. We were now going to call on the captain. He was going to give us a little bit of advice.

He stood there looking at us and he said, "Well, I don't know very many of you. I remember you though; your name is Benson."

I said, "Yes, sir."

I wanted to add, "No, it hasn't changed." But I just said, "Yes, sir." I thought that would be enough.

He then looked us over with those cold eyes of his and then he explained something and said nice to have you aboard and all that sort of thing and we marched off. Gee, I was delighted, here I had a chance to meet the captain. That was fine.

I asked a very renowned Naval Academy athlete, I forget his name now, but he was the second Naval Academy graduate to make the football Hall of Fame, I asked him, "What are the pluses and minuses of a star athlete when he goes out into the fleet as an ensign?"

He said, "Well, you have the advantage that everybody knows you. Every single person on board that ship knows exactly who you are. They will observe everything you do. Now if you can arrange it such that everything you do is fine, that's all well. But if you ever do anything which isn't quite perfect everybody on the ship knows about it right now."

Well, of course, it is a minor example, but you can be sure that Sinclair Gannon had his eye on me, because he didn't know any other name there, but he knew mine. He couldn't help inquiring now and then, "How's that guy Benson doing?" Couldn't help it, I would think. He would know that name.

Q: What were the other officers like on board the NEW YORK?

Adm. B.: Oh, they were fine. I first got into communications on board, there. I became the assistant radio officer. That was a very interesting sort of thing. One year after I had gotten on board the signal officer was detached and so I became the signal officer.

Benson #1 -52-

This might be a good point to talk about Naval aviation for a second. We've all heard the talk that the Army and Navy sort of ignored aviation. They didn't pay much attention to aviation back in those days, say 1929, 1930. Well, here's an example of the extent to which the Navy paid attention to naval aviation. Every member of my class, and I presume this is true of the classes before and after, every member of my class who could pass the aviation physical exam, and that was probably all of us, had to go to elimination flight training. If you're in the Atlantic Fleet you went to Norfolk and if you're in the Pacific Fleet you went to San Diego. There you had ten hours of dual instruction followed by a couple hours of solo if you checked out for solo, which everyone did. Then you went back where you came from. If you want to go to further flight training you would have already asked for it because you left Norfolk or San Diego. You would then at some time, perhaps a year later, you'd be ordered to Pensacola for flight training. This was how the Navy was neglecting naval aviation. That's not very much neglect.

Q: Well, this was toward the end of the 1920's and the Navy had perked up in this area. Were you interested in aviation?

Adm. B.: No, I really wasn't. Anyhow I passed the aviation physical exam and I went to Norfolk and did the ten hour elimination flight training and solo. When it came to filling out the form whether you wanted further flight training I put down, "No."

I had had in mind since I was in high school or even younger that what I wanted to do was go to the Orient. This was what I really wanted to do. However, I did have another dream at about the same time I went to flight training. I was interested in lighter-than-air. I thought that lighter-than-air would be the way of the future. So, I had written to Goodyear and told them that I was interested in lighter-than-air and did they have any suggestions of what I ought to do. They came back and said "Apply for lighter-than-air training in the Navy because they do have some training in the Navy. Apply for that and once you do finish that course, then if you ever are interested in coming to work for us maybe we will have a job." But I wasn't so interested in getting out as I was interested in this thing that looked pretty good to me, lighter-than-air. But you couldn't apply for that until you were three years out of school. The same as submarine school.

Anyhow, I went back to the battleship NEW YORK having had my little flight training and about a year or so later here was a set of orders. By that time the NEW YORK had transferred to the Pacific.

Q: Was Gannon still with the NEW YORK?

Adm. B.: No, Gannon had departed. He had made flag rank and departed and I never had any run in with him. I suspect that he probably kept an eye on me and I certainly didn't do anything that he would be very unhappy about as far as I could see. But, I really wasn't a playboy. I was a pretty serious sort of a guy.

A set of orders arrived for me to go to Pensacola. So I went down to the executive office and said that I don't want to go there. I want to go out to China. So, they sent in a request that the orders be cancelled but came back, "Carry out the orders." And so, in early 1931 I was detached to Pensacola, got down there and they had interviews. One of the things they were presumably trying to find out in the interview was: were you psychologically tuned to this sort of thing or not?

Q: Did they have gliders? Did you have any experience with gliders?

Adm. B.: Now, these were very much like, you know the airplane that's flying from the overhead of Dahlgren Hall? It very much like that. It was a single engine biplane. You started the engine by cranking which started this great big cylinder rotating and you'd plug in the engine and that would start it; instead of turning the prop. We had gotten beyond that.

I was in the midst of a little bit of this flight training and I guess I'd probably gotten in two or three hours when I had my interview. I explained to the interviewer how it was that I was there.

He said, "You still don't want to be here?"

I said, "That's right." I said, "I still would like to go to China. I don't particularly care to go to flight training. I might be interested in lighter-than-air."

And so, they got hold of the Bureau of Naval Personnel and I got a set of orders to go to Asiatic Fleet.

Q: That's one way to be persistent.

Adm. B.: Yes, I really wanted to go there. I thought it was a good idea.

Q: So your career in naval aviation was very brief indeed?

Adm. B.: Very brief indeed. Looking back on it from time to time I think I really did enjoy it and I wonder, maybe I did make a mistake.

Q: Did you have any further opportunity to go to or investigate lighter-than-air?

Adm. B.: No. I got out in China and I got sort of absorbed in what was going on there. Then about, yes it would have been in the middle of 1933, that we were down in Tsingtao, China. We normally summered at a place called Chefoo. We had nineteen destroyers out there and we would go down to run high speed target for the submarines. There were twelve submarines based at Tsingtao, China. We'd go run high speed target for them. Once, while we were down there, I ran into a classmate of mine.

He said, "Hey, why don't you come for a ride on a submarine with us sometime?"

Fine. I took it up with the skipper of my ship.

"Sure, okay."

The next morning I was on board this old S-type submarine. This classmate of mine was the so-called diving officer. What the diving officer does is, one of the things he does is when they order "Rig for dive," every compartment is rigged for dive and he goes through and checks that everything has been done that's supposed to be done. Then when you hit the diving alarm he is the diving officer. I went along with him and watched what he was doing and all that sort of thing. Fascinating! Gee, this looked great to me. So, I put in for submarine school.

-58-

Interview No. 2 with Rear Admiral Roy S. Benson, U.S. Navy (Retired)

Place: Arnold, Maryland

Date: Tuesday, 11 March 1980

By: John T. Mason, Jr.

Q: Well, Sir, when we broke up last time you were at the point of joining the Asiatic Fleet (or we called it the Station in 1931). Now, you take up the story at that point.

Adm. B.: Well, you recall that I had left my battleship and had gone to Pensacola for a little bit of flight training and did not want to be there. I was quickly detached from Pensacola and I got my lifelong dream. I got to go out to the Orient. I got on board a Dollar Steamship Company ship in Los Angeles and we proceeded out to the Orient. The first stop for me was in Hawaii, where I acted as a beachboy for two weeks.

Q: A beachboy being what?

Adm. B.: Young fellows who run up and down the beach and surfboarding and all that sort of thing. I had taken a ship two weeks in advance of the one I was scheduled to so that I could have two weeks vacation in Hawaii. A place I very definitely wanted to visit.

Then I caught the next ship. These Dollar Steamship Line ships went all around the world and they were two weeks behind one another. They would stop about three days in each port. The ports we visited on the way out to my ship were, leaving Hawaii we went to Kobe, Japan; Shanghai, China; Hong Kong, and I got off at Manila. I took the ferry to Cavite, about a half hour ride on the ferry across Manila Bay. And there was the ship that would be my home for the next three years. This was a four pipe destroyer.

Q: The USS SMITH THOMPSON.

Adm. B.: The USS SMITH THOMPSON. She had a hull number 212, the Fahrenheit boiling point. I became the junior officer on that ship. A matter of fact, probably the junior officer on the Asiatic Fleet. I got the conventional jobs for George, that's the name in the Navy for the junior officer. I became the communications officer and the commissary officer. You recall when I was on the battleship NEW YORK I was in radio and then in signals. This fitted me very well for my communication job aboard this destroyer.

Q: What sort of a complement did she have?

Adm. B.: Oh, we had six officers and seventy-five enlisted men, perhaps. She was about the length of a playing part of a football field. She had almost the same amount of horsepower in her propulsion plant as one of our old battleships. With four boilers on the line she could make almost thirty-five knots. She could make twenty-seven knots on two of the boilers.

For all practical purposes this was an engineering plant with very few accommodations for people. The whole bottom was an engineering plant.

Q: That wasn't emphasized in those days, was it? Accommodations?

Adm. B.: No, that wasn't very important.

It might be interesting, perhaps, to review what we had on the Asiatic fleet at that time.

Q: Who was the commander-in-chief?

Adm. B.: A four star admiral by the name of Taylor. M. M. Taylor I believe it was, anyway, he was a real old timer. He would probably have been at the Naval Academy class back around the turn of the century.

We had nineteen of these four pipe destroyers out in the China fleet. And we had a destroyer tender which was a mother ship. You could get repairs beyond the capability of the ships force, and food and fuel and so forth. Then there were twelve old S-type submarines with a submarine tender. Then up the Yangtze River there were about half a dozen gunboats. They had actually been built in Shanghai, most of them. Then there was a cruiser. When I first got out there this cruiser was a coal burner and had four stacks. I think the name was USS ROCHESTER. It was a real old timer. That was the flagship of the admiral.

Now our normal modus operandi was we wintered down in the Philippines, really in Manila. The summertime we spent in China. There was a song "When We All Go To China In the Springtime, When We All Go To Manila In the Fall."

When we went to China the destroyers and the destroyer-tender went to a place called Chefoo. Chefoo was about fifty miles away from where the British Asiatic fleet spent their summers in Wei-hai-wei.

The submarines based at a place called Tsingtao which was around a top of the Shantung promontory. Strangely enough

Tsingtao was the only place in China in which they drove on the right hand of the road. The reason they did was the Germans had held Tsingtao for many years and had imposed right hand drive while the rest of China and the Philippines was all left hand drive.

At that particular time, 1931, Chiang-kai-shek was trying to be president of China. He and a character by the name of Mao Tse-tung had both been number one assistants to Sun Yat-sen. When Sun Yat-sen died his number two assistants, as so often happens, went their separate ways.

China militarily had been trained by the Russians. And why? Because when they needed help and asked for it, they didn't get any anywhere else. But the Russians helped them train their military.

Anyhow, they went their separate ways. Both Chiang-kai-shek and Mao Tse-tung had been to Russia, I believe, for training of their own.

Q: And indoctrination.

Adm. B.: Indoctrination yes. So Mao Tse-tung went one way and Chiang-kai-shek went the other. Chiang-kai-shek somehow was called the president of China.

Mao Tse-tung and his people at that time, 1931, were in South China around places like Foochow, Amoy, Swatow. They were down there on that South China coast. They hadn't started their long march out to the west.

There was another phenomenon going on and had been for many years and they were called warlords. Now for example, and only an example, I don't know if there were two dozen or if there were fifty warlords but there was a warlord up there around Chefoo where our destroyers were based. And there was one down around Tsingtao.

Q: They were simply local commanders, but independent practically.

Adm. B.: Local commanders and practically independent, took their direction from no one. But while we were in Chefoo, probably in the summer of 1932, the warlord from out in the sticks somewhere decided that he should take over the area held by the warlord for Chefoo. And according to what we heard they had a meeting; they came to an accommodation. Chinese are very good at that;

they come to some kind of accommodation, each side hoping that the near future will tip the scales in its direction. But they don't want to fight about it very much. Apparently they came to an accommodation, and the warlord up around Chefoo and his army all embarked and went somewhere. The new one came in and we noticed in the personnel of the local police there were new individuals, they came in and took over. There was a lot of cholera out there at that time and I remember being in Chefoo when they had a cholera epidemic. Many people died in Chefoo. The U. S. Navy around Chefoo lost one. One enlisted man got cholera. For the rest of us, our shots were very effective and only one person got cholera.

Q: And sanitary arrangements--

Adm. B.: Sanitary arrangements were very poor. Chefoo had no sewage system. Just throw the stuff in, we used to call (the stream), "Rose Creek." That was a good name for it, a good euphemism, it wasn't quite like roses.

Now, why did we have an Asiatic Fleet? Well, the most important reason for our being out there was to show the flag and hold down difficulties just like a police car driving around a bad neighborhood might hold down a little bit of the terrorism.

Q: Sometimes called "brush fires."

Adm. B.: Show the flag and people might slow down a little bit. They might cool off a little bit. That was the number one reason we were there. However, we were also there, perhaps, because other countries had ships there.

There was an Italian ship now and then and there were some French ships, and there was always a British fleet out there.

Q: Well, there was the incentive of trade, was there not?

Adm. B.: Yes. Standard Oil Company was extremely important. Everywhere you went there was a Standard Oil compound. By compound we mean sort of like a fort, but it was wooden.

Of course there was missionaries everywhere. One of the things we had to be prepared to do was to evacuate U. S. nationals in the event of trouble. There were always plans for each location as to how you go about doing it. Plans not very good perhaps, but they were plans and we were aware of the fact that we had to prepare to do this.

In addition, the ships in the Asiatic Fleet carried out the same training exercises and their personnel competed for promotion and so forth along with the rest of the Navy in the

Pacific and the Atlantic fleets. In other words, if there were certain training exercises of gunnery, torpedoes, engineering and so forth that were done on the East and West coasts of the United States a similar type of ship out in China was in competitio with these as a type.

Q: So there was a coordination in the fleet?

Adm. B.: Oh yes. When we were out there for two or three years we did not miss out on what was going on in the fleet. We knew exactly what was going on.

Ships stayed there. When I arrived out there those ships had been there for perhaps ten years. The ships stayed there and the people transferred. When I went out there it was going to be a two-year tour of duty.

Q: Was that the normal tour?

Adm. B.: Two years was normal at that time. At the end of one year, just before one year was up, they changed it to three years. So, a lot of us who had just been out there for one year threw ourselves a party welcoming ourselves to the China station. We had been there a year, but now we had a two-year tour coming up.

Q: Now you say the fleet units stayed on and on; what about refitting, where did they refit? In Manila?

Adm. B.: Down in Cavite, near Manila. There was a naval shipyard down there and that's where we had our work done. As I told you originally, on anything generally beyond the capabilities of the ship's force, the destroyer tender or the submarine tender helped. But then, when it came time for an actual shipyard overhaul or in an emergency, some major thing beyond the capability of those tenders, it would be done in the Cavite Naval Shipyard.

Q: Now, was there some special reason for retaining the ships there; was there some adaptability of ships to that locality?

Adm. B.: Not that I'm aware of. I don't know why they did that. When I'd been out there about a year they sent some of them back to the United States. But they did not replace them; they simply decided to reduce the number a little bit.

In addition to being up in Chefoo in the summer and down in the Philippines in the winter we destroyers also augmented the gunboat business. The gunboats, which I mentioned, were built in Shanghai.

Q: They were river boats?

Adm. B.: River boats. They were built out there and they stayed there and I'm sure they didn't go to Cavite for repair, they came to Shanghai to a commercial repair yard. We destroyers augmented the gunboats. These river gunboats on the Yangtze River, did not go to other ports along the coast of China and various places. We destroyers did that.

Our squadron of destroyers, of nineteen destroyers, was divided into three divisions. When it was your division's turn to go gunboating, three of them would join the Yangtze Patrol; and three of them would constitute the South China Patrol. The South China Patrol would be Foochow, Amoy, Swatow, and down around Canton. I believe there was a gunboat of some kind down around, one of ours, around Canton, but I'm not quite sure.

Q: Did the British maintain gunboats also?

Adm. B.: The British had gunboats on the river and they also had quite a few other ships, and they also had a few cruisers out there on the Far East station. They operated, of course, from Hong Kong and Wei-hai-wei. But they would also show up in these various ports and so did the Japanese. Matter of fact, beginning around 1932-1933, wherever we went with our destroyer, when it was our turn to be on gunboat duty, if we went to Foochow, for example, right behind us came a Japanese ship. They were with us all the time and sometimes it would be the same one. We'd go down to Swatow and in they'd come. We'd make and return calls and we'd move to Amoy and do it all over again.

Q: Were they observing and spying on you or what?

Adm. B.: I suppose so. Every so often they would challenge us to a boat race or something. But only in case, I'm sure, if they had their star crew on board ready to give us a licking. So, we tried to avoid that.

I made a note to myself to tell about the landing force officer. Remember I had mentioned that we had to have plans everywhere for the evacuation of our U.S. nationals in the event of need. There were three kinds of nationals generally; they were businessmen of which Standard Oil Company is a real good example; there was another set the consul, and his assistants and their families; and the third were missionaries.

It's all well and good to make up a plan for the evacuation of U.S. nationals and you have a place where they all meet; usually the Standard Oil Compound. If you have a drill, everyone will get there, but no missionaries. It's very difficult to convince the missionary that things are really bad and "we want to help you get out." He doesn't want to get out. He wants to teach Christianity and, God bless him, that's his job and he sticks to it. Regardless of what comes up he's going to stay there and help the people.

Q: He has an innate feeling, I suppose, that God will take care of him.

Adm. B.: That's correct. I mentioned that Mao Tse-tung was now along the South China coast. He and his people, and they were communist terrorists, and they would make raids here and there. We used to hear about these rumblings every so often--. I was landing force officer. I was "George." Any jobs that came along they decided, I guess, good training for the junior officer, so give him the job and he does it real good. So I was the landing force officer and my land force consisted of about, oh, maybe ten bluejackets. We'd get all dressed up in our dungarees and so forth, we'd go and save the world.

I remember very well in Amoy there was a real threat there apparently and I remember we spent two or three days and nights ove in the Standard Oil compound to protect the compound but also to protect U.S. nationals who would be gathering there. But nothing

Benson #2 -71-

happened, so it was all right. Some years later, you remember, that Mao Tse-tung and his gang proceeded from there out into the west.

Q: Were they hostile to foreigners at that time?

Adm. B.: Not that I'm particularly aware of. They just wanted to raise a little bit of the devil here and there I guess. Just be active. Perhaps you remember in September of 1931 the Japanese took over Manchuria one night. Took it away from China, and from then on Japan was always pushing out in the Far East. Actually I believe that World War II really started that night in Manchuria. You recall that the then-called League of Nations met and talked about it and decided that the Japanese should get out of Manchuria. Whereupon Japan marched out of the League of Nations. They never got out of Manchuria until World War II was over. They kept pushing. In January of 1932, believe it or not, the Japanese armed forces attacked the city of Shanghai. They didn't attack other places; they simply decided to have some little exercise down around Shanghai.

Shanghai was made up of three cities. One was operated by the Consul Body, that was the international settlement and was governed by the foreign consuls. There was the French Concession.

The French Concession, according to French beliefs, was just as much part of the Republic of France as Paris was. It belonged to France. Then there was the rest of the city, which presumably belonged to the Republic of China.

The Japanese were attacking that Chinese city. We, down in Manila, were told to proceed posthaste up to Shanghai. About, I'd say, a half a dozen of us destroyers proceeded up from Manila to Shanghai. What we were going to do there I'm not sure. I guess the same as we'd always done, show the flag and you're ready to evacuate U.S. nationals. After we'd been there for a couple of weeks my destroyer and another, the PARROTT I believe it was, proceeded up to Nanking.

Nanking is a city a couple hundred miles up the Yangtze River. When you go up the Yangtze River you get a native pilot. He sits up there on a high chair and he actually steers the ship himself. You try to follow where he's going by looking at the chart and you're wasting your time. That river meanders all over the place. Perhaps it's the same in the Mississippi. It meanders all over the place and he knows where the river is.

Q: He knows where the channel is?

Benson #2 -73-

Adm. B.: Yes. He knows where you can go. So, we proceeded up to Nanking. At Nanking, a couple of hundred miles up the river, ships there at anchor swing to the tide of the Pacific Ocean. I suppose that's true of other rivers. Now, up there at Nanking at anchor there were about six Chinese naval ships and a half dozen Japanese. There was one British ship and two American destroyers. The British destroyer and our destroyers anchored between the Chinese and Japanese ships. That was a very strange thing with the Japanese and Chinese ships right there in Nanking, and two hundred miles down the river there's a fight going on in which Japanese troops and Japanese ships with their gunfire are attacking the city of Shanghai. Two hundred miles up they are sitting there with their guns trained but not shooting.

The day before Washington's birthday 1932, as the custom was, I didn't realize this, that if you're in a foreign port and you're going to full dress ship the next day, and we were for George Washington's birthday, you invite the foreign ships to full dress ship if they would care too. You'd consider it a great honor if they would. So, I put on my full dress, frock coat down to my knees, the gold pants, sword, sword belt, the swabs, that is the epaulets, the fore and aft hat and the white gloves. And here goes "George". It's winter out there and of course you can't put an overcoat on top of this and it got a little chilly. I proceeded over to the senior ship of each of the other navies and explained to them, "We are going to full dress ship tomorrow for George Washington's birthday, the father of our country. If you'd care to we would be honored if you would also full dress ship."

Q: You being, in advance, in full dress?

Adm. B.: Yes. I proceeded back and the next day we full dress ship. Flags flying all over the place. Signal flags from bow to stern. The same with the other ships. So the day after George Washington's birthday I get on my rig again and away I go to thank them for having done it. That day the weather turned terrible, so bad it was impossible to get a boat alongside of the companionway; people often times call gangway. So they had rigged what they call a jacob's ladder. That is a rope ladder hanging down the side of the ship. In my fore and aft hat, and my swabs, and my white gloves and my sword, the gold stripe down the side of my trousers and everything, away I went down the jacob's ladder into the boat and away we went. I thought we were going to founder on the way. Terrible weather and I proceeded to each one of these ships; thank them for having so greatly honored us. As I was leaving the Chinese ship one of my epaulets fell off and fell into the Yangtze River and went straight to the bottom. I looked up there and I thought the Chinese officer was absolutely going to split. I think he's still laughing.

In July 1932 I made Lieutenant Junior Grade. I got promoted. In those days you took promotion examinations for every promotion, I don't believe you took examinations for either Captain or Admiral, but you took promotion exams for everything else. The promotion exams were drawn up in Washington and were sent out.

I had taken my examinations about the time we were up in Nanking; ten subjects. They went back to the examining board in Washington and, if you passed them, you were ready to become the next rank when there was a vacancy.

Q: Simultaneously were you taking extension courses with the Naval War College?

Adm. B.: Not yet. You could take them but that didn't enter my life for quite a few years later when I was teaching school at the Naval Academy. There were only a few subjects you could take. You could take strategy and tactics, and you could take communications. I forget the rest, but there were two or three subjects you could take. If you finished the course you didn't have to take the exam in that subject. It was also very good for your record having taken these various courses. It was sort of like going through the chairs in some other organizations.

Q: It's an indication of ambition too in a young officer to do this.

Adm. B.: That's right. It means a great deal to his career. You become known if you try to help yourself. One big advantage of standing high in your class at the Naval Academy is when you arrive on board ship you are known by everyone. If you are then to do a good job everybody notices and this is a leg up.

Let's return to China. Foochow is on the old river Min. Foochow is twenty-five miles inland and halfway up there is an anchorage called Pagoda anchorage. There's a tremendous pagoda there and that was as far up the river as our ships were permitted to go because of the depth of water. Of course, we always took a native pilot if we could on some of the infrequent visits; at least someone who could advise where the river was.

Q: Because of the silting, I suppose?
Adm. B.: Surely.

I remember we all went to to Foochow one night and the American Consul up there threw a party, a tremendous party. Well, the chief of police that evening said to my commanding officer—my commanding officer on board that ship was Commander E. B. Lapham. Then a year or so later he was relieved by D. C. Edger, who was relieved by Scott D. McCoy during the three years I was there. I was junior officer during the whole three years.

We were at this big party and the native chief of police of Foochow said to my commanding officer, "We think that you should visit the great big Buddhist monastery which is up on the top of a mountain near that Pagoda anchorage."

Obviously, then the thing you say is, "Why, that's very nice of you."

If you don't want to do it obviously, there is some reason why your ship has to get under way first thing tomorrow morning. You can't turn them down without a real valid excuse. The only one you can really think of is you're not going to be there. "Very sorry about that."

Anyhow, my skipper was an athletic type. He had found out that you had to climb the side of this mountain. He accepted the invitation and the chief of police said, "You may bring one of your officers with you." And of course, who went? George! Me!

The next morning we were ready; we had four armed guards.

We had four police army people just bristling with rifles, swords and all kinds of things.

Q: Well, it was dangerous to travel through the countryside.

Adm. B.: That's the idea. So, up we went. These were stone steps I don't know how high it was; a few thousand feet perhaps. It was very exhausting. We climbed up with these armed guards and met the person in charge of the monastery and had some tea with him and then we bid him goodbye and down we went. That was almost as difficult as going up. That was quite an incident and the fact of the armed guards is an evidence of how unruly things were or they thought they were.

Q: What was the general attitude of the native Chinese? Toward Americans?

Adm. B.: Fine as far as I could tell. However, there is another good point. There was extraterritoriality out there everywhere in all of the so-called treaty ports. They would include all of the ports I've mentioned, Hankow was another. In all of these ports the customs service was run by the British. There was nothing that a non-Chinese could do which the native police would object to. Exclude the Russians because they were not recognized as a government by anyone. There was nothing that a non-Chinese could do that would be so bad that a Chinese policeman would even consider arresting him. Never even think about it. Maybe outside these ports they'd more than think about it. Down in Shanghai and in Hong Kong most of the police that we saw were Sikhs. The north Indians. The mode of transportation (actually there were some automobiles) was the rickshaw. For instance, up in Chefoo and in Tsingtao as an Ensign in the U. S. Navy, I arrived at Chefoo. Immediately some Chinese fellow with a rickshaw wants to be hired by me. Everyone had his own rickshaw and rickshaw boy. Every time I came ashore there he was sitting ready to take me anywhere. I paid him, I don't know what it would be, I imagine the equivalent of five U. S. dollars for a month.

Q: That's what he lived on?

Adm. B.: That's what he lived on. Correct. If he didn't get a steady customer he didn't get any business. Everyone had a rickshaw. We used to race up and down the beach. That is us young bachelors. We'd have a good race and then--of course the rickshaw coolies wouldn't get any refreshment after the race. We'd go into

Benson #2 - 80-

Chefoo Club and the fellow who owned the rickshaw who'd done the worst paid for the beers. But I fooled them. I brought some grease and oil and all that sort of thing, and paint from the ship. One afternoon we proceeded to take that rickshaw of his apart and grease up all of the bearings and that sort of thing. So, that rickshaw was as light as a feather. If that fellow coul run faster than the rest of them he'd win. But he didn't have anything holding him back. We never lost. I never bought the beer.

The best way to be a tourist, this is true in all sorts of things, is to be attached to a ship and the ship go somewhere. Because then, when the ship gets there you put on your glad-rags and you hit the beach and at the end of maneuvers ashore you go back to your nice clean ship and your own accommodations.

Q: And this is contrast with land travel.

Adm. B.: That's right. This is magnificent even in the tourist right today. My wife and I have made several of these trips where you get on board the ship and the ship goes somewhere, you go ashore and you come back.

Q: That's your hotel?

Adm. B.: Yes, but be attached to one of these ships for three years and have the ship go everywhere. On one trip we went as far up the river that goes by Tientsin and Peking as we could and there we went along side of a pier. Then we went to Peking by train and went up and looked at the Great Wall. We went absolutely everywhere. We went to Hangchow. We went to Tsingtao. We went to all of these places and even Canton. We were down to Singapore and we went to a place then called Batavia which was part of the Dutch East Indies now called Djakarta on the island of Java in Indonesia. And we went to several of the biggest cities of the Philippines including Zamboanga, Iloilo, Cebu, Subic and of course Manila, and up to Baguio.

You know, there was a floating drydock at Olongapo. Olongapo is up in Subic Bay where we now have a Naval Air Station. Subic is the next bay to the north of Manila Bay. That floating drydock, the Dewey Drydock, was built on the east coast of the United States and was towed all the way across the Atlantic, around the south end of Africa, and all the way up to the Philippines and there she was in Subic Bay.

Q: Capable of taking how large a vessel?

Adm. B.: Our destroyers and the submarines. I don't know whether it would take a cruiser or not. But, there it was and surprising enough it was built in three parts, and any two parts could drydock the third part. So, it dry-docked itself to scrape off barnacles and repaint. There are two things you're trying to do with underwater painting. You put on antifouling paint that has poison in it that will repel and destroy the barnacles, but you also paint with rust inhibitant.

Q: That was a big problem for the Navy for many years, wasn't it? Development for ships' bottoms?

Adm. B.: Oh yes, and the barnacles building up on your hull will slow you down tremendously.

Q: In what period of time would they build up?

Adm. B.: If you stay in salt water and particularly if you're in the tropics, if you are capable of making twenty knots with a clean bottom, I dare say at the end of two years you're probably making sixteen using the same energy. Now, however, if you're so fortunate as to go and spend some time in fresh water, like way up the Yangtze River, and various places where there is fresh water, barnacles don't like fresh water. They die and drop off. You recover some of your speed.

Q: The improvement in paint was due largely to old Henry Williams, did you know him?

Adm. B.: Yes, I remember him very well.

Q: He made this a special study. Now, you mentioned going to various places and being a sightseer, also in a sense an ambassador of the U. S. What provision was made for the crew, the enlisted men? Were they instructed as to what they might expect when they went ashore? Were they given any particular attention in this area?

Adm. B.: Not a great deal that I recall. I would have known about it. No, they just went ashore on their own. We went ashore on our own also. There was always something to see everywhere. But there wasn't very much of anything to do.

Q: No, but the things to see, were they informed in advance of what was to be seen?

Adm. B.: There was no program like now on board cruise ships advertised by travel agencies. Some places there was a YMCA and certain of the crew would go over there and they would know things. I know that up in Chefoo I went on several day-time tours in which they had several old broken down buses that took us to look at various things in and about the city. Quite a few of the enlisted men took advantage of that YMCA organization.

Q: Now, what does the communication and commissary officer do? What are some of the things that get into his life?

Adm. B.: You recall that I had been in the communication business that battleship and I got into the same business on board this ship. You also recall that I said we conducted the same exercise on our ships out there as were conducted in the rest of the Navy. One of those that affected me most was the communication competition. Once a year, if I remember correctly, at least once a year they used to have tests that we would compete in. When I got to that destroyer I was not only the radio officer, I was also the signal officer, I was also the code and cipher officer. All of the rated enlisted men (radiomen) had to be test to see how well they could do in sending and receiving of radio messages like telegraph. Messages were transmitted to them and they transcribed them. Also they had to transmit, again like telegraph. The radio officer was also tested and he was tested at the same speed as third class radiomen. This made the communication officer (radio officer) on every one of these destroyers all through the whole Navy learn how to send radio and receive radio and be able to do it well. You know that one of the basic elements of leadership is, if your mark and your crew mark are going to add together for the ship's mark, you must make sure that your performance is at least as good as the average of the enlisted men. In other words, you're not going to pull down their marks. You have got to make sure that your performance does not pull down the scores; that would be poor leadership.

Okay, we covered radio, now we get into signals. The same thing, the officer has to be tested as if he were a signalman third class. In what? Semaphore, receiving and sending flashing light same as the Morse Code. Flashing light, receiving and sending. Then, remember the signal flags flying from the halyard up there? All right, we had a general signal book which gave meaning for various flags. For instance if you want to change course to such and such there are certain signal flags that you put up. When you pull them down the ships do it. You could also transmit message of certain stereotyped form by signal flags. They test your ship in this also. They raise the hoist on another ship and within forty-five seconds from the time they have it all the way up you must have read it and explained to the examiner what it meant.

Q: The examiner being somebody from another ship?

Adm. B.: All 19 destroyers out there were in a destroyer squadron. The squadron communication officer presided over these tests.

Q: They took one ship at a time?

Adm. B.: Yes, they took one ship at a time. The squadron communications officer with help from ships' communication officers would examine your outfit and assign a score. The result was your ship's standing in communications in competition with every similar ship in the Navy.

Q: How often were they given?

Adm. B.: At least once a year. I don't know if you know a retired admiral over here by the name of Brook Schum. He and I were always vying for first place in the Asiatic Fleet in the communication competition.

We had the same thing with torpedo firing and gunnery firing and in engineering. In engineering the competition was based on energy saving. How many miles did you steam on a certain quantity of fuel. Very complicated. Also breakdowns, they affected your score.

There was one very interesting phenomenon that I'd never heard of: a casualty "real or imagined." In other words, if you shut down your engines because you thought something was wrong and nothing was wrong you would still get a penalty. There was a penalty because you stopped doing something with that engine which you were supposed to be doing.

Q: Under false premise?

Adm. B.: It was okay, therefore you fixed it quickly because there was nothing to fix. The fixing time was zero. But the time it took you to find out there was nothing wrong, that counted. Otherwise, if there was something wrong, how long did it take you to fix it? This all went into the score. Again, this competition was very keen. As with all ship's functions the competition reflected in the fitness reports of the commanding officer of the ship and his heads of departments. In other words, if the engineering plant of your ship did poorly in the engineering competition, that's one reason you don't like that engineering officer that they gave you. He needs some guidance from you so that he and his people will do better. This applied to all the competitions throughout the Navy. They kept us on our toes.

Q: Did they have at that time the system of E-awards?

Adm. B.: Oh yes. E-awards came from these competitions. If you could have painted "E" on the smokestack or on the guns, etc., it was certainly "excellent." Of course, there was always people who want to beat the game.

Q: And do!

Adm. B.: They do indeed. There were two kinds. One kind was, I believe, perfectly all right. It is the careful reader of the rules governing the competition and taking advantage of fine print, etc.--what many people refer to as "loopholes" in income tax returns. It gives an advantage to the person who tries harder, is more thorough.

The other kind of "beating the game" was out and out cheating; manufacturing a gear wheel with one more tooth than the one it replaces so that it is registered that your ship went 105 miles when, in fact, it went 100 miles. This would be deliberate cheating. There were few, if any, of this kind of "beating the game." The competition throughout the Navy and in as many as practicable of a ship's functions were good for us. We are a competitive people. It inspires us to try harder.

Perhaps we have covered my duties as communications officer, particularly the competitions. The everyday duties were rather obvious.

Should I explain some of the duties relating to my duties as commissary officer?

Q: Please do.

Adm. B.: The duties related to feeding the officers and crew of the ship.

The Navy's Bureau of Supplies and Accounts in Washington, D.C., submitted budget and received funds to feed the Navy's personnel. Instructions were issued which allowed a certain amount of expenditures by each type of ship per man per day. Monthly commissary returns were submitted by the commanding officer of each ship to the "bureau" in Washington. Overspending was not permitted. Under-spending gave the ship a cushion to use in following months.

The ship obtained its food by purchase from a naval store activity, a supply ship, some other ship and in the civilian market. Very little of the purchase was by money. It was by paperwork, but it amounted to the same. In the Asiatic Fleet we obtained food from our destroyer tender, other ships or purchase on the local markets in the various Chinese cities.

The commissary officer of a destroyer was responsible to his commanding officer for appropriate feeding of the crew and the related paperwork. He could be rather certain that the enlisted men under his command would do a fine job of obtaining the supplies and feeding the crew, but he had to depend on himself relative to the monthly reports and not overspending. His commanding officer was depending on him. If you let him down you were not being loyal.

When you were at places where we could obtain supplies from our destroyer tender and other Navy sources, the process was quite simple. In places like Foochow, Amoy, Swatow, Nanking we had to buy our supplies ashore from Chinese merchants.

Q: So you had to bargain from the local market?

Adm. B.: Yes. From the local market. The chief commissary steward, the chief petty officer (an expert in this sort of business) and the commissary officer would proceed ashore. You had made up a list of what you want to buy and then you go over and get these people to bid on them. And they bid on the individual items. You had to get at least three bids on each of the items. So you'd look over the various produce. We'd buy things like tomatoes, and cucumbers and other produce but also bread.

Q: On the basis of three bids?

Adm. B.: Yes.

Q: But you couldn't go directly to one stall and buy? You had to go to three or more different stalls and get their prices?

Adm. B.: You had quite a few copies of your shopping list and you'd go around to a store and look at their produce. You wouldn't let them bid on an item unless that item looked pretty good. If they had some old rotten-looking tomatoes you wouldn't let them bid. They didn't have to bid on everything. We used to buy bread over there in the same way.

Q: You could vary the diet, then, and if you're a good bargainer you provide a superior table, couldn't you?

Adm. B.: Yes; we used to do the best we could. Of course, the first thing merchants wanted to do as soon as you arrived was to try to ply you with strong drink which you, obviously, would turn down. You'd have no strong drink 'cause you're going to keep yourself in good shape to get some proper bids.

Q: What was their strong drink?

Adm. B.: What they offered us was not native. They probably had some Scotch waiting to give us if they could. I doubt if their motives were other than hospitality. However, business is business

Q: The Orientials didn't generally drink, did they?

Adm. B.: No. They drank their own sort of rice wine. They would always say "gambe" (bottoms up) but you don't want to do that. You don't want to go out on official business of this kind and drink anything anyhow. So, you'd get all these bids and you'd get all this food. These were in specific quantities. When you were ready to leave that port you'd get their bills. Their bills would be made out in Chinese currency. Generally what you'd do was to turn the bills over to the U. S. Consul. The U. S. Consul would then pay the bills.

Q: For the ship?

Adm. B.: For the ship, for the United States. When you came to make up your commissary return at the end of the month you'd make that up in U. S. dollars. But these bills were in Chinese money. Now, how much did you really pay for them, what was the rate of exchange when the consul paid the bills?

Q: Well it was fluctuating quite a bit wasn't it?

Adm. B.: Fluctuating every day. So, what would you do? The U.S. consul would pay them when he wanted to pay them (most favorable to the United States) and send those papers back to Washington. They would send the papers over to the Navy Department. We would receive a copy of the consul's voucher so that we would know what he paid. But when would we get it? Well, maybe he paid the bill next month. Maybe he paid it when the exchange rate was most favorable. Anyhow, what we did at the end of the month was to assume the rate of exchange. We would guess at it as best we could and make the reports up based on that. Sometimes we would have been to Amoy; we may have been to Foochow; we may have been to Nanking. We might have two or three of these in one month's commissary returns. We would assume what the rate of exchange was and make up our returns based on it. Then, when we finally received the voucher showing what they paid, we would make an adjustment. In other words, we sent a correction to that old report. Now, the thing that amazes me the most about this was that here I was, the junior officer on board the ship, and I made these reports up and brought them in once a month for the captain to sign. He signed, and off they went, and no one checked what I was doing until the papers all got to Washington, and there they checked. No one checked me on it at all.

Obviously, if I had made mistakes the commanding officer would be informed from Washington and he would have given me some guidance.

Q: It's interesting. Now it occurs to me, as you tell this story, that the person who really suffered was the small merchant who had a stand at the market. He couldn't afford to carry all this for a month, could he? He should have been awarded money immediately, out of your pocket.

Adm. B.: You made a good point that I had never heard before. Obviously, at my level, we followed regulations. Now there was another little wrinkle out there called a special disbursing agent. SDA, special disbursing agent. If we were going to be gone from our destroyer tender or any supply corps disbursing office long enough so that payday would appear, and it would usually appear, someone on board the ship, namely "George" would be designated special disbursing agent. How did you choose the officer on board the ship to be the special disbursing agent? The person who had the communication ciphers and codes; he had the big safe in the wardroom. He had it because we had all these secret codes and ciphers. All kinds of classified material was in this safe. If you're going to have official money on board, you'd better give it to the officer who has the safe.

So, on this particular ship, which was probably true on most of them, the junior officer became the special disbursing agent. I was give instruction by the supply officer on board the destroyer tender who had cognizance over our matters. I'd get a list from him of all the people in the crew and how much they should get on payday. He'd give me this list, a modest amount of American money, and then he would give me a paper called "bill of exchange" and I would go over to the bank. I would obtain Chinese money. The Chinese money I obtained was in silver dollars and was called Mex. Many of those silver dollars actually said Republic of Mexico on them. Apparently Chiang-kai-shek's government somehow had purchased great quantities of Mexican coins before they got around to coin their own. They were the size of our silver dollars and you got them over in the bank.

If the members of the crew had indicated I could give them all their pay in American money, in Chinese money, or a mixture. But I had to find that out before I went to the bank.

Chinese money would be in straw bags. I don't know how many coins there were in each bag. They counted them by weighing them. When you bought something with one of those coins they would throw it on the counter and hear it ring or they'd try chewing on it.

Q: To see if it was valid?

Adm. B.: Try to see if it was really proper 'cause sometimes the counterfeiters made them out of lead and put a little silver plate on them and try to get rid of them.

You'd then take all of this money with you and when it came time to have payday you'd proceed to pay them what they were supposed to have. We used to advise them that generally they should not draw more money than they really need. It was better to leave it on the books than to draw more than you really need because of possible thievery. Because I owned the safe I was also authorized to hold on deposit certain of this money. Later if the person wanted some or all of his money he could have it.

Q: You had to be a banker and maintain separate accounts?

Adm. B.: That's right. I had to maintain separate accounts. When I drew this money and got it out to the ship I immediately made up envelopes, one envelope for each individual. Then he could have as much out of that envelope as he wanted. The rest of it went back into the safe.

Q: That was a time-consuming job, wasn't it?

Adm. B.: Yes and I had a few other things to do.

Obviously then, another by-product, and I'm not sure if they did this on all the ships, it's very nice, you know, when you're in a foreign country, if you're going to write a letter home, you can put a local stamp on it instead of mailing it by a U. S. system whereby it might end up with a U. S. stamp. To put on a Chinese stamp, that's pretty neat. So, I sold Chinese stamps and Philippine stamps; stamps of the country where we were. I also could exchange money. If we arrived in Hong Kong I went over and got some Hong Kong money and I was the money changer. They could also go ashore themselves and exchange money. I always had some that I could exchange money for.

Q: Not only was it time-consuming but it was a real responsibility

Adm. B.: When I think back on it I am absolutely startled that an Ensign or a Junior Grade seagoing sailor man line officer had this kind of responsibility. I would have thought that if you're going to have that sort of thing you'd at least give the job to a Lieutenant, but the only Lieutenant we had was the Executive Officer. But, these kinds of responsibilities startle me really when I think of it.

Q: Well, it's part of training, isn't it?

Adm. B.: Tremendous training. You remember that I mentioned that many years before I had taken a commercial course in high school. I mentioned that I found it very convenient. I certainly did. That I had had bookkeeping in high school was tremendous in these jobs that I found myself in.

Q: This went on for three years?

Adm. B.: For three years. Those three years were not devoted entirely to communications and commissary. We had courses on board these ships that had been prepared by the Navy. When I first arrived on board not only did I become communications and commissary officer but the skipper decided that I should take the engineer's course. That was a course for makee learn to become engineering officer of a four-pipe destroyer.

Q: Now, does this say that in that day the Navy didn't have the extensive schools that they have now on shore?

Adm. B.: That's right, hardly any.

Q: It was all on board ship?

Adm. B.: Almost all.

Q: There were little schools on board ship.

Adm. B.: There certainly were, but not really formal enough to warrant the name "school."

We had courses on board ship and you had to have someone on board each of these four-pipe destroyers, in addition to the engineering officer, who was either taking the engineering course or had finished it. Similarly, there was a course for torpedo officer, there was a course for gunnery officer. One of the first things that happened to me, when I'd come aboard and I'd gotten these two jobs, communications and commissary, I was "volunteered" to take the prospective engineering officers course. So, I started taking this course and was amazed at how complete it was. Sometime during those three years I took all of them. I took the engineering course, I took the torpedo course, and I took the gunnery course. There was also first lieutenant course, which I took. What did first lieutenant mean?

The first lieutenant was the officer in charge generally of the upkeep, repair, cleanliness, and so forth in eveything but the engineering spaces. He was responsible for all the rest of it. The anchor gear, boats, etc. all belonged to the first lieutenant.

Q: Was there any attempt to combine training in special areas with the training of men from several ships?

Adm. B.: No.

Q: If you had a particularly good instructor was there not some thought of combining the classes?

Adm. B.: Well, we didn't have that. We did not have instructors as such. There were study courses for all our enlisted men and before they could be considered for promotion, even back in those days, they had to take the course for the next step up.

Q: But it seems to me that since it was done on individual ships that there must have been a great difference in the end product.

Adm. B.: Bound to be. In some ships, you know very well, there would be a rather poor training program. Poor in some of them and excellent in others. I believe it depended more on the student than it did on anything else. The student, whether this was the young officer, Ensign, taking the prospective engineer's course or a radioman second class studying the radioman's first class course, there wasn't an instructor. The book was the instructor. If he didn't have the get-up-and-go to study and learn it, obviously he wasn't doing very well, and when he came up for examination for promotion he would fail. If he finished the course, he'd probably do very well on the exam also. If he didn't do the course very well, he probably wouldn't be promoted. It was really up to the individual. That was true also in our officer's course on board the ship. The individual's supervisor could be a big help.

I took all of these courses. I figured this was what I was supposed to do, so I was a busy young fellow.

Q: Obviously you were. Do you want to talk for a moment about the discipline on shore? What about the crew members when they had leave on shore? Was there a shore patrol?

Adm. B.: Yes, we had a permanent shore patrol on Shanghai. There was a permanent shore patrol in Manila. Permanent cadre and each ship would be required to produce certain numbers of personnel to augment the permanent cadre. They came back when liberty was up and went ashore when liberty started. There was no overnight liberty. Shore patrol always made contact with the local police. In small cities like Amoy, Swatow, Foochow, we wouldn't have an actual shore patrol; merely make good contact with the local police. The system worked well.

Q: Did the men get into great difficulties on occasion?

Adm. B.: Not really great difficulties. In Chefoo shore patrol was one officer and a few enlisted men from one of the ships. I had it once there for a week in Chefoo. A young Chinese officer and I each had a rickshaw. We would drive around town and we'd go in and look around all the various cabarets. There was a lot in Chefoo, Tsingtao, and Shanghai, all these big cities, the cities that were accustomed to having our forces around.

They always had a lot of five cents a dance places, bars, and all kinds of things. That was something to do and whether you did it in moderation was up to you.

Q: What was the extent of venereal disease and that sort of thing?

Adm. B.: There wasn't much because in places like Chefoo, Shanghai, Tsingtao, places that we were accustomed to being there was a red light district and every entrance and exit was barricaded except one. Any person who tried to get out of that district got a prophylactic for venereal disease even if he'd gone in just to pick the flowers. No great difficulties because there was a lot of emphasis on taking care of yourself.

Q: What was the role of the chaplain in the fleet at this point in time?

Adm. B.: We had for the destroyer force, the destroyer tender and nineteen destroyers, one chaplain. He was on board the destroyer tender. I remember this fellow particularly well, he was a Roman Catholic, he was a Lieutenant Junior Grade. He had a real hard time getting us to go to his church but he was a real good guy and if anyone wanted to shoot pool, play softball or something why he was right in there. He was very popular with all of us and I'm sure he did a good job in religious matters for those who wanted his services. The fact that he was a pleasant person was important but I recall that his performance in advising people and carrying out more formal roles of the priest was also excellent. I assume that other chaplains did likewise. My opinion of chaplains in the Navy has been most favorable. I recall when we were in one of the Chinese ports and there was a French ship there. The word came over from the French ship that invited officers and crew to come over for divine services on Sunday morning. So, the captain said, "Now, let's see, we've been invited and this is going to be a Roman Catholic service on board this French ship at eleven o'clock on Sunday morning. Any volunteers?" No hands.

The skipper said, "Well, you know very well we're not going to say 'No thank you.' We're going to say, 'Yes, thank you.' We need to have two officers and half a dozen enlisted men to go to church."

The skipper then asked what our denominations were and there was an officer by the name of "Dutch" Deutermann who was Roman Catholic. Does that name ring a bell?

Q: Yes.

Adm. B.: Harold something Deutermann, "Dutch" Deutermann. He was on this destroyer and when we first started out he and I were the bachelors on board. Then he got married.

On this particular occasion--Dutch Deutermann was a Roman Catholic. So when the captain found out that Dutch Deutermann was he said, "Dutch, she's yours and you need another officer to go."

So, I put my hand in the air, I might as well because I was going to get told. We went and where in the world Dutch Deutermann got the half dozen enlisted men I don't know. Maybe all of them wanted to go.

Off we went and we had a great time for, on that French ship after church, they fed us lunch and supplied us with wine and so forth. We had a great time. I think others missed out on a good party.

Q: What about organized sports in the fleet?

Adm. B.: Oh yes, we had organized sports. We had competition in pulling boats. We had on board each ship one lifeboat. It was made like a lifeboat and actually instead of having a tiller it had a steering oar. The person in the stern steered with a huge oar. Strangely enough there were three oars on one side and two on the other. I guess that was because he had a steering oar and also propelled. We would have competition between all of the destroyers. I don't know what they did in the submarine business. We also had basketball teams. We had softball teams. I remember well that we had soccer teams. Everywhere we went, and this is true in the world today, if you have a soccer team on board your ship you'll always get a game because soccer is played all over the world. Every little kid everywhere in other parts of the world plays soccer. They call it football. All you need to play it is a ball.

On one particular occasion it had gotten up to the point in soccer where there were two ships that were going to fight it out for the championship of the destroyer squadron. Naturally, being George, I was the athletic officer on board the ship. I was in charge of the sports.

Q: Did this include being a coach as well?

Adm B.: Well no, I didn't have to coach them. No one did. I remember refereeing a basketball game down in Manila once and I didn't know any more about basketball officiating than nothing.

But on this particular occasion in Chefoo we were playing for the squadron championship of the destroyers in soccer. You remember my classmate Jerry O'Donnell? Well Jerry O'Donnell, he was George on one of the other destroyers. Neither one of our teams had done very well so our teams weren't involved in this championship. We were told to be the officials. Neither one of us knew very much about soccer but we figured that the rules that applied to basketball ought to be pretty good so we started playing.

Gee, they played and played and nobody could score. Finally we called them all together and we said, "We've been playing for about forty-five minutes; we propose that we have a sudden death. We're now going to start playing. We're going to have no timeouts. We just keep on playing until somebody scores. When that somebody scores, he wins, the game is over."

They thought that was great. You know, strangely enough, it lasted only about two or three minutes. They wanted to get out of there too.

So Jerry O'Donnell and I umpired. We did not have organized sports but we did have sports.

Benson #2 -109-

Q: But there was emphasis on it?

Adm. B.: Oh yes. Find out where there's a softball field, get your teams over there and start playing. That's great stuff.

To the north of Manila there is a place called Baguio which is a beautiful resort. It was up high and therefore it was cool but the sun was hot so you'd better keep yourself covered. That was magnificent for getting out and playing golf.

Q: We've reached the year 1934. You're about to leave the Far East and you were to report at the submarine school in New London, Connecticut. Will you tell me about your trip there by way of Suez and other places?

Adm. B.: Yes. You recall that in 1931 I came out on a Dollar Steamship Company's ship and it went to various places and I got off in Manila. Strangely enough, three years later, I was going to go back to New London, Connecticut, and I was to go via the Pacific and by train to New London. I requested permission to take myself home via the Suez and Europe at no additional expense to the government. I had had no vacation for the three years I was out there. So, I had three months' vacation on the books.

Q: You had a travel lust?

Adm.B.: That's right. So, I got on a Dollar Steamship Company ship at Manila, where I'd gotten off three years earlier and away we went. You recall those ships carried a lot of cargo and carried passengers, and when they went to a port they were usually there about three days. This was excellent.

From Manila we went to Singapore and then Penang in Malaya, and then to Colombo, Ceylon. Outside of Colombo there is a place called Kandy where Buddha's tooth is on exhibit and where I rode an elephant with one of these fancy elephant hats. Then we left there and went up to Bombay where I had a chance to observe a fight between a mongoose and a cobra. We went to the Zoroaster funeral place; and rode around in a Victoria, having a great time. We came up the Red Sea. One Sunday was Easter.

Q: It wasn't really observed in that part of the world, was it?

Adm. B.: No, but this was on board a ship. On board this ship coming up the Red Sea, Easter occurred. There was a clergyman on board and he was going to have divine services. I think probably he was a Roman Catholic. He asked me if I would help him. What I was supposed to help him do was at certain times I was supposed to ring a little bell. We were both dressed in vestments of some kind.

Q: You were an altar boy, an acolyte.

Adm. B.: Suddenly it occurred to me that I had lost track of my bell. I didn't know where it was, but fortunately I found it before the magic words for me to ring the bell were spoken.

So we proceeded up through the Suez Canal and I got off at Port Said, the northernmost point of the Suez Canal. I had hand luggage and no itinerary; no hotel reservations and no travel reservations. So I proceeded to such places as Cairo and I spent about a week up in the Holy Land; Damascus and all over the place. And a place called Jaffa, which used to be called Joppa. Jonah left from there and had his adventure with the whale.

Q: Did you have any difficulty with the language in all these places?

Adm. B.: No difficulty at all. I became a good friend of some missionaries coming home on board our ship and were going to the Holy Land so I went with them. They had hired a tourist company representative to show them around. So, I went with them and stayed at the same pension and this Arab guide and I became friends; he wore a fez with a business suit. I got a fez and wore it with my business suit. We wandered all over the Holy Land. I remember on one occasion we were stopped and he said, "Come on, get out here fast! Here come some tourists." He had an old carpet and he laid it on the street. We got out there, the tourists stopped the bus and got out with their cameras and they took pictures of us praying toward Mecca. They took movies of us and I wonder who has the beautiful movies. Obviously, I was another Arab in my fez.

I got on board a ship at Alexandria that went up to Istanbul, Rhodes, and we went to Athens. We went everywhere. I got off this ship in Italy and went up through Naples, Rome, Florence, Vienna, Venice and Berlin to Copenhagen. I have first cousins who live in the south-central part of Sweden. My mother's sister was still living and I went up to see them. Then I went to Stockholm and then down to Copenhagen again. That time I went to visit second cousins who were living at Elsinor, near Hamlet's Castle, just a very short distance from Copenhagen. Finally I got on board the German ship BREMEN and came across the Atlantic.

Q: That was quite a "cook's tour" wasn't it?

Adm. B.: Yes indeed. What an adventure! The BREMEN was completely full of Hitler youth on their way to the Chicago World's Fair.

Q: Oh, really?

Adm. B.: Three young German fellows and I had a room together. The four of us and four German girls ate together in the dining room. Every evening after dinner we would gather around and wear our hats as if we were Heidelberg college guys. We would drink beer and we'd sing songs by the hour. I was disappointed that the trip lasted only four days and nights. I would have liked to have stayed about a year. That was a very delightful cruise.

Q: Yes, because of the companions.

Adm. B.: They were great; no politics. The ship's engineer showed me all through the engineering plant. There wasn't time enough.

When I arrived in New York, I went up to New London, Connecticut. I arrived up there in about early May. But, submarine school wasn't going to start until the day after the fourth of July. So, what do with me? I was attached to a submarine USS R-14.

Q: With any specific duties?

Adm. B.: Well, the only other officer on board was the captain and he was a Lieutenant by the name of M. M. Dana, D-A-N-A. The only other officer attached had just been detached. So I became the only officer that "Heavy" Dana had on board his submarine.

Q: Why would you call him, "Heavy?"

Adm. B.: That was his nickname. We had, I would say, maybe, twenty-five, maybe thirty-man crew. These were little submarines. The purpose of those submarines was to take students, both officers and enlisted, out for training. So, I found myself second in command of a submarine taking students out for training and I hadn't been to submarine school yet.

Q: But, you learned quickly?

Adm. B.: Well, it was great, positively great. "Heavy" Dana and I became the finest of friends. Naturally we were very close. You'd have to be if you are the only two officers on board ship.

What jobs did I have? I had all the jobs. I was engineer officer. I was the diving officer. Well there was everything. "Heavy" Dana was everything and I was his assistant.

The submarine school was magnificient. That was a great experience. There were thirty-six members in my class. I was the senior of the students.

Q: Would you tell me about the R-boats? They were quite old, they dated from the 1920's, did they not?

Adm. B.: Yes, they were built, oh I would say, I doubt if they were built before World War I, but they were certainly built shortly after. They were probably part of a building program that was started up because we got into World War I. They were, maybe, a hundred and fifty feet long. They displaced something on the order of four hundred tons.

Q: Were they Holland Boats?

Adm. B.: Yes. They were Holland Boats. Let me state that I am continually amazed at your knowledge. They were built by the Electric Boat Company in New London, Connecticut. Their diesel engines were also built by that company. The engines were called Nelsecos. But they were built right there. You could not back down on them. I'm thinking now. Yes, you could not back down. Before you backed down what you needed to do was to ring up "all stop" and instantly the people on the controls down below would not only stop, but they would put in some pins which made it impossible to move them into reverse. They automatically shifted to electric battery power. From then on until you said, "Get ready on engine such-and-such," otherwise you were on batteries with electric motors with the same propellers.

You ring up "all stop" and they'll say "All stop, pins in." And they've got the pins in and you can't back down. Cause otherwise you'll have cast iron thrown all over the engine room.

Toilet facilities on board that ship consisted of one place and a person could stand throttle watch on the main engines and still be going to the bathroom. There were no bathing facilities on board at all.

Matter of fact when I reported to the R-14 we were just finishing a shipyard overhaul at the Electric Boat Company in New London and the ship didn't look very good. No ship in a shipyard overhaul looks very good, but this submarine looked worse. Someone pointed to my "pride and joy" and said, "Do you think you're going to be able to salvage that wreck?" Obviously

I didn't like that cause this was my pride and joy. You have got to feel this ship is the most important thing in the world. Really got to feel this! This is very important. In order to run things properly you've got to have enthusiasm for your job and consider that no assignment could be better--until you go to the next one. Then you transfer the whole business right there.

These submarines operated only for training at submarine school. When we got into World War II we brought in an older type of the O-boats. I think the R-boats were transferred from there down to Panama at the beginning of World War II and continued to operate.

We had a positively great time going to submarine school. The instruction was magnificient.

Q: How long a period was it?

Adm. B.: It was almost six months, about five months, July to December just before Christmas. We took diesel engineering. We took electricity including the storage battery. We took torpedoes. We took the principles of how to control a submarine. The compensation. For instance, when you take on a thousand pounds of food you have to pump out a thousand pounds of water. You have to keep yourself compensated, not only overall weight but fore and aft trim so that when you go to sea and you sound the diving alarm you go down and if you've done the compensation properly you will end up in a perfect trim, you are being buoyed up with the same amount of force that the weight of the submarine is being held down, but also you have a fore and aft trim. You're not heavy fore or aft. I can't imagine a more thorough school because we studied all these things and it was a great community. You had thirty-six students in a class and you're doing important things and interesting things. You go out there on submarines and actually do things, that's great! I enjoyed that thoroughly.

Having just come back from China obviously, I was full of China stories, as you can imagine. I was full of China stories and I used to bend the ears of those other thirty-five students, none of whom had been to China. And about half a dozen of them requested to be sent out to China. But, I had the same experience when I was teaching at the Naval Academy. I got a lot of those people to get into the submarine business cause I used to splash salt water and battery acid all over the classroom, figuratively speaking.

Q: I expect you were a good exponent of all these things.

Adm. B.: Oh yes. I have always been enthusiastic. You've got to do this. When we finished submarine school I wanted to go back to Hawaii because I had had two wonderful weeks on the way to China. I got orders and drove across the country and got on a luxury liner going out to Hawaii. Out we went and I became attached to a much larger submarine, but small in today's submarines, of course. This was the USS S-42.

Q: The S-boats?

Adm. B.: Yes, the old S-boats.

Q: They were an improvement over the R-boats though.

Adm. B.: They were a considerable improvement. Instead of being about a hundred and seventy-five feet long they were about two hundred and twenty-five, if I remember correctly. They were longer and they were heavier, they had more battery power. They still had two engines and the engines were Nelseco engines, perhaps more powerful than the ones we had on the R-boats but the same company.

We ran into an interesting phenomenon there I hadn't heard of yet relative to diesel engines; maybe this is true of all engines. When you're running at a certain speed there are vibrations such that if you are not careful you might shear off your propeller shaft. I hadn't heard about this in the R-boats. They probably had it in the R's, but in the S's through the whole range of speeds of the engines about half of it was in critical ranges. When you're speeding up to go from one to the other you went through the critical range rapidly. You didn't hesitate there. You went from one speed of the engine up to the next one as quickly as you could. Naturally the reason that I became so familiar with this, when I reported on board the R-14, was that I became the engineering officer who was also the diving officer. I forgot to mention that at New London, Connecticut they had the great big tower. They also have one in Pearl Harbor submarine base. That tower is a hundred-foot-tall cylinder of water. What you learn there is how to get out of a submarine that cannot surface.

Q: This is a safety measure?

Adm. B.: This is a safety measure and the Momsen Lung was what we were using at that time.

Q: Oh it was in being at that time?

Adm. B.: That's right. M-O-M-S-E-N, "Swede" Momsen. We were taught there how to use this Momsen Lung. This was, really, a rescue breathing apparatus in which you could breath in and out while you were down in the water.

Q: It also proved to be a morale builder to think that you could do.

Adm. B.: They also trained us first to learn it a little bit and to go down to a little bit. Before you finished your training you came all the way up from a hundred feet. You'd go through the door lock coming out at the bottom and you would come up with the Momsen Lung all the way up. You were supposed to keep yourself from popping up. What you want to do is hold yourself down.

Q: So you avoid the bends.

Adm. B.: Yes, because if you just go ahead and pop to the surface you are apt to get the bends; the nitrogen bubbles in your blood stream. If you come up more slowly your system will be able to absorb the nitrogen bubbles as they are formed instead of causing a blockage in one of your veins or arteries. We had very extensive training and there was a very important psychologic thing here. People often times ask, "Don't you have claustrophobia in this iron box down under the water?"

Q: And the atmosphere was not very good?

Adm. B.: No.

I'd say, "No, you can't go through the training with that hun foot tank and the Momsen Lung, you cannot successfully do that if you get claustrophobia."

You haven't got stability enough to serve in a submarine, if you could not come up in that 100 foot tank.

Q: Was there any test at the beginning of a man's training in submarines which would eliminate a man who was afflicted with this?

Adm. B.: Not really. When you requested to go to submarine school you had to get a physical examination by a physician, a Navy physician, and he would turn in the regulations to the proper page and make sure that he checks you on items having to do with submarine training as it was with aviation training. You had to take a special exam. But it wasn't psychological. That psychological business, I believe, was taken care of by the training in escape with a Momsen Lung.

Q: It was a great factor, I've heard submariners say.

Adm. B.: Officers and enlisted personnel get into submarines by requesting it and being chosen.

Q: It's a volunteer service?

Adm. B.: That's right. People ask for it. It's more than that; volunteer means to me that we've got something awful to do and we need some volunteers. We are talking about people of their own desire asking for this duty. There are still two ways to get out of the submarine even in the middle of World War II. If you were attached to a submarine and did not want to be there, all you had to do was either ask to get out or do a no-good job. Either one would get you out. That refers to all the officers and all the enlisted men. You do a no-good job and they're not going to put up with you very long.

Q: Well, that pertains in other parts of the service, too.

Adm. B.: Certainly, except that when you enlist you have a certain obligation, but if you get into the submarine business you can get out right away if you want to get out of the submarine business.

You'll be in some other part of the Navy, but you don't have to be in the submarine business.

Maybe there are times when people are assigned to submarines, but I'm not aware of it. Naturally there were people drafted into the Navy during various periods of time, World War II and so forth. Then they ask for submarine duty. They were never drafted directly to submarine duty.

Q: Well, another incentive was additional pay.

Adm. B.: That's right. There was additional pay.

Q: In the old days in the R-boats and the S-boats you got additional pay for every time you dove.

Adm. B.: That's right, I'm surprised that you've heard of it. They used to get a dollar a dive. I never knew of that one; that was before my time. We used to get (the aviators got fifty percent), we got twenty-five percent more pay.

I'm reminded of another strange one. Do you know that a qualified submarine officer wore a submarine pin? But when he went to some other duty, which was not submarine, he took off his submarine pin. When I was teaching school at the Naval Academy and I was "qualified to command a submarine" I didn't wear my submarine pin.

Q: You didn't wear your dolphins?

Adm. B.: Couldn't wear them. Violation of "Uniform Regulations."

Q: What did you wear?

Adm. B.: You were just a naval officer. Interesting isn't it. I had forgotten all about that.

We are far afield from my arrival at Pearl Harbor from submarine school. I reported to the S-42. That particular class was six feet longer than the rest of the S-boats. Why? I don't know. There were certain differences about it. The commanding officer of the S-42 was named John Longstaff. T. G. Reamy out of '25 was the second in command. Soon after I came aboard Longstaff was transferred and Reamy became the Skipper and I became second in command. We called that person, "the second," we didn't call him the executive officer, we called him the second. We had one officer also on board junior to me. Of course, I enjoyed that duty very much. We operated in and out of Hawaii.

Then about the summer of 1935 I went off to the hospital. I had a cyst at the base of my spine. It was operated on and I've never had any difficulty since. That is what now? Forty-five years, fine. Except that after the operation the incision would not heal. And it wouldn't heal, and it wouldn't heal and I was in the hospital for almost six months. I then went back to my S-42.

Q: You must have been discouraged.

Adm. B.: Yes. I certainly was.

Q: Did you think that your naval career was coming to an end?

Adm. B.: Well, the timing was terrible. I had gone to submarine school a little bit later than my class. I went to submarine school in 1934. I didn't know it, but my class was due to go to post graduate school. They were supposed to go in 1936. That was their year. It was only two years, but I did not know that.

Anyhow, in the summer of '35 I found myself in the hospital and six months later I came out and I had not qualified in submarines yet. For some reason the S-42 class were going to go down to Panama and they left me there and I became the second in command of the S-27. I had done all of the work having to do with qualification in submarines. Then one of the skippers came with the submarine and we went out for a day's operations. You showed that you could rig the ship for dive and take it down and you could do all these various things. Then you'd man the periscope and they would have a target out there and you'd show that you could handle the periscope and you could fire a torpedo. Then you were designated as "qualified in submarines." Then you'd start wearing this pin. Aviators wear their pin when they leave Pensacola. You have to be out of submarine school for a year. So very quickly I got that. But, I was in a hurry. My class was going to go to PG (post graduate) school. There was no use in my trying to go. It was too late. So I requested to remain in my present job for an additional year. I had to because I'd gotten into this business of submarines and had run out of time.

Q: You seem to have a great ability to request specific duty and to get it. Wasn't that unusual?

Adm. B.: Well, I tried to plan it. I have not always succeeded; some disappointments. When we get to my last tour of duty in the Pentagon in 1962 we're going to recall an item that has to do with Claude Ricketts which bears on this exact subject.

Interview No. 3 with Rear Admiral Roy S. Benson, U.S. Navy (Retired)

Place: Arnold, Maryland

Date: March 18, 1980

By: John T. Mason, Jr.

Q: All right, Sir, we resume your story this morning by dealing with your request for an additional year of duty in Hawaii. You must have liked the climate out there.

Adm. B.: Well, yes, but that wasn't the reason I requested it. I requested it because I had been in the hospital and I needed some more submarine time at that particular point in my career.

The S-42 to which I had been attached, she and the rest of the submarines of that division, six of them, were ordered to the Canal Zone, Panama. So, they decided that I should stay right where I was. So I stayed in Hawaii but I transferred to USS S-27.

Q: She being of the same class?

Adm. B.: Generally the same class, very similiar to the older boats we've talked about, the R-boats and the O-boats. The Commanding Officer, Lieutenant C. W. Wilkins, had a nickname, "Weary." "Weary" was no name for Weary Wilkins, because he was very energetic and one of the finest people I've ever worked for.

He was never hurried or harried or worried or discourteous. He was magnificent. I stayed with him, however, only a few months. He was transferred to some other duty and was relieved by a Lieutenant by the name of Robert H. Gibbs. Why he in turn got transferred very soon thereafter I don't know. But he was relieved by a Lieutenant James D. Taylor III. You recall the reason that I wanted to stay there and what I really worked at on board the S-27 was that I had not been out of submarine school long enough to get my submarine dolphins which you do not get when you graduate from submarine school. You get them when you have finished one year of operations in the submarines. Then it is a very strict procedure to get you qualified anyhow. My time in the hospital did not count or, if my ship had been in a shipyard overhaul, that would not have counted. A year, not necessarily in one lump, but a year operating in a submarine and you had to be recommended for "qualified in submarines" by the commanding officer. Then you had to work on a very exhaustive notebook in which you had to trace out all kinds of pipelines, all sorts of things on board the submarine. You'd better know how to man the engine throttle. How to make the adjustments on the torpedo. How to make the adjustment on the torpedo tube. When you had finished your notebook and had finished the required time the division commander appointed a board of three commanding officers, none of them your own, who'd be a board to examine you and find out how much you really knew about submarines. They would take you from stem to stern and they would ask you all sorts of questions. Then you'd get the submarine underway and you'd handle the submarine and once you got out you'd handle all sorts of stations. You'd be down on the electrical controls or you'd be back on the throttle of the engine, and you'd be up there preparing torpedo tubes. They had a target and you would take the periscope and would make an approach to fire an exercise torpedo. Than you'd bring the submarine in and put her alongside the pier. Then they would decide if you could handle a submarine all right.

I forgot to mention, obviously, you were the diving officer when you dove and you were the undiving officer when you undove. You also rigged the submarine for diving; everything. Very exhaustive. Then you had earned your precious submarine pin.

Q: Well, you had really won your spurs?

Adm. B.: You had indeed. Well, there was another qualification.

Any time after that your commanding officer could recommend you for, "qualified for command of a submarine." That would go up through the chain of command and almost immediately that I got my dolphins and having been qualified in submarines he recommended me for qualification for submarine command. So, with a couple of snaps of the finger I'd gotten through my qualifications which I would not have if I'd gone to shore duty in the summer of 1936.

My duty aboard the S-27 was not much different from the S-42. A very interesting thing happened, however, in Hawaii. They wanted the large ships on the West Coast to be able to come out to Pearl Harbor and to come in and go alongside. Apparently these heavy ships, carriers and battleships and cruisers, had not generally gone to Hawaii. But they did a great deal of construction around there including those big concrete berths that the ARIZONA, etc. were alongside. In preparation, in addition to the physical construction and dredging of the channel, after they had finished this they brought quite a few of the large ships, battleships particularly, there to practice. Strangely enough, there was only one Pearl Harbor pilot. A

Civil Service pilot. With half a dozen ships arriving to try out the facilities more pilots were needed. So they took submarine commanding officers and made them pilots for the battleships; a lieutenant advising a very senior captain.

Q: Why would they be particularly qualified over the others?

Adm. B.: Because they were going in and out all the time from Pearl Harbor and they were familiar with the channel. So, here comes a battleship, obviously a four-stripe Captain in charge, and here comes this lieutenant from the submarine to be the pilot. He is going to advise where the channel is and what this buoy means and this sort of thing. We devoted quite a bit of time to that project.

Q: Did you do some of that?

Adm. B.: I wasn't a commanding officer, but we all worked at it hard to make sure we understood where the channel was. We hadn't paid much attention because submarines were not very large and so you just go in and out, no problem. But these great big things coming in, you want to make sure that you do, indeed, know the limits of the channel.

Q: Was this about the time they brought out the big dock, the Ten-Ten Dock?

Adm. B.: It might have been. I don't recall.

Anyhow, at the end of a year, we'd come to the end of the summer of 1937. I now had my dolphins and qualification for command and I was then going to go to shore duty. I got the job that I asked to get. I wanted to go to the Naval Academy to teach navigation.

Q: Why?

Adm. B.: It was an interesting subject and certainly a seagoing subject; ought to be interesting and fun to go back and teach. Well, some of my friends back there were teaching English, and other people were teaching mathematics and various things. I wanted to teach a more seagoing subject.

So, I arrived at the Naval Academy and was assigned to the Department of Navigation.

I forgot to mention that in the spring of 1937 also I checked off my examinations for lieutenant. Examinations in those days were ten subjects. You were examined on ten succesive days. These exams came out from Washington and you worked them out under the supervision of a proctor. Usually they had quite a few people taking the exams at the same time. The examination papers went to Washington and if you passed you were ready to make Lieutenant when a vacancy occurred.

I wanted to get all these things out of the way, so I checked that one off also during that extra year in Hawaii.

Soon after I arrived at the Naval Academy I started wearing my two stripes of a full Lieutenant.

Q: You exercised a certain degree of planning, did you not?

Adm. B.: I tried. I still try to plan. All plans don't go right. But, I've always felt, I think most people will agree with this, it is much better to have a real good plan and carry it out poorly than to have a no good plan and carry it out well. I really think that you'd better have that plan.

My boss in teaching navigation at the Naval Academy was a Commander by the name of F. C. Denebrink. D-E-N-E-B-R-I-N-K. One of the smartest people I have ever known. He told me a very interesting thing once upon a time there. He said, "Never make a decision until you have to." He said, "Don't think that I mean you should vacillate, no. If you can see in the distance that a particular subject, an important decision needs to be made, don't make the decision until you have to. However, start collecting the information. Get yourself a piece of paper and a pencil or a notebook and think about it and put down the pros and cons of the alternative courses so that you are ready when the time comes that you must make a decision, then make it and don't ever change your mind after having made it."

Well, I'm not sure about that one. I think that, obviously, in spite of all the planning, if you find that you've made the wrong decision you'd better back off. Often times it's extremely difficult to back off once you've come to this "Y" in the road and started down one; it's very difficult to go back to the intersection and start in again. So, you'd better be sure, look at the road map before you give left rudder.

It was very interesting teaching at the Naval Academy.

Q: You had never taught before, had you?

Adm. B.: I had never taught anywhere before.

Very interesting. Naturally my students were approximately ten years younger than I. They thought I was about seventy years old, I guess. They didn't realize that I was running around with the same girls they were.

They had changed the system of midshipmen's cruises, summer midshipmen's cruises. In my day, you recall, all three of the upper classes went out on cruise together on battleships. Now, they had determined that the new juniors, that is the people that were starting their third year at the Naval Academy, would spend the summer, not along with the new seniors and sophomores, but would be on their own with other things. They spent one month at the Naval Academy. They then spent one month on board a destroyer, almost exactly like the same type that I had served in for three years in China. They spent a month on board this destroyer cruising around and they also spent another month going to New London, Connecticut, and flying down to Pensacola and various places to become acquainted with what the Navy is ashore other than the Naval Academy.

The first chore I had was teaching new juniors. We taught them hydrographic survey. It's very much like a land surveyor except it has important differences and great use.

Q: Was there some originality to it, I mean were you plotting areas that hadn't been done adequately?

Adm. B.: Not really, what we were teaching them was how to do it. They would do it out in the yard of the Naval Academy. What we did here was to teach them to use some of the same instruments used by a land surveyor. We taught them, also at the same time, how to adjust and use a sextant. Also, very interesting, I had never heard of them and that is taking horizontal angles with a sextant. A sextant is built to do this vertically, bring the star down to the horizon by mirrors. It was a fascinating study and I had never had anything to do with it before. I had a great time with the midshipmen learning all about this. Also we taught them the magnetic and the gyro compasses. The use of them is fairly easy. But, what are the basic principles behind them? Do we understand what we are trying to do?

Q: How large a class of men was this?

Adm. B.: Well, you'd have about fifteen or so in a class. After one month I was told that I was going to go on one of these destroyer cruises. So, away I went. We had thirty brand new juniors on board one of these destroyers. These were not the same men I'd had in my hydrographic survey.

That class was the class of 1939, there were approximately six hundred of them at the time. So, if you had a class of fifteen or if you took thirty out on this destroyer, that's an awful lot of classes, awful lot of classrooms, and lots of ships. They had about a half a dozen destroyers. So, we went to various places. Among the places we went was Newport. We were there at the time of the America Cup Races.

Q: Well, the destroyers were based at Newport at that time, were they not?

Adm. B.: Yes, there were destroyers based there. That was a magnificent month out with these midshipmen and I knew quite a bit about this type of ship.

The commanding officer was an officer by the name Lieutenant Commander Hugh Hadley.

Last evening, when I was looking over all these papers, all at once it dawned upon me that except for, just before I retired, and was working for the Secretary of the Navy, I had never worked for anyone who was not a graduate of the Naval Academy. The reason it came so much to my attention was this Hugh Hadley, I checked him in the book. We have the register of graduates.

So, we had a wonderful cruise and then the third month teaching hydrographic surveying again to the new juniors. A different group, of course. Then academic year started and the football season and all. What a great experience!

Q: Where were your quarters? Where were you living?

Adm. B.: I was living out in town. I was living just outside of the main gate, the Maryland Avenue gate there on Hanover Street. Fortunately, when I went out for that month the people said, "You're not really living here so we won't charge you rent, but you leave your things here."

That was very nice, I appreciated that greatly. Very nice people.

One of the things we had at the Naval Academy in all departments was an extra instruction system. That is, between four-thirty in the afternoon and six, if any midshipman felt that he would like to have some extra instruction in some subject or some part of the subject he could go to that particular building and there was always an instructor, a professor there who would explain things to him.

Q: This was a tutoring sort of thing?

Adm. B. Tutoring, yes. And often times you'd have the whole classroom full of people asking questions and you'd be up at the board explaining.

Q: I suppose there was a cross section. Some of these boys were really weak in the subject and they were trying to bolster themselves and others were eager to learn more.

Adm. B.: Yes. There was a psychological point also. We were required to keep records of who came for extra instruction.

Q: For what purpose?

Adm. B.: Well, in our department they were put on the bulletin board and I know that it is very easy for one of our navigation instructors to go over and take a look at the board and here is one of his poorer students, he's coming to extra instruction every day. You're apt to be a little lenient toward a fellow who's really trying.

Q: But this was completely voluntary, wasn't it?

Adm. B.: Completely voluntary on their part. The psychological bit referred also to examinations. They all had a time limit but you could leave when you were done. Anyone who felt uneasy at all at how he's doing should not leave early because the time was recorded when you left. If you did poorly on the exam having left early could have been a psychological disadvantage to you. So, you'd better sit there and do what you want to, twiddle your thumbs if necessary, but you'd better not leave early.

Q: If you were exceedingly bright you could walk out?

Adm. B.: Easy, nothing to it, if you've got that much confidence.

Being a bachelor at that time I told the married navigation instructors "anytime that you have anything that you've got to do some afternoon and it's your turn to have extra instruction, I'll take it if my afternoon is free." Often times I would be in there two or three afternoons a week. I enjoyed it. I always liked to help people just like I liked to be helped if I needed it.

Our boss, Commander Denebrink, came up with a new idea. "Instruction for officers at the Naval Academy." There were always promotion exams going on for various officers for promotion to the next rank. Denebrink said, "One of the subjects they have to be examined in is navigation. So, why don't we one night a week from, say, seven to nine, have extra instruction in navigation for officers who are at the Naval Academy? They can then come over here and we'll explain navigation all the way from "A" to izzard if they want to spend that time here."

So we started and several of the other departments followed suit.

Q: Did you have takers, and what was your part?

Adm. B.: We had many people who came to our courses. I was the expert on the magnetic compass. I always seemed to become the expert just about the time something became obsolete. I was told to learn all about the magnetic compass. This is one of the things that Commander Denebrink did. He would say to one officer, "You find out all about tides and currents." You become an expert on this and you become an expert on that. Denebrink was quite a guy. He eventually became a Vice Admiral and lives out in San Francisco, a very fine gentleman.

The next thing on schedule was the summer of 1938; time for the midshipmen's cruise. This is the end of my first academic year as a teacher. Two or three battleships were taking out all of the new sophmores and the new seniors, going on a European cruise. I had my hand in the air, of course, to go on the cruise. We had officers from the Naval Academy who would augment the officers on board and would conduct the midshipmen's training.

Q: Classes?

Adm. B.: Not much. It was a practical work at sea. In navigation they could practice determining the ship's position by the stars; also by the sun, moon and planets.

Q: A real application.

Adm. B.: A real application. I had the pleasure of going on the cruise and another navigation instructor went with me. We went to the battleship USS TEXAS. He was an officer by the name of Burrowes, Thomas Burrowes. He was a Lieutenant, as was I.

At the Naval Academy at the time, we had about a dozen navigation instructors and two of them live here in Annapolis today. One of them is Rear Admiral W. F. Fitzgerald, "Dolly" Fitzgerald. The other one is a Rear Admiral by the name of W. C. Ford, they call him Henry, of course. They both live on Prince George Street.

Well, off we went on the midshipmen's cruise. Before we went to Europe it was decided to take the ships up to New York. Why, I'm not quite sure. Anyhow, these three battleships arrived in New York and they were supposed to moor. By mooring, as opposed to the expression anchoring, we mean to put down with two anchors so that the ship will move around where the two anchor chains meet at the ship. One anchor over here and one anchor is over there. If you're simply anchored with one anchor the center of your circle of swing is the anchor. While with two anchors the center of swing is where the anchor chains meet.

Q: And there's not that much swing.

Adm. B.: That's right. Unfortunately one of the battleships ran aground.

Q: In New York?

Adm. B.: Right off Grant's tomb on North River (Hudson River). They got the ship off rather promptly, but there was an Admiral in charge of our division of ships and he told the senior Officer from the Naval Academy, "I want a very thorough survey of this part of the North River to determine whether the charts were accurate."

Q: Because there had to be a board of inquiry over this?

Adm. B.: Oh yes, there would be some kind of a board and he wanted this kind of information because, obviously, if the charts were accurate that's one subject. If the charts were inaccurate that's another one. So, obviously--I don't know why I am always chosen, I didn't put my hand in the air, but I did indeed make it. I got the assignment and this was on a Friday and we worked all over the weekend on this. I got the job and about a half a dozen first class midshipmen, new seniors, and we went to work. What was it? It was hydrographic survey, just what I had taught during the summer of 1937.

Q: Naturally it was. Was the skipper of the battleship claiming that the charts were inaccurate?

Adm. B.: No, but they hadn't had the board of investigation. The convening authority, that Admiral decided, "Yes, let's have a survey to see whether the charts are accurate." It was the first time that I'd seen a practical application of this subject, I'd just heard about taking horizontal angles with sextants. That's the way we plotted the position of our boat. By "our boat" I mean the ship's boat in which we worked. We would cruise slowly against the tidal current so that we would be practically stopped. We'd put the line down and at the same time that we're getting the depth of the water with the line, we also want to know where we are. The way we found out where we were was to take two horizontal angles on some prominent landmarks. Something that was on the chart. We could determine exactly where we were. We also had to correct the depth we got on the leadline, for the state of the tide.

Q: Tides are very strong in the North River, aren't they?

Adm. B.: The tidal current at their maximum speeds are indeed strong.

This is a complex subject and I do not believe that I should try to explain it completely; just a few essentials. We used the tide tables; we assumed that the tide tables were correct and we could look in there as to the time of the tide. We also asked the Coast Guard to please check to see whether the actual depth of the water is in agreement with the tide tables.

One thing I determined from the beginning; there's no use in collecting a lot of data and once you've collected it return to the ship and find that there is something wrong with it. We plotted the whole business while we were doing it. If there were any spaces where we don't have any data we could get it. When we finished by the end of that Sunday afternoon it was done. I took it over to the flagship and delivered it.

Q: What was your verdict? Were the charts accurate?

Adm. B.: The charts were indeed accurate.

The commanding officer of this ship had made the mistake, which is very easy to make, he assumed that "high water," when the tide had gotten as high as it's going to be and then starts going down there will be no current flowing in the river. As the tide goes down the current will be flowing out. It just happens that that's not true. It just happens that at that particular time in that location, if I remember correctly, the time of maximum flood, that is water is flowing up the river, coincides with the high tide. Yet the height off Grant's Tomb is getting less and less all the time; finally it gets to its low water stand and starts up again. You'd think that when you had high water the current would be minimum and as the water receded it would go out, but it didn't. It continued to go up the river all the way to Albany. I said that this whole subject and hydrographic surveying are complex.

Q: Well, was it any different there in the North River from what it would be anywhere else?

Adm. B.: No. If you have a river like that where it goes all the way up. For example, in the Yangtze River in China we must have the same sort of thing. There you swing around your anchor way up in the Nanking and that's two hundred miles up the river. It must be true in all of the rivers.

Q: The captain really should have known?

Adm. B.: Yes. Maybe he didn't know, I don't know what went wrong. Anyhow, what happened was he dropped the first one and then he tried to back down and drop the second one; really trying to back down into a current is a very perilous thing to do. You'd better not do it--maybe the Admiral was at fault. He, with advice from his staff chose the time of arrival. We should have arrived at slack water, that is no current either way. We arrived at the wrong time.

Anyhow we had a good time with it and had a chance to try out hydrographic survey. In my classes the following year I always explained, up on the blackboard, what we did and how we did it and why we did it and this, that and the other. It was part of the instruction. It wasn't in the book but we explained it anyhow.

We proceeded on our European cruise and went to Le Havre, to Portsmouth, England, and to Copenhagen.

In Copenhagen one bright afternoon I proceeded up the Danish Riviera to visit my cousins. My father's first cousin and her husband living in Elsinore. The city where Hamlet's Castle is.

Q: You exercised your ability with the Danish and Swedish language?

Adm. B.: Yes. A second cousin of mine and I took the ferry over to my father's hometown of Helsingor to visit other cousins; there is a ferry that takes fifteen minutes to go across into Sweden.

May I tell about teaching West Pointers who were with us aboard our ship for this cruise?

Q: Please do.

Adm.B.: At West Point, at that time, new juniors got the whole summer off. Three of them asked if they could spend the summer on the midshipmen's cruise. This was granted and they reported for duty on our ship (USS TEXAS). When asked, they gave as reason for their request that they wanted, on graduation from West Point, to be in the Army Air Corps and, therefore, they wanted to learn "navigation by the stars". They were assigned to me. Right down my alley!

What was their background which would help? They had had mathematics including trigonometry, logarithms, astronomy, land surveying among their many subjects. All I had to do was to put their knowledge together in a new way. In a week they were able to take sights with the sextant and compute the position of their ship by the stars, celestial navigation.

After the start of my second academic year I offered my services to the yacht club to teach celestial navigation to boatsmen. Teaching them was not as easy as teaching the West Pointers; not the same background.

In about October 1938 a privately owned cargo ship had run aground off the Florida coast. Commander Denebrink was asked to be a consultant to the steamship company. In those days outside employment required permission of the Secretary of the Navy. Commander Denebrink got permission for himself and me. The suit related to the reliability of the ship's magnetic compass. The ship did not have a gyro compass. I have the experience of working, then, with a real expert at analysis and at appearing in court as an "expert witness." Commander Denebrink was a real master. He retired in the early 1950's as a Vice Admiral; lives in San Francisco.

My tour of duty at the Naval Academy was supposed to be three years. But in the spring of 1939 Europe started looking more and more perilous. Orders came out to most of us seagoing sailor men on duty at the Naval Academy to be detached in the summer of '39 instead of the third summer of 1940. So in 1939 I drove across the country again as I had in 1934. Drove across and became executive officer of a four-pipe destroyer. This was a very familiar sort of a thing. She was identical to the SMITH THOMPSON in which I had served in 1931-34.

Q: Had she been in mothballs?

Adm. B.: She had recently come out of mothballs.

Q: What was her condition when she came out?

Adm. B.: Rather poor. It was a challenge.

Q: She was the HOVEY?

Adm. B.: Yes, H-O-V-E-Y. I served in that type for three years and had made a midshipmen's one-month cruise in that type of ship; here I was executive officer of the ship. We seemed to be typed, as it were; I was supposed to be a submarine officer. I've got more than three years in this type and it looks like I'm going to have a fourth one.

During the time I'd been out in China I had taken all the courses, you recall, and I also had when some officer got detached and his relief hadn't arrived yet I'd find myself with that other fellow's job. So I had had all the jobs on board there except the captain and the exec. I'd never been captain or second in command, but I'd had every other job. So, I knew those types very, very well.

The commanding officer was a Lieutenant Commander. I've now got myself a commanding officer who is a Lieutenant Commander and I'm a Lieutenant, so we're going up. The commanding officer was a Lieutenant Commander by the name of Thomas B. Dugan.

I don't remember all the details, but very soon after I'd arrived on board Dugan was detached. He was relieved by a fresh caught Lieutenant Commander, the expression "fresh caught" means he's just become a Lieutenant Commander. Dugan was relieved by Lieutenant Commander Rufus Rose. One of the smartest people I'd ever worked for.

Q: Smarter than Denebrink?

Adm. B.: Different type. Denebrink knew--had a breadth of knowledge in practically everything. It didn't matter what you wanted to talk about, Denebrink seemed to me to have knowledge in it, all across the board. Rufus Rose was more academic and strictly professional Navy. He had never been commanding officer, executive officer, or a head of department of any ship in his life, as he had always served on battleships and cruisers. He hadn't gotten senior enough for any of the senior jobs while I had had all these jobs in much smaller ships. We were a real good twosome. Maybe they arranged it that way. I knew a great deal about that type of ship and he knew nothing but he learned it very quickly.

Less than a year after that he was relieved by a Lieutenant Commander by the name of John E. Florence. About that time we were sent to Mare Island Naval Shipyard to be converted into a high-speed minesweeper. About a dozen of us were to be converted.

Q: What was back of that decision? Was the Navy lacking in minesweepers?

Adm. B.: Yes, indeed!

Q: And suddenly became aware of the need to have--?

Adm. B.: Yes, the Germans had started to lay mines over there to the approaches to the English Channel and to the Thames River and so forth. This was a new sort of business. Minesweeping and minelaying are very apt to be neglected during times of so-called peace.

Q: What is the rationale for that?

Adm. B.: Well, it's not very exotic. Flying planes or shooting torpedoes and doing dynamic sort of things are more interesting. This thing that you just put down on the bottom and it just sits there and waits until something goes by, it's not very sexy. I suspect that right now (1980) we do not give mine warfare a high priority.

The Germans had started laying mines so we'd better learn how to sweep them. You recall, they had been also laying "magnetic" mines. Let me explain. In moored contact mines you had a mine and you had a cable; with an anchor on one end and the mine floatable on the other. A ship would go by and get snagged on the cable; he'd bring the mine to the ship to go off. By getting snagged on the cable he'd bring the mine to the ship and "wham" she'd go. These contact mines could be on the surface or just below it. Drop them over the side. They'd go down until the anchor hit the bottom. When it hit the bottom the mine would ease up until it got to the depth you wanted. You could set the depth desired; unique. Very clever.

But these "magnetic" mines--you lay them on the bottom.

Q: Magnetic mines were a new technique, were they not?

Adm. B.: Yes. I believe the Germans were the first to lay them (1939-40). If a ship goes by, the ship's steel disrupts the magnetic field. The magnetic needle is deflected and sets off the mine; explosion directly under the ship and blows a hole in the bottom of the ship rather than blowing a hole in the side of it.

We'll discuss this more in submarines (1942). If you can have a torpedo that would take the bottom out of a ship instead of hitting the side and exploding or like the aviator's bomb coming down which blows a hole in the top. You can make a hole in the bottom of the ship; a good way to get the ship to collapse and go down, break in two.

They gave us equipment so we could sweep moored lines. We also had equipment to sweep magnetic mines. The way you sweep a magnetic mine is to generate yourself a change in the magnetic field. Our ship wasn't big enough to do much deflecting, but we could have a magnetic field making apparatus on board so that we could cause the needle to deflect and explode the mines. Obviously we had it blow up at a safe distance from ship. The way we did this was they installed in the after torpedo workshop a tremendous number of high capacity truck storage batteries. Then we put in some great big diesel engines and these diesel engines would either be stopped or they'd be going full speed. When they went full speed they charged the batteries. You had two electrodes and when you threw the switch these two electrodes they would cause a magnetic field. But the batteries, all these truck batteries, we had a hundred of them, would go from fully charged to practically no charge in a couple of seconds. Like a tremendous electric chair I suppose. As soon as the magnetic field had done that the switches were flipped and the diesel engines would start full speed and charge the batteries.

Q: This outpouring of energy from the batteries would tend to detonate the mines in the area?

Adm. B.: Yes. The electricity would go around a solenoid and produce a magnetic field. It deflected the magnetic needle which exploded the mine.

Q: And that's when the mines would go off?

Adm. B.: Yes.

Q: Did you practice with actual mines?

Adm. B.: No. What we did was get the ship converted and then we went out and operated.

Q: How long did it take for the conversion?

Adm. B.: It would take three or four months, something in that order.

Q: Did it detract from the speed, the original speed?

Adm. B.: Original speed, yes, because we lost two of our boilers. We were now limited to two boilers, but these ships could make twenty-seven knots on two boilers. That's where they put these big diesel engines in the space where the two boilers had been. When you were back in the battery room at the time you were operating you've never seen so much metal flying around. Those batteries were taking an awful beating. The switches were automatic; the switch would operate, and the battery would go from full charge to nothing, practically, in a matter of a few seconds. Then the switches would go the other way and the diesel engines would start roaring away to charge the batteries. You recall often times when you operate a switch there would be a little spark? This wasn't a little spark; it was a big spark. I don't know how they ever held up.

Q: You would think the batteries wouldn't stand this sort of thing very long.

Adm. B.: I don't know how long they would stand it.

Q: Sounds like a very makeshift design.

Adm. B.: I agree with you. I don't know what they finally did. We had barely gotten started with this when I was detached.

Q: So you weren't with the minesweeper very long, then?

Adm. B.: I was there for the conversion in the shipyard and I was there for the initial operations; then I was detached and where did I go? I became executive officer of the submarine NAUTILUS.

Q: Let me ask you another question about the minesweeper. In your knowledge, did they continue to use this mechanism for very long?

Adm. B.: I believe they did. I don't know in detail but I believe they used it in various places in the Pacific. We didn't have as much mine difficulty in the Pacific as they had over the English Channel. Most of our mine warfare in the Pacific was laying them. The Army Air Corps closed off the Japanese Inland Sea toward the end of the World War II. I don't believe we ever tried to sweep them until sometime well after the war.

Q: Would you explain degaussing.

Adm. B.: Yes. The idea of degaussing was to reduce a ship's magnetic field. If a ship has no magnetic field, the ship can go through an area where there are magnetic mines and not explode them.

Q: It nullifies this?

Adm. B.: To degauss a ship you install cables around the ship. Electricity is sent through the cables. The amount of electricity depends on the heading of the ship. You must compensate the degaussing system on various headings. You'd go over a degaussing range and they would measure your magnetic field and whether good enough. That's degaussing.

Q: Now, would you also explain British paravanes?

Adm. B.: We had those when we came out of this conversion.

Q: They were British originally, weren't they?

Adm. B.: That's right. You remember that I mentioned that we had magnetic mines that the British invented. But, before we had moored mines. Paravanes have surfaces on them like the rudder on airplanes so that when the ship is proceeding ahead these paravanes will be held out from the side of the ship.

Q: They were antennae, were they?

Adm. B.: Yes. There was a steel rope from the bow of the ship and the paravanes held it out. Along comes a moored mine and the cable of that moored mine comes against this steel rope going out to the paravane. Instead of being pulled into the ship the mine cable is pulled out to the paravane. When it gets out there an apparatus cuts the cable to the mine.

Q: It doesn't detonate the mine?

Adm. B.: No, it cuts the cable.

Q: So it just sinks to the bottom?

Adm. B.: Or comes up to the surface, and if it does you give it a burst of gunfire to explode it.

Q: With a moored mine, what is the area of destructive power?

Adm. B.: If you could succeed in going by a moored mine without hampering it in any way or bothering it, you haven't done anything. You are safe.

Q: Yes, but if it detonated, how far away does the ship have to be and not be harmed?

Adm. B.: Oh, I would say that you'd better be at least a hundred feet away from it. Something in that order, I suppose. It has to be fairly close to cause tremendous damage. It depends on if the mine is off to the side or whether the mine is directly under and how deep. If you're going to explode a mine you like to explode it right under the ship and not very far. Obviously any explosion dissipates as it goes in distance. This is quite a subject and I don't think we do very much about it even today.

Q: Again we've neglected it today, haven't we?

Adm. B.: Probably.

Q: And we say today that minelaying is done largely with helicopters and so forth. So there is not that much problem. You can lay mines on short notice.

Adm. B.: Yes. How you sweep them is still a problem.
The Americans and British laid down quite a few mining barrages in the North Sea during World War I. Then after the war was over they had to sweep them. It was a big job.

Q: In this day and age it is the Russians who are credited with being so skilled in this area.

Adm. B.: I wouldn't be surprised. I wouldn't be at all surprised if they were very skilled.

Q: Shall we go to the NAUTILUS?

Adm. B.: Okay, now we arrive on board the submarine NAUTILUS.

Q: Was this a happy event for you?

Adm. B.: This was a very happy event. This was great! Back to submarines.

Now the strange thing was that I had heard, and I suppose that most of our submarine people had heard, that there were two ways to do things in the submarine business. One was the way the NAUTILUS did it and the other was the way everybody else did it.

Q: Now, would you explain all this?

Adm. B.: Well, it's a strange thing, that's what we'd heard,, she was sort of left-handed.

Q: Tell me about her as a submarine.

Adm. B.: Well, she was tied with three other submarines at that time for being the largest in the world.

Q: That being how large?

Adm. B.: Well, she was almost four hundred feet long. She displaced three thousand tons on the surface and four thousand tons submerged. She had two six inch deck guns. She had two main engines, they were both German-made MAN's and each one of them weighed forty-seven tons. They had been built when the hulls were riveted rather than welded. There was a little bit of difficulty there.

Q: What was their age at that point?

Adm. B.: She was commissioned in 1930 and so I thought at that time she was very old. But, I don't think so anymore.

Q: 1930 to 1941.

Adm. B.: Eleven years old, we don't consider that very old anymore. Generally, what we try to do in the Navy, because we have to, when we build a ship, we're not building a ship for a single purpose and if technology changes all you can do is scrap the ship. We build it as a platform which will last many years because we know it has to last many years. Then we can shift the apparatus and the equipment on board, but that hull is going to be with us for a long time.

The three submarines tied with one another in size were ARGONAUT, the NARWHAL and the NAUTILUS. They were sister ships except they had built into the ARGONAUT the capability for laying moored mines. She could lay them over the stern. These ships were not very fast, but they were pretty good ships. They were comfortable ships.

The fourth ship for this four-way tie was a French ship submarine by the name of SURCOUF. She was about the same tonnage on the surface and about the same tonnage submerged, but she was a little shorter. She had one eight-inch gun, instead of the three American ones being twin six-inch guns. They were the only ones we could put six-inch guns on.

Q: Was the SURCOUF built in the same shipyard or was she built by the French?

Adm. B.: By the French.

Q: But she was copied after the others?

Adm. B.: I don't know that she was copied. I never saw the SURCOUF, but just about the same size. Of course we build submarines now so large that the NAUTILUS would be considered very small.

The Commanding Officer of the NAUTILUS when I reported on board was a Lieutenant Commander by the name of L. D. Follmer, F-O-L-L-M-E-R. As you've noted the same refrain, I had barely been on board a few months when we got a new commanding officer. That commanding officer was Lieutenant Commander Joseph P. Thew, T-H-E-W. When I was in submarine school, he was a teacher in diesel engines and a very good one. He had a master degree in engineering. Very capable individual.

Q: What was the complement of the NAUTILUS?

Adm. B.: We had seven officers and about 100 crew. You recall that old R-14, there were two of us. One those S-type we had something on the order of three or four officers. Now, we've got seven officers on board this ship. The engineering officer and I were the only Lieutenants, the rest of them were all JG's (Lieutenant Junior Grade).

One of the officers on board you may know, Chick Clarey. Chick used to be Commander In Chief of the Pacific Fleet. And others named Herman Kossler and Frank Hess and Steve Gimber. The other Lieutenant was Tom Hogan. We had a lot of talent on board that submarine. So much talent that when we got into World War II it wasn't very long before every officer who served on the NAUTILUS in 1941, I would say, by 1943 they all had submarine commands.

Q: The NAUTILUS was stationed in the Pacific, wasn't it?

Adm. B.: In Hawaii.

Q: Torpedo tubes, how many did she have?

Adm. B.: She had only six torpedo tubes. The newer submarines that we came out with during World War II had six torpedo tubes forward and four aft while the NAUTILUS had four forward and two aft.

In this narrative we are going to re-engine and bring up to date the NAUTILUS, she's only eleven years old. But, before that we need to mention another thing that is of great interest.

A Lieutenant, retired by disability, by the name of Jasper Holmes had written articles in the Saturday Evening Post, I forget his pen name. This was well before World War II. But he wrote one in which the Japanese in this story used the French Frigate Shoals, which is half way between Hawaii and Midway, used French Frigate Shoals as a fueling stop for sea-planes; Japanese sea-planes, which in this story as I remember it, they were carried on board ships. Sea-planes, came to French Frigate Shoals and also submarines came to French Frigate Shoals and those submarines could carry aviation gasoline and they refueled the flying boats at French Frigate Shoals. Then they took off and bombed Hawaii; according to the Saturday Evening Post story.

Q: Jasper had an active imagination, didn't he?

Adm. B.: He did indeed and showed it in World War II and even now.

The strange thing is that somebody picked this idea up. Whether they picked it up from Jasper Holmes or Jasper Holmes picked it up from somewhere else, or not connected.

The NAUTILUS and NARWHAL, the sister ship of the NAUTILUS, were both changed such that they could carry aviation gasoline in the submarine. We tested this concept. We actually proceeded to French Frigate Shoals and seaplanes from Hawaii flew out to French Frigate Shoals and there we refueled the planes. We spent two days getting there and that morning after we'd arrived at French Frigate Shoals the aviator had breakfast, kissed his wife goodbye, got in his plane, flew out, refueled and came home for lunch. We spent two more days coming home.

Q: There was some question about whether the Japanese had been inspired by this, but I think it was discounted.

Adm. B.: That's what I understand. It was in Jasper Holmes' book.

Q: Incidentally, his name was Alec Hudson, his pseudonym.

Adm. B.: That's right. Do you know everything?

Very soon, in the fall of 1941, we were ordered back to Mare Island to be re-engined to get rid of these great big German rock crushers and in other ways to be remodernized. It looked like, maybe, a war was coming along. Back to Mare Island was something to see. There was so much going on. There must have been about half a dozen submarines undergoing overhaul. Various of our submarines were being upgraded or fixed or just plain repaired. There were about half a dozen submarines in all stages of being built.

Very soon after that there was a launching of a submarine there at Mare Island. I got permission to ride the submarine down the launching ways. I had never done that. I'd never been on board a ship when she was launched. I wanted to do that, so I did. That submarine, by strange coincidence, was the submarine TRIGGER. By coincidence, several months later I became her commanding officer.

So we went ahead with all this work.

Q: What kind of engines did you get in place of MAN's?

Adm. B.: We got some General Motors engines. Very similar to the engines we had in the other submarines. They used the space to put four engines. These big diesel German engines were direct drive. By direct drive I mean that the engines turned over and the power went through reduction gears and then that turned the propellers. This is the same as the old S, R, and O types. The submarines that we used almost entirely during World War II had four diesel engines and their electricity turned over electric generators. The generators generated electricity and then put it into the main motors and the main motors turned the propellers. You'd say, "Well, this is a strange way to do it." It gives you tremendous flexibility. You run your engines. You can run one, two, three, or four engines and you can put all the electricity into the storage batteries or you can put any amount into the storage batteries and the other amount onto the propellers, as you please. You can run one engine or any number of engines. The propellers don't know how many engines are running. It's a very fine system. Really what we had was electric reduction gears. The engine generally turns over much faster than the propeller, so you need to reduce the speed in some way.

I remember watching them pull those forty-seven ton engines out of there. We were glad to get rid of them because we'd had great difficulty. All three of the ships had difficulty, the ARGONAUT, the NARWHAL, and the NAUTILUS.

Q: They were always breaking down, weren't they?

Adm. B.: Very difficult to keep going. Very unreliable. There was another type that we had during World War II that was even worse. That was built in the United States and that was the HOR engines. They were terrible. They had to re-engine every submarine that came out with HOR engines.

The engines that we had during World War II were generally of two kinds. We had the General Motors engine and we had the Fairbanks-Morse engine. The General Motors engine was not quite as repair free as the Fairbanks-Morse, but the General Motors engine was very accessible. When they had something wrong you could get to it while the Fairbanks-Morse was very reliable but if something went wrong we had a terrible time. Very difficult to get to. So they each had their pluses and minuses and both types were magnificient. Very good, we loved them. Each one of those engines had fifteen hundred horsepower. We could make just about twenty knots on them. On one engine we could make around ten or eleven knots. By the time we get four of them up to full high speed we had multiplied the power by more than four, not quite double the speed.

Benson #3 - 174-

Q: You were virtually flying.

Adm. B.: Yes. So we went to Mare Island and we're re-engining and everything is getting done pretty good and along comes Pearl Harbor Day. Now, what in the world was I doing when the attack came on Pearl Harbor? At Mare Island, aboard the NAUTILUS and it was a Sunday morning and I was down on board the submarine. Whether you have your ship repaired by people who are not attached to the ship because it's beyond their capability, whether by submarine tender or destroyer tender or some other base, whether you're having it done at a naval shipyard or a commercial shipyard, it really doesn't make all that difference. They are going to do a good job, yes. But if you want a job to be done and on time you had better watch that job being done. In the first place, if they observe that you are observing them, they are apt to bear down a little more. They are just people, human, this is a human story. If you ignore it, they will go and work on something else, on another ship where somebody is watching them. You spend a lot of time watching what they are doing and every officer on the ship goes around the whole pile of these work requests that have been approved. You are watching all the time as to how they are doing because you want to make sure that they are going to do them all; keep an eye on them. You want to get these things all done and you want to get them done right. They are going to require you to inspect the job-- you better inspect the job while it's being done rather than after something is all buttoned up. Keep your eyes on it. You'll get better work if you spend your time checking how they are doing. All of the ship's officers and many of the petty officers are doing exactly that during a shipyard overhaul. That was quite a harangue; warranted. While you are making sure that work is properly done, keep your cool. Getting angry does no good.

Q: The same thing applied elsewhere in life.

Adm. B.: This is routine; you can't walk away and leave it.

Well, what was I doing on board that submarine on Sunday morning? There were various things on board the NAUTILUS that were not going to my satisfaction. So, I had a date on Sunday morning when the workman were not working. They were not working on Sunday mornings at that time. I had a date with this person from the naval shipyard. "Let's go over everything in the submarine and discuss what's going on, what we should do, and so forth." So, we were down in the pump room, down below the control room, we were down in the pump room in the submarine NAUTILUS when a message came. I read it and I didn't say a word, nice poker face, handed it to the person from the shipyard. He read it and said, "My God, we'd better go to work!"

I said, "Yes, before you go to work, let's finish going throug the submarine and decide what we're going to do."

So, obviously they did go to work. They had been working all the time, but they started working twenty-four hours a day. We got squared away pretty well.

In January of 1942 I became a Lieutenant Commander. This was the first rank in which you were actually selected for promotion when a vacancy occurred. The fall of 1941 I had been selected and in January 1942 a message came out saying all people on selected lists promoted. So I was a Lieutenant Commander.

Q: Was the NAUTILUS completed by that time?

Adm. B.: She didn't complete until, I'd say, April. In January of 1942 a very strange thing happened. A Lieutenant

Commander by the name of W. H. Brockman--oh, before I say about Brockman, the commanding officer Joe Thew had gone up to the hospital at Mare Island for something wrong with him. I don't remember what it was, but he was up there. Somehow the word got back to Pearl Harbor. He hadn't been transferred to the hospital for some lengthy stay, he was simply up there for, maybe, various kinds of tests. Somehow the world got back to Pearl Harbor and they sent Lieutenant Commander W. H. Brockman to relieve him as commanding officer. So, Brockman arrived with orders to relieve Thew as commanding officer, but he, Thew, did not have any orders being detached. So, I was in the middle of this one because Bill Brockman was a smart guy and an energetic guy and the first thing he wanted to do when he arrived was to, "Let's line up all the officers and crew, I'm going to read my orders and take over." Before I had a chance to do that and I was not about to do it, Thew was my boss, he was going around telling people what to do; "I want to do this and I want to change that," and so forth.

I said, "Now, Bill, I think that we ought to go up and see Captain Thew. Let's get it squared away."

Well, we did go up to see Thew; it did get squared away and Brockman did become the commanding officer.

Q: And what happened to Thew?

Adm. B.: He was transferred to become the engineering officer on one of the submarine squadron's staffs. I'm sure he did a very valuable job there.

So, Bill Brockman became the skipper and we continued, I'd say around March we'd finished most of our work and we started having various sea trials around there and to try out various kinds of equipment. The first time we made a dive we made it in San Francisco Bay, first time after the overhaul. Compensation hadn't been very good because we sounded the diving alarm, opened up the main ballast tanks and were supposed to go down, we didn't go down. If my memory doesn't fail me, they had forgotten about these tanks that had gasoline. During the re-engining and overhaul a decision had been made that we're not going to have this gasoline any more. So, we removed the gasoline from the tanks, but then, I guess somebody didn't quite follow through, those tanks were empty.

Q: So they were buoyant?

Adm. B.: They were supposed to be converted back to main ballast tanks so that when you opened the floods and opened the vents they would fill also. So, we hit the diving alarm, opened the vents, opened the flood valves, and she didn't go down.

When I speak of flood valves and vents I refer to the main ballast tanks, which are the differences between whether you are submerged or surfaced. In order to submerge you fill what we call the main ballast tanks completely full of salt water. If you are properly compensated and have done your arithmetic properly you should go down with a neutral buoyancy. You should weigh exactly the same as the size of the hull is pushing you up. You should then be compensated and also fore and aft. The way you do this is you have great big valves in the bottom of these main ballast tanks. You also have valves in the top, we call these the vents. You open the flood valves, you open the vents. Usually, if you want to dive fast you open the flood valves and leave the vents shut. You're then riding the vents. Then when you want to dive, "ooogh, ooogh," you open the vents and down you go. As soon as you open the vents the air in the tanks can go out and the water can come in. During World War II we did away with flood valves. We stopped having them because you don't need them. So, we go around these great big holes in the bottom of the submarine, but the air ballast tanks is entrapped by the vents. When you want to dive all you do is open the vents. In comes the water and down you go.

The flood valves were removed because they were not needed and one had hung up off the Japanese coast and the submarine could not dive. Fortunately repair was completed before detection and attack.

About early May we left Mare Island to go out to Hawaii. We're all done and everything is great. So, away we went and when we are about half way or so somebody pointed toward the stern and said, "You know, I've been looking at this for some time and it looks like we're leaving a path behind us."

Sure enough the sea was nice and clear and looking toward the stern we could see our track all the way back.

Q: Oil?

Adm. B.: Yes, we were leaking oil. So we go to Pearl Harbor--immediately.

Q: On the surface?

Adm. B.: Yes; right on the surface, but we'd dive once a day. Until we got nuclear power, a submarine really had to be a surface ship capable of diving. You couldn't get anywhere submerged in a submarine of World War II vintage; diesel driven. If she had a battery completely full of electricity and she dove and ran at full speed, in one hour her batteries would be dead. She had moved eight miles; she now had to surface to charge batteries. If she went her lowest speed, we'll say a knot, about a mile an hour, that battery would probably last twenty-four hours. So she had now moved twenty-four miles. So from the time she dives she can proceed as little as eight miles or as much as twenty-four miles. She can't go very far submerged. So, obviously, if you want to go somewhere what you need to do is go on the surface. Then you dive when you see a target. You're almost a moveable mine.

When we left the West Coast to go out to Hawaii aboard the submarine NAUTILUS, obviously we were on the surface and we could see that oil slick. That was all right for peace time, but can you imagine taking that submarine out to the Japanese coast and have a slick like that coming up while you're submerged, also?

Q: That was a sign of death for you.

Adm. B.: It would be. You recall that these were riveted hulls. I'm told that that's much more difficult to make them tight while welded hulls are much better.

Q: So then I assume it was a common occurrence of submarines of that period?

Adm. B.: I would think so.

Of course, we had a lot to learn when we got into a war. We had an awful lot of things to learn. When we got into this war and started to go out to the Japanese coast, we'd leave Pearl Harbor and we'd come home two months later. We would have been without a doctor, without any way of getting more torpedoes, more fuel, more anything. We had an enlisted pharmacist's mate who was specially trained, but it wasn't the same as having a physician. But we were on our own. What made us think that we could go out for two months like this and do that Had we tried it? No. We simply did it. Nobody told us that it was impossible, we so we just went ahead and did it.

We arrived at Pearl Harbor with the oil slick. Obviously

we went immediately into the dry dock and they did the necessary repairs. They found out what the difficulty was.

Q: It wasn't anything very serious?

Adm. B.: Nothing very serious. Toward the end of May of 1942 we were ready to go out to Japan and to sink targets if we could find some. But, we didn't go there directly. We proceeded to Midway. This was only a few days before the battle of Midway.

Q: Was your timeliness due to the fact that a battle was imminent?

Adm. B.: We knew when we left Hawaii that we were supposed to go by Midway but we did not know exactly what was going to happen.

Q: You didn't have sealed orders or anything?

Adm. B.: No. But we had about twenty submarines leaving Pearl Harbor at about the same time and that certainly was unusual. You can communicate with them very easily, simply by sending the message. They don't have to disclose their presence. You encode the message and the enemy, we hope, doesn't know where you are when you received it or that you did receive it or that it was addressed to you. Receiving it on the radio doesn't put out any kind of a signal.

So as we proceeded out to Midway, we didn't really know what was going on. There were at least twenty submarines, I would say. These were placed in a circle around Midway, about a radius of fifty miles. We were assigned these positions all around Midway. The idea obviously was to give early warning. I didn't know whether we knew that they suspected a Japanese force was coming along, but I suppose we were simply told that we should report anything that we see. So, we were all set.

At dawn on the fourth of June, we were in the NAUTILUS and located to the northwest of Midway. In the right direction. It happened that the submarine, TRIGGER, which we heard about and was aboard when she was launched, was over on the eastern side and unfortunately in the middle of the night she ran aground. They did get her off.

Q: Ran aground what, shoals?

Adm. B.: Yes. I really don't know but she did run aground; didn't do any harm except that the so-called flood valves, that I described, the flood valves in the forward part of the bottom of the ship; from then on never would close properly. But that was all right; you remember that a year or so later they did away with them anyhow.

Before dawn we had submerged because it was getting light enough to be detected, but it still wasn't light enough that when we dove we'd be able to see through the periscope. There's a time when they could see you if you surfaced, but if you're submerged you can't see anything, because you can't see through the periscope.

Q: Was there any evidence of any other ships being present?

Adm. B.: No. Not when we submerged. We were submerged because of the coming dawn. Very soon after we submerged the sonar operator underwater sound apparatus operator, heard sounds of the propellers of ships. We couldn't see anything, but it was in a northwesterly direction. As soon as it got light enough that we could see through the periscope, we stuck the periscope up and, my goodness, there were ships all over the place. We were in the midst of a great number of ships. I don't know how many. Immediately we made ready--

Q: Were they enemy ships? Could you discern this?

Adm. B.: All we knew was that they were ships and we assumed that they were enemy until we could get a better look. We got the torpedo tubes, all six of them, ready to shoot. We came up and the skipper took a look and he determined that they were indeed enemy and he started shooting torpedoes and didn't hit anything.

Q: How many torpedoes would you carry?

Adm. B.: Oh, I would think that the NAUTILUS probably carried maybe twenty, something like that. They had put two torpedo tubes forward and two aft up in the superstructure during our time in Mare Island. It was too difficult. In order to operate them you had to get up on the surface. There were some controls inside but they didn't work very well.

Anyhow, we fired some torpedoes but didn't hit anything. Immediately we had destroyers making a lot of noise and so we went deep.

Q: You had made your presence known to them?

Adm. B.: Yes, and that was the first time that anyone on board had been involved in firing a torpedo war shot, that is, with an explosive head. Immediately we also had a baptism in depth charges and what they sounded like. We hadn't heard these before so we had a chance to listen to depth charges.

Q: And you dove how deep?

Adm. B.: We were down about two hundred and fifty feet, I guess. The limiting depth of a submarine at that time was three hundred feet.

Q: So you were below the danger of depth charge.

Adm. B.: Well, not quite sure. They could have been lucky enough to put one right next to us and that would have been curtains. We were lucky enough and they were not lucky enough. Anyhow, there were no results from the first encounter. Then they proceeded elsewhere.

When we then came back up they had all disappeared. Soon we saw in the distance an aircraft carrier. She was lying to in the water and didn't look as if she was moving. Some kind of a ship was near her bow and we presumed an effort was being made to take her in tow. She was stopped and she was burning.

Q: She was disabled?

Adm. B.: Disabled and she was maybe going to be taken in tow. So we proceeded over in that direction. I'm not sure why we didn't fire first at the ship that was trying to take her in tow. However, the stopped, burning ship was an enemy aircraft carrier; a choice target.

Q: Was the other ship a war ship also?

Adm. B.: Yes. In the report we called it a cruiser but it might have been a destroyer. My memory gets a little vague. We got over there and fired. I think we fired all the bow tubes and turned around and fired all the stern tubes. Maybe, but I'm not quite sure. But, we fired torpedoes anyhow and we got three explosions.

Q: At what distance were you from her?

Adm. B.: Oh, I should say maybe a little under two thousand yards. Two thousand yards would be one nautical mile. We got three explosions and there was increased smoke and fire. Then aircraft flew over and dropped bombs. We sneaked away.

Now, later on in the war we wouldn't have done everything exactly the way we did. We'd never have sneaked away. We would have stuck around, but you have to learn. In some of the early patrols, submarines would go all the way from Midway to the Japanese coast running submerged all day long and on the surface at night. Well, it would take forever to get there; and we never did that. Once we got into the war and learned a few things we would proceed from Pearl Harbor and Midway all the way to the Japanese coast running on the surface day and night except for the daily check dive. When we had the coast of Japan clearly in sight, then we would start submerging in the day time and running on the surface at night to charge the batteries in addition to being able to see.

As we were sneaking away, there was one tremendous explosion and we came up to periscope depth and took a look in that same direction and there was an awful lot of smoke and fire. Then shortly after that we took another look and there wasn't anything there; not even smoke or fire. Obviously, she had sunk.

Q: What about the screening ship, where was she?

Adm. B.: Don't know, never saw her after we fired. We got credit for sinking the S-O-R-Y-U,--oh before we fired we looked through the identification books with great diligence. We were not going to fire torpedoes if there was any possibility that the targets were ours. The ones we'd fired at in the morning could have been our own. Heaven forbid! But, before we fired at that aircraft carrier we looked through the identification books, not only tried to make sure that this couldn't possibly be one of ours, but we also wanted to be certain we identified the exact ship, the HIRYU and the SORYU (sister ships); it was one or the other.

At the same time we were engaged in sinking an aircraft carrier the total Battle of Midway was going on; a great victory for the U. S. Navy (all four Japanese aircraft carriers present were sunk by Navy aircraft and our submarines).

About a day later we went into Midway harbor. We topped off fuel and started for Japan; assigned the area containing the entrance to Tokyo, Yokohama and Yokosuka. Soon we sank a Japanese destroyer and took pictures of her sinking and of the famous mountain Fujiyama. Both pictures came out in LIFE magazine. We sank also two cargo ships and were supposed to fire our guns at an important railroad tunnel (main line from Tokyo to Kobe and Osaka). It would have involved actually entering Tokyo Bay. We had been damaged in enemy depth charge attacks such that we were noisy. Also every time the rudder was moved, "CLUNK". We decided to forgo the gunfire attack on Atami Tunnel. We headed for Pearl Harbor, Hawaii.

There was great jubilation when we arrived at Pearl Harbor. Among many others, Admiral Nimitz was there to meet us and awarded the Navy Cross to our commanding officer, Lieutenant Commander Brockman, and a signed commendation from Admiral Nimitz to each officer and member of the crew.

Soon thereafter we started planning for the attack on a Japanese island, named Makin, by "Carlson's Raiders," headed by Colonel Carlson, U.S. Marine Corps. His Chief of staff was the President's son, James Roosevelt. The two submarines, NAUTILUS and ARGONAUT, were to be used to carry the (about) 200 marines.

Before departure I was transferred to take command of the new submarine TRIGGER. She had been commissioned in 30 January 1942. After the Battle of Midway she went on a patrol in the Aleutian Islands near Alaska. The commanding officer caught a cold and, on return to Pearl Harbor, was sent to the hospital. They had had no encounter with the enemy, so when I took command, I was a veteran in their eyes.

Interview No. 4 with Rear Admiral Roy S. Benson, U.S. Navy (Retire

Place: Arnold, Maryland

Date: March 25, 1980

Subject: Biography

By: John T. Mason, Jr.

Q: Last time as we broke off you were about to take charge of the TRIGGER, the submarine TRIGGER; that was the twenty-ninth of August 1942. You told me to remind you, to have you repeat what you said to your exec (executive officer) on that occasion.

Adm. B.: I told my executive officer, Lieutenant Commander E. C. Schneider that I had been second in command of five ships with eleven commanding officers and this is my first command, but that he could be sure that I knew his job of being second in command, the executive officer, far better than he did and there was no use in trying to fool the "Old Man."

The TRIGGER, perhaps you recall, was the submarine that I rode down the building ways on in the fall of 1941 at Mare Island, California. By happenstance here I command the submarine that I had part in launching.

Q: Let me follow through on what you said to your exec. Did he try to fool the "Old Man" on any occasion?

Adm. B.: I didn't detect it. So either he didn't or he was very skillful. Believe it or not when I was executive officer on one ship, and I'm not going to name the ship or its skipper, but he was not very easy to get along with. I used to try to fool him because if I could keep away from him, everything is all right. He would make no distinction between some minor difficulty and running the ship aground. That's a slight exaggeration, but this fellow was a very hard person to get along with. I tried to be a buffer between him and officers and crew.

The executive officer was supposed to be the mean guy and the skipper everybody's friend. Finally, I became the skipper; everybody's friend.

Very soon after I took command we proceeded on my first patrol in command of the TRIGGER. We went out to the coast of Japan. The area assigned us was the area of the principal Japanese Islands, but not as far north as the one I'd made on the NAUTILUS. This one included the eastern entrances to the Inland Sea, Bungo Suido and Kii Suido.

Just before we left on this patrol, being commanding officer of a submarine going on patrol, I went over to see our friend,

Jasper Holmes, to be briefed on the area to which we were going.

Q: Well, why would he brief you on that area?

Adm. B.: Well, he was in the intelligence business and he had perhaps some things to tell me about the area we were going to or anything that they thought was going to go on in that area.

Q: Did he also brief you on Ultra and what he would be sending out?

Adm. B.: Oh, yes. Briefed me on that whole concept. Actually, we were also briefed at submarine admiral's headquarters from the submarine tactical point of view. What had occurred there on previous patrols. Where targets might be.

Well, we proceeded out to the Japanese coast and we had almost gotten there when we sighted this small cargo ship.

Let me now go back to when I first had this interest in submarines. Sometime in the 20's I read a book that told about German submarine operations in World War I. One of the things that they did was to do a lot of gun shooting. Instead of firing torpedoes at ships, small ships, they would get up on the surface and open up with gunnery and sink the ship by guns. I thought this was a good idea.

Q: Because they had nothing to come back to you with.

Adm. B.: That was the idea. We like one-sided combats. So, we were almost out to the Japanese coast and we saw this small cargo ship; let's try it. So we surfaced. We had been submerged at first, when we first detected him. When we'd gotten so that he was pretty close to us we surfaced and manned our three inch gun up on the forward deck.

Q: He had no armament whatsoever?

Adm. B.: No, not in our minds. But, we had barely started shooting when he started shooting. When he started shooting, why, we decided the thing for us to do was to get out of there. So, we dove and I promised myself never again, I'm not going to try that one.

Q: You were in the wrong war.

Adm. B.: I was in the wrong war; that's good.

Q: Incidentally, did you do anything further with this small ship? Did you try to torpedo it?

Adm. B.: We tried to, but she finally got away from us. She could run faster on the surface than we could. I don't know what kind she was 'cause she was a pretty good one. Submerged, of course, we couldn't keep up with her. So we never got anywhere with that ship at all.

How did we conduct our patrols?

We would be assigned an area, a geographic area on the Japanese coast or wherever we were. That area was ours and anything that appeared in that area was an enemy. If it wasn't an enemy, well that was too bad for him because there was a war going on and this area was right on the coast and we can presume it was the enemy. We ran on the surface all the way until we got to the Japanese coast and when we would submerge during the day time and we'd surface at night for two reasons. One, we had to recharge the batteries and also we wanted to be able to see. Being able to see through a periscope at night is almost a waste of time. You can see something on a moonlight night but generally there is nothing to see. So, you'd stay up on the surface; you could see and charge the batteries. When we submerged we would make practically zero speed because we don't want to wear out the storage batteries. If we ran into action with the enemy we may need all the power we've got in that battery for endurance, if nothing else.

On the coast of Japan they have something very much like our Gulf Stream. It goes right by the Japanese islands at speeds from one to four knots to the northeast all the time. Now, during the night while charging batteries and looking for targets you've got to get yourself to where you want to be the next morning, because if you dive, if you head into the current, the current is probably going to be a little stronger than your speed so you gradually move northeast anyway. But if you go on any other course you go faster to the northeast. So, get yourself where you want to be the next day or a little bit to the southwest of it. And where do you want to be? You want to be all day so that the coast of Japan is in sight and you want to be off a big harbor or any entrance so that ships trying to go out or in will have to go by you.

Q: Was there any danger of underwater entanglement with rocks and coral?

Adm. B.: We never paid any attention to that; charts were apparently pretty good. Well, they're very good up around Japan. Down south in the southern part of the Pacific, not as good. But, those are the chances we take. We do the best we can.

A good question always is, "Was our peace time training appropriate for war time operations?"

Yes. Of course there were a lot of things about war time operations that we didn't know, that we had to learn, that would be different when we're entering war, and different in every location. But our fundamental training of submarines was magnificent. No one was in the submarines that didn't ask for it. They were specially chosen. They were specially schooled. They knew how to operate all the instruments, machinery, and so forth; equipment on board the submarine. They knew their stuff in regard to submarine operations. All they had to do was to learn the specifics having to do with that war in that place.

Q: And some of that was imparted to you by Holmes and others who had this knowledge?

Adm. B.: Oh, yes, and also reading the patrol reports from submarines that had already been out on patrol and came in.

Q: How much of that did you do in advance?

Adm. B.: You read a great deal of that. You read them very carefully. You are motivated. One of the things you did before you went out on patrol was talk and listen to people; particularly people who had been out in the area where you were going. You read up yourself, you were briefed by the Admirals and their staffs, you were briefed by Jasper Holmes. When you went out on patrol you were really up to here in information on where you're going.

Q: Now, was this the skipper and his exec. too?

Adm. B.: No.

Q: Just the skipper?

Adm. B.: Just the skipper.

So we proceeded close to the Japanese coast; having learned not to shoot guns, although some people tried it later in the war and did very well.

Q: Had this shown up in any of the reports you'd read?

Adm. B.: No.

Q: It was an innovation that you added?

Adm. B.: Well, I was going to give it a try. It might have worked.

So we proceeded to the Japanese coast and I'd say maybe

an hour or so before dawn and there was a moon. That moon was to the westward, therefore the Japanese coast was silhouetted against the moon and we saw something over there on the coast that looked like it might be a ship. A dark shape. Well, we had no way of measuring how far it was to the target or his speed. In other words, we did not have any kind of range finder up on the surface. We had a stadimeter arrangement in the periscope, but we're talking now about night time. So, we saw this ship and we ran over closer. Remember he was on the silhouette side and we were on the dark side. When we got a little bit closer, maybe, three or four miles, then we paralleled him. We can assume that he was on a course going up the coast so we can take that off the chart. He is a coast hugger. Then we got over and went parallel to him and jockeyed our speed until he seemed to be remaining on the same bearing. We were going about the same speed that he was. This tells us approximately how fast he's going. We then put on higher speed and run up the coast. We're trying to get up on his bow, maybe forty-five to sixty degrees. Then turn toward him. You're at battle stations torpedo and all the lookouts are looking in all directions. So, you head right for him. You don't know what the distance is, you can guess; running in like motor torpedo boat until he looks like he's a little bit too close and you're breathing a little heavily. Then you let fly and it seems to me that we fired a spread of three torpedoes hoping that we'd get at least one hit. Don't shoot unless you're going to hit. If you have to spread more, go ahead and spread them more. Put in more torpedoes in the spread, but don't fire any torpedo just for the fun of it. If you're going to shoot, shoot to hit him at least once. If you can hit him once, that's pretty good. Most ships, except for the very biggest and most protected, cannot survive one hit. One will take care of an ordinary cargo ship. We hit him twice, I believe, and down he went.

Q: What size was he?

Adm. B.: Oh, I would say a six to eight thousand tonner. Fairly large but certainly no giant.

Q: So one out of your three hit him?

Adm. B.: Well, two of them, I think. Anyhow, he sank like a rock. We moved up near the entrance to the Bungo Suido and stayed submerged all day long watching for any targets trying to get into the Inland Sea or to come out. We didn't see anything.

Q: Were there any searchers looking for you?

Adm. B.: Not that we know; at that time. But then, I recall, writing in my patrol report that "at dusk we surfaced, close to the entrance to the Inland Sea in the hopes of picking up a target in the afterglow." I believe those were my words, "Our hopes were fulfilled to overflowing because here comes a destroyer." We had been barely surfaced when all at once here comes this guy with the bit in his teeth heading straight for us.

Well, now let me go back and tell about something that happened just before we left Pearl Harbor. While we were waiting to leave Pearl Harbor on patrol I was sitting around chatting with some other people about my vintage in the submarine business. We were talking about various things, arguing and so forth. The three people were an officer by the name of Mush Morton, one by the name of Sam Dealey, and one by the name of Mackenzie. While we were discussing tactics someone brought up a "down the throat shot."

Now, let me describe the "down the throat shot" a little bit. If the enemy destroyer or escort vessel is heading straight for you, you then submerge or maybe you're submerged even before he started heading for you. He's heading straight for you so you take your course so that you are at a very slow speed heading for him. When he gets to a distance of maybe a thousand yards you let fly with three torpedoes, not spread, three of them, right down his throat.

Q: Very narrow target?

Adm. B.: Yes, but if he has the courage to do it, he will not alter his course the slightest bit, he'll hope that he can thread his way. You know those torpedoes were steam driven and they had bubbles that you could see on the surface. If he was strong enough he would maintain his course and try to thread his way among the torpedoes and have them go down his sides. It took courage. He might not get hit and he also might pass right over the submarine and let him have a good salvo of depth charges. If, however, he doesn't do this or hasn't thought it out, he might put the rudder over and this is what you're inviting him to do. When you turn the steering wheel of a car the car turns, but the ship pivots approximately one third of the distance back from the bow. Approximately at the bridge. When he puts over the rudder not only does this part stand out, the bow part, but the stern part moves out in the other direction. The target gets wider. So, if he puts over the rudder, he makes his ship wider and he makes it more certain that he's going to get hit.

Q: Yes. What would be the wisdom of his action in turning the rudder?

Adm. B.: No wisdom; just impulsive action.

Q: It is obvious that the ship would be a bigger target.

Adm. B.: Well, just all at once he sees the torpedoes and he puts the rudder over without having thought it out.

This Japanese captain on board the destroyer; I don't know what he did. I can tell you what I saw. Very soon after we'd fired the torpedoes we had a tremendous explosion. Then a few seconds later we had another tremendous explosion and we had another one. As soon as we heard the first two explosions. I couldn't possibly go deep. I just had to see this. So here I am hanging on the periscope looking out on this bright moonlit night, and I expected to see sections of destroyer obliterated like slices of baloney. I had to see this one. A good friend of mine Clemenson actually saw this one year later in the war. He did this one and actually watched the ship being sliced off like pieces of baloney. Anyhow, I hung on the periscope and when the turbulence of the sea subsided so that I could see, lo and behold, there is the target except that he has turned tail and is heading for the barn. Apparently what happened was that our first torpedo exploded as soon as it was armed at a distance of five hundred yards. Then the other two exploded as they ran through the turbulence of the first one.

Q: None of them hit him?

Adm. B.: None of them hit him, but I found out then that the Japanese could scare too. He had turned tail and was headed for the barn, that night Tokyo Rose explained on the radio that this destroyer had polished off the U.S. submarine near Bungo Suido that had sunk the ship further down the coast that morning. So, Tokyo Rose explained this to us in great detail. We loved it.

Q: Now, you had to assume that the skipper of the destroyer knew that you were out there somewhere.

Adm. B.: Yes.

Q: He was searching for you.

Adm. B.: Searching because that ship had been sunk. He assumed that we would be there and he was out to find us. I'm surprised that the Japanese didn't send out submarines to look for us.

Q: What about planes?

Adm. B.: Planes are not quite as dangerous. Especially at night time, we'd be on the surface and they couldn't see us. But put a couple of submarines out in those areas and just have them sit around looking for us at night. I should think that that might work very well.

Q: Except that their submarines were occupied, I understand, in conveying cargo and all sorts of things.

Adm. B.: They did a great deal of that. It's too bad from their point of view. Of course, I suppose they had no choice. They should have tried to get some of our submarines. Our submarines did them an awful lot of damage.

Q: Since this was early in the war they weren't so hard up at that point in supplying their land forces.

Adm. B.: I agree with that. I don't know what their submarines were doing. I never tried that "down the throat shot" again. I don't know if it is a good idea to do it or not. I decided not.

Q: Well, I would think if your torpedoes had been better you might have succeeded.

Adm. B.: I agree. It might have become standard practice and escorts might have been more wary of us. Of those three other people who I sat around talking with, Sam Dealey did it successfully several times. But, then when he went out on the last patrol on his submarine he, his officers and crew didn't come back. Maybe he tried it once too often. But he did succeed in sinking something like two or three destroyers on one patrol. He did try this maneuver at least once.

Mush Morton lost his submarine, the WAHOO, up in the Sea of Japan; he may have tried it. Morton and Dealey sank many ships.

Q: He was lost too?

Adm. B.: He was lost with all hands. Mackenzie was lost also. So I am the sole survivor of that discussion in the summer of 1942. I'm going to tell you what I think may have happened to Mackenzie on a later patrol.

A few days later, after this "down the throat" shot, we were still on the coast at the entrance to the Inland Sea and we saw this destroyer come out and run up the coast. We couldn't get into a favorable firing position. He ran up the coast and he almost disappeared, all at once there he is coming back again. So, we assumed he was making some kind of speed trials. When he came back again as soon as we detected that he apparently had turned, we went over to where he had been when he went up the first time. When he came down that time we were in good position and we let him have it. I have a picture; he was hit twice, one of them right under the bridge, and I have a picture in which the rest of the destroyer is the usual position of a ship and the whole bow has jack-knifed up and then they sank.

Q: You didn't hear from Tokyo Rose?

Adm. B.: No, not that time. I don't recall any other particular things that went on during that patrol. We headed back for Pearl Harbor.

Q: What was the duration of a patrol like that?

Adm. B.: From the time we'd leave port until we'd get back again was two months.

If you were going to leave Pearl Harbor or Midway and you're going to go out to the Japanese coast, it would take you almost two weeks to get there. Then you'd spend about a month out there and then it would take you almost two weeks to get back again.

Q: That brought you into October?

Adm. B.: That's right. I don't believe that I've explained before the operation of the Royal Hawaiian Hotel. When we got into World War II some very smart people, and I don't know who they were, on both sides, both the Matson Navigation Company/ Royal Hawaiian Hotel and naval authorities got together. Obviously there wasn't going to be any tourist business, during the war, at the Royal Hawaiian Hotel. So, that hotel was leased and was made into a submarine rest camp. When you came in from patrol, everybody, officers and crew, went to the Royal Hawaiian Hotel for the two weeks duration of the refit of the submarine.

Q: That was on Waikiki Beach was it?

Adm. B.: Yes. Waikiki Beach. They had relief crews so that your submarine had some officers and crew on board that belonged to the division commander. They were relief crews and they were supposed to do the ship's work. Anything that could be fixed by the ship's force, they'd fix, for anything being fixed by the submarine base or the ship yard, they were supposed to oversee. Of course, it didn't work out quite that way. I've said before that when anything is being done on your ship you'd better spend some time watching what's going on if you want it to happen right. So, if you're commanding officer or anyone else in a fairly high position on board, even though you're resting at the Royal Hawaiian, you'd be out to the submarine almost every day watching very carefully.

Q: And most of the crew just played during the two weeks?

Adm. B.: It was magnificent, a great idea and I imagine of great mutual benefit. The Matson Navigation Company got back at the end of the war a very nice refurbished facility. It was primarily a submarine rest camp but they allowed other people in all services to use the facilities to the extent that they were not being used.

We now start out on the second patrol of the TRIGGER. This time we were sent to the area which contained the entrance to Tokyo Bay.

Q: This was to be a minelaying operation.

Adm. B.: Yes. This was going to be a minelaying operation but also torpedo shooting. This is the same area we went with the NAUTILUS in our first patrol. This is the area that contains entrances to Tokyo Bay which go up to Tokyo, Yokohama, Yokosuka. Why were we going to lay magnetic mines? Well, the rumor was that there was a shortage of torpedoes. Well, that could have been. Anyhow, no one was on board our submarine that had any experience with laying mines. So, we had a course to learn a little. You recall that in 1940 I had to learn minesweeping as second in command of a destroyer.

Q: This was one of the first efforts, wasn't it?

Adm. B.: Yes. The mines we were going to lay were of the same diameter as the torpedoes. We laid them through the torpedo tubes. Same diameter, twenty-one inch, but one-half as long as a torpedo. Therefore, we could put it into the torpedo tube. We could also store two mines in a position where we could normally store one torpedo. Let me describe a little bit about our particular mine.

Its explosive was something called torpex and the, as I recall it, it was just under a thousand pounds of explosive with an explosive equivalence of one ton of dynamite. That's an awful lot of explosion.

As I said these were magnetic, therefore, they are going to sit on the bottom, and a target is going to go over and the target's metal is going to upset the earth's magnetism; it's going to deflect the magnetic needle and explode the torpedo. From the time you laid the torpedo until the time the torpedo was ready to explode was a period of fifteen minutes. Then it was "ready." Also the click mechanism from one to ten. If, for example, it was set at one and the first target went over and deflected the needle--the explosion would go. If it were set for ten, nine targets would have to go over and simply deflect the needle, no explosion; the tenth target would explode the torpedo. The clicks were randon.

Q: What's the rationale for that?

Adm. B.: The rationale for that is if they sent out minelayers and they find a mine they might be able to sweep the whole lot. But, it would be an awful job to try to sweep all those mines when some are waiting for later targets.

Q: Were they any more dangerous than torpedoes in launching? Could there have been a mishap in launching and they would have been detonated?

Adm. B.: I would think that that would be possible. There was another little hazard which gave us some thought. You lay them through the stern tubes as you are proceeding slowly ahead and you drop the mine, obviously you were pulling away from it all the time it was settling to the bottom. You also launch them out of your bow tubes and they go out and as they are getting down to the bottom you are proceeding right over them. Hopefully you will not be over them when they are armed. And if they don't wait to arm the fifteen minutes, you've had it unless the click mechanism saved you. So, that was a little worrisome but there was nothing you could do about it.

Q: It all depended on the mechanism working perfectly.

Adm. B.: That's right, and it had better work perfectly. None of us had had anything to do with this minelaying so we had to learn a lot.

Q: Did you feel more insecure in minelaying than in torpedo use?

Adm. B.: Well, you always have a little bit of fear in the things that you're not familiar with. Of course, being the skipper you don't even let the thought get out because anything you even think about is spread through the crew, just like an epidemic. So you must always make sure that even in your thoughts everything is great. I don't worry much anyhow.

Q: It is like the power of positive thinking.

Adm. B.: Yes, and you can be sure that your officers and crew are watching you all the time. Their future is in your hands.

Q: And everybody is living on tenterhooks.

Adm. B.: I guess so. I don't think it bothered us. Well, where do you want to lay these mines? You want to lay them close to the coast. You don't want to lay them in water deeper than about a hundred feet.

Q: Is that where they are most effective?

Adm. B.: Yes, because beyond about a hundred and twenty feet the deflection of the meter will not be sufficient. But you certainly don't want to run your submarine aground while you're laying these mines. You want to lay them when you can see so you know where you are. You don't want to lay them in the day time, of course. Actually, you don't want to lay them while you are on the surface at night. You don't want coast watchers, if there are any, to see that something is happening there. You want to do this real secretly.

Q: And so you have to be submerged while they are laid?

Adm. B.: Yes. You really would prefer to lay submerged on a moonlit night close enough in so the depth of the water will not be more than a hundred and twenty feet. Yet, you're going to run aground at sixty feet. You plan all this together. Of course, they chose a place which they considered good, a place called Inubo Saki. It was about a hundred miles up the coast from the entrance to Tokyo Bay. Okay, so we're off on the Inubo Saki now; all is well.

Q: If I'd been skipper of that submarine I would have tried to lay them by the stern only.

Adm. B.: Well, how would you get them there? Each mine weighed nearly a ton. It's very difficult trying to move them through the submarine. I'm not sure if you could turn them around or not. There wasn't enough room to stow them back there anyhow. But we had about twenty mines and some ten torpedoes on board. Our instructions were that we were supposed to lay one line with about half of them going in toward the coast. Then run down the coast a couple of miles; then turn and head for the deeper water laying the other half of the mines. These are sort of parallel lines, a couple of miles between the lines and they're all in water between sixty feet and a hundred feet. You lay them all down and everything is fine.

When you start laying mines, as soon as you shoot one out immediately you're going to reload and this thing is pretty heavy. A mine weighs, oh, three quarters of a ton. They will be reloading the tubes because you're going to keep on laying them. The diving officer has quite a job keeping track of all these weights because he has to maintain a neutral buoyancy of his submarine, not only in overall weight but fore and aft distribution. So he's got a ticklish job. We hadn't practiced at this at all. We had discussed it plenty and planned how to do it.

Q: Was this somewhat different from the torpedo problems?

Adm. B.: Same idea but with some differences. Usually, you fire a spread of torpedoes say 3 or 4 and then you generally would not, unless there were a lot of targets out there, try to reload at that moment. With mines you have to be reloading these mines as you lay them. You're trying to lay them all that evening. You try to get every one of those mines out of the ship that night.

Well, so, we got into position and it was pretty good, a bright moonlit night, could see pretty good. So we started laying these mines and every--this was going great. We finished the first line and started moving to the southward. We'd rigged up our sound gear cause we didn't want that taken off. We were practically scraping the bottom. Naturally if we should scrape a little bit on the bottom we can always come up a foot or something. We were at slow speed. We went down the coast a couple of miles and we turned heading into deeper water cause we're still going to lay the other line between sixty and a hundred feet of water. We'd barely started laying these mines when we sighted something, sort of an object, might be a ship down the coast. So, we continued to lay them. Here comes a Japanese ship.

Q: Not a war ship?

Adm. B.: Not a war ship, but it turned out she had one escort ship with her and here she comes. We were nowhere near close enough to do anything with torpedoes, besides we hadn't loaded torpedoes yet. We were getting rid of mines. So, anyhow, we kept watching him and suddenly I saw some motion over there, then a great big explosion, and that cargo ship was apparently right over one. What an unlucky guy! He arranged to arrive at the time when we were there, and I believe this was the only periscope eye that actually laid mines and watched a target go up in the minefield. But I watched him, and he was an unlucky guy. He arrived there while we were there so I could look. By bad luck, he went right over one of our mines that the click mechanism was set for one. It could have been set for five or anything, but it was one. He went right over the one that was set for one and it had been down the prerequisite fifteen minutes and therefore was armed.

Q: It had been more than fifteen minutes?

Adm. B.: Yes, but not much. He arrived there just in the nick of time to get polished off real good. We heard this tremendous racket about the same time. I could see the whole center of the ship jackknifing up until the whole ship was practically two pieces standing up; they disappeared. You couldn't count to five and the whole thing was gone.

Q: How large was she?

Adm. B.: Gee, I don't recall at all. I really ought to look through the records and find out these things. Well, it looked like a pretty good sized ship. And she did have an escort.

Q: What about the escort ship?

Adm. B.: As we were heading into deeper water, we had four mines still on board but we decided that we wouldn't bother with them. We'd laid half a dozen in that second line and that was all right. No, we've still got a lot of mines there ready to go if a target wants to run over them. Well, as we were proceeding outward all at once we heard another explosion from that direction. But we did not see anything. So, I presume that the escort set off one. Maybe he didn't, I don't know.

We then departed from that area. We thought that there might be a very big party up there. So we got out of there and headed toward the entrance of Tokyo Bay. Right at the corner when you come out of Tokyo Bay to head north there is a peninsula called

Nogima Saki. There's a big lighthouse out there. Of course, they didn't have any lighthouse burning. When we had been down near that part of the area for a couple of days, a big cargo ship came out headed north but he didn't get there because we sank him, right there at the entrance.

Q: With a torpedo?

Adm. B.: With a torpedo. We then proceeded up to Inubo Saki again. We decided that we'd go up there and see if there was any activity. Naturally we took position far enough out there that we weren't going to make the mistake of running into the mine field. We gave that real good clearance.

We could see from a distance that there were six columns of smoke coming down from the north from smokestacks of ships. Six of them in column and when they got to the bearing of our mine field there was a big explosion and one of the smokes turned into a great big amount of smoke. So, I assumed that another ship had been sunk in the mine field.

We then departed and proceeded back down again to the entrance to Tokyo Bay; this was around Christmas time. We stayed around there for several days and the weather got terrible. So we headed out a little bit. We found that trying to maintain periscope depth and trying to see was a waste of time. So we'd go out further and patrol on the surface 'cause at least we could see. We could also get drowned, open bridge, terrible weather.

So we took a position, oh, I'd say thirty miles from the entrance to Tokyo Bay and on the line from Tokyo Bay to the island of Truk, down in the south seas of the Pacific. We figured that anything that was going out might go in that direction. There was a big important Japanese naval base down at Truk.

Q: More than that, it was a bastion, wasn't it?

Adm. B.: Yes. So, we took our position there and patrolled on the surface in this terrible weather. New Year's Eve, I'd say in the middle of the afternoon, suddenly we saw a ship in the distance. We observed a little bit to see which way generally he was heading and we got to a point where we were ahead of him. He was not zigzagging but going in a straight course, and we were ahead of him, maybe at a distance of, oh, five miles, maybe, in the terrible weather. We dropped down to periscope depth and we couldn't see and so we simply surfaced. We're still on the bridge, but most of the submarine was submerged. We're all set to jump down the hatch and "pull the plug" and also close the hatch anytime. Finally we got into a pretty good firing position and we let fly. I don't recall how many hits we got, but he sank very, very quickly. He had an escort with him and that escort was completely useless. The weather was such that he couldn't possibly do anything in manning his guns and trying to do anything with it. It was a waste of time and he wasn't a very large escort. He turned around and headed home.

Q: Is that the OKIKASI, the destroyer?

Adm. B.: I don't know, but don't think he was a destroyer; he was a small ship of some kind. He didn't hesitate around there at all. He just turned around and headed back to Tokyo Bay. That ship had a lot of deck cargo and also among the deck cargo were a lot of airplanes that were all tied down on his deck.

Q: This was destined for Truk, you believe?

Adm. B.: Yes, and he got destined for Davy Jones Locker in great order. We then proceeded back to Midway.

Q: Now, you have neglected to mention something, a very touching little subject which adds color to your duty there and that was the Christmas Eve affair; the playing of the carols.

Tell me about that.

Adm. B.: I don't recall very much about it. We simply played Christmas carols--

Q: You surfaced didn't you?

Adm. B.: Yes, to play Christmas carols. It was a touching sort of thing to do, yes.

Q: Ned Beach wrote about it later.

Adm. B.: Yes, that's right. It was a very nice place to spend Christmas Eve, Christmas and New Year's.

Q: Wonderful weather.

Adm. B.: Oh, great. We went back to Midway. I had grown a beard during that patrol of two months.

Q: Why, to keep warm?

Adm. B.: No, I grew it because I think everybody would like to grow a beard at one time in his life. So, I grew a beard those two months. When we got to Midway my intention was, during the two weeks at Midway, to continue to let the beard grow and then go out for another two months. So when I came back I'd really have some whiskers. But, I couldn't do that because when we arrived at Midway there was a message that submarine admiral, Admiral Lockwood, wanted to see me at Pearl Harbor. So, the next thing I did was to get rid of my whiskers because certainly I wasn't going to go back to Pearl Harbor to see the Admiral with those whiskers.

Q: This was prohibited?

Adm. B.: I don't know, but there were no whiskers around Pearl Harbor at that time. So I--if you're going to be different from people, you should make sure that in your difference you're better. Don't be different and worse. So, I proceeded back without my whiskers. When I got back there they had a great interrogation with regard to minelaying. I knew more about minelaying than anyone back there.

Q: None of your peers had done it?

Adm. B.: Not yet. Some of the submarines were still out on patrol and they were also laying mines, which I didn't know at the time. Apparently I was the first one to come back, so they interrogated me at great length because I knew more than those at Pearl Harbor did. They should have brought my whole crew back because I'm sure that a lot of knowledge by individual members of the crew knew a lot that I didn't know because of their expertise.

Q: What was the gist of the questioning; what were they trying to ascertain?

Adm. B.: How you handled the ship and the mines in it. They weren't concerned about how the mines operated because that was technical business in which they had experts who had been brought in. I didn't know that. They had been brought in specifically to get our mines ready.

Q: From BUWEPS?

Adm. B.: I don't know. But they were very much interested in what sea conditions, depth control, difficulties. They were asking some questions that I couldn't answer, but at least we were learning something about this minelaying business.

Q: Was there any questions of the merits of minelaying in coastal areas over the merits of having torpedoes and using them?

Adm. B.: Oh, generally the submarine force was opposed to laying the mines. They would much rather put the torpedoes on board and go out and hunt for targets instead of just laying mines around.

Q: They were more versatile with the torpedoes, I suppose?

Adm. B.: Also more chance of seeing some results, because if our target had not been so unlucky as to have arrived at the right time we would not have known, perhaps never have known that anything happened there. Maybe the post-war stories might have told us something. But probably not.

Q: Before you came back they had knowledge of your success. You had communicated this?

Adm. B.: Oh, yes. When we were out on patrol like that, I forgot to mention, we were always at complete radio silence. The only time we would open up on our radio was when there was a real need to open up and say something, or you were on the way back and you were two or three days run away from the Japanese coast. Then you would open up the radio and you'd tell anything that you wanted to say of value to them and also when you expect to arrive off Midway. If any ship or submarine arrived off Midway and wasn't expected she might get bombed. So we'd always tell when we're coming.

We had a very interesting system, a sort of neutral zone. I think we called it that. We had a rectangle and when we were moving that rectangle moved with us. In other words, oh, maybe twenty miles each side of that and maybe fifty miles fore and aft. No one is going to attack anything in that zone. That moves with you. Of course this isn't something physical that moves, this is on the charts. Any target in that particular rectangle is immune from being attacked.

Q: Well, this was an open sesame as far as the enemy was concerned. They could utilize this for their own safety.

Adm. B.: Yes indeed. So we kept quiet on that one. While I was at Pearl Harbor I was to be awarded the Silver Star medal and they were going to give it to me in Pearl Harbor. I said, "No, let me take it home, back to Midway, and we'll have a ceremony in which all my officers and crew can be present."

Q: They had earned it, too.

Adm. B.: I hope so. Back to Midway. The senior submarine officer at Midway was a captain by the name of W. V. O'Regan. We had a big ceremony and he presented me my Silver Star.

We had a system relative to awards that the Submarine Force Commander, the Admiral, had an awards committee and for every patrol that came in they looked over the results and recommended to the submarine Admiral what, if any, awards should be made. The Submarine Force Commander never wanted the authority himself to approve and award decorations to his people. His awards committee recommended things to him and he sent his recommendations to Admiral Nimitz. Admiral Nimitz had an award board. Admiral Nimitz did have the authority to actually award them in the name of the President. But the Submarine Force Commander sent his recommendations up there and that awards committee would look them over and would approve or change or turn down and so forth. But they also had another gimmick that, for example, I got this Silver Star medal. I could recommend something on the order of two of my officers or crew to receive the Bronze Star Medal and maybe three or four officers or enlisted men to receive Admiral Nimitz's commendation. These were not hard and set rules. You could recommend anyone on your ship for anything or you could fail to recommend anyone on your ship for anything.

Anyhow, back to Midway with my Silver Star medal, I sat down and wrote recommendations for the other people. All I had to do really was to scribble it out in some rough form and the people back in Hawaii would embellish it so it would read properly. Any time you recommended a person for a decoration obviously you had to come up with some suitable wording. Then, they have people who can sling the language better and they'll draw up the final papers.

At Midway, where did we stay? We stayed at the Gooney Bird Lodge there on Midway. There wasn't anything to do except you'd have great big tables and the bar, serving only beer. The commanding officers of submarines who were in from patrol or on the way through would all sit around one table and the seconds in command of submarines would sit around another. I recall one sitting there at Gooney Bird Lodge and somebody behind me at the second in command table, the executive officers' table, was telling some weird story; there were a lot of weird stories there. This fellow was telling about the submarine he had just come in from. I could hardly believe it and I turned around and found that the story teller was my executive officer! And where he got that story from I don't know, but it was a great one, a great yarn that he was telling. He must not have been on the same submarine that I was. A miracle.

Benson #4 - 230-

Q: That was the time for sea stories?

Adm. B.: Oh yes! You know there was a lot of gooney birds, big albatross, on Midway. Sometimes you'd come into your little room, which wasn't much of a place and somebody had thrown a gooney bird into your room, that was handy, quite a job to get him out.

Our "Gooney Bird Lodge" was built by Pan Am when they were flying seaplanes between California, Hawaii, Midway, Wake, Guam, Philippines and Hong Kong (later 1930's).

Q: Clippers?

Adm. B.: Yes. That was one of their stops.

So, we then started out on the third patrol of my command of the TRIGGER. We were then sent out on a very interesting concept.

Q: What was the date of this one?

Adm. B.: This would be getting around to January, I would say. Probably the end of January of 1943. Let's see, we left from Tokyo around New Year's and in two weeks got to Midway, that's the middle of January. Two weeks refit, the first of February, yes. Around the first of February.

We're heading now for a Round Robin. We're getting more and more submarines all the time. When I got back to New London a year later I found that they were launching and also commissioning a submarine every second Sunday. They were building them also at Portsmouth. They were building them at Mare Island, California. They were building them at Manitowoc, Wisconsin.

There's an article in the latest <u>Naval Institute Proceedings</u> by Captain Nelson, about building them up at Manitowoc, Wisconsin and bringing them down the Mississippi River.

They had already started this Round Robin. Submarines one week apart. When we headed out there was one that had left Midway a week before and when we'd been out a week another one would be leaving Midway. First you'd go to Wake. What are you going to do at these places? Reconnaissance. You're going to look it over. Attack ships if any. You're going to observe and when you leave there you're going to open up on your radio if there's anything to say. With regard to the radio I mentioned that we kept total radio silence. The people in Hawaii could communicate with us anytime. They'd send it out on a very low frequency circuit. We could copy that whether we were on the surface or submerged. They would send it two or three times, say four hours apart on a regular schedule. We would get these messages but we didn't have to say anything. They would assume that we got it.

We went to Wake. We went to Truk, both the north pass Truk and around the corner to the south entrance and observed. At every one of these places you'd spend two or three days. Keep to the schedule unless there was something special. You're following the leader. There were other places including Palau and then you came back. You were out for two months, but you went to these various places and looked things over. If you saw a target you had to judge whether you want to attack him and disclose that you're there. Maybe all you want to do is look and report what you saw. Sometimes you want to do one, sometimes you want to do the other.

While we were on this patrol we received a message from back in Pearl Harbor that a convoy consisting of, if I recall correctly, five ships and two escort ships was leaving from somewhere going, of course I do not recall those details, to somewhere. They specifically told us that we were on the line between where they came from and where they were going. So, we would expect them at such and such a time.

They gave instructions in these messages to each individual submarine that was going to be on this line to try to get this convoy. The one before me was about a half a day's run of the convoy. In other words, a couple of hundred miles southeast of where we were. This was the submarine TRITON. The TRITON was coming up to bat about a half a day before we were coming up to bat. The skipper of the TRITON was my friend Mackenzie, one of the four who discussed "down the throater" in 1942. Mackenzie sent a message that he had detected them and enumerated that there was five ships, two small escorts. So they were all there. The next day when they came by and we sighted them they were all still there. We succeeded in bringing ourselves into position where we were between the two columns and polished off the leader of each column. We fired from the bow tubes this way and the stern tubes that way and got them both.

Q: These were merchant ships?

Adm. B.: Merchant ships. I don't know how big, but then the escorts held us down until the ships had gotten safely out of the way.

We proceeded to Palau. When we arrived at Palau there wasn't time enough, to reach the entrance on the western side that day. It would still be dark, so we decided to take a look at the eastern side where there wasn't supposed to be any entrance. We'd barely gotten up there when a ship came out of what wasn't supposed to be an entrance. Apparently they had dredged an entrance there, an entrance and exit.

Q: This was into the lagoon?

Adm. B.: Of Palau. We observed this ship coming out. Well, we couldn't get into position to shoot at him, so after he was safely out of the way so he couldn't see us we surfaced and started running after him. If we had enough speed and endurance we could do what was called an "end around". He would be cruising along and we would run around him far enough away so he couldn't see us until we were up ahead of him and then we would submerge and wait for him to come and let him have it.

Q: His speed was very slow then?

Adm. B.: Maybe making something like twelve knots or so. It was a lengthy process. We started doing that, then along came some rain clouds and where he went I'll never know. We couldn't find him so we went back to Palau and took a look at both sides again and then it was time for us to go home.

It really was time for us to go home because we were running very short of fuel. We'd used a lot of fuel running around this fellow with all four diesels churning away. So, we then decided to go back to Midway. We couldn't afford to run on more than one engine and even then at a most economical speed. It took us a long time to get to Midway. I'm surprised that we actually made it. We must have been awfully low on fuel. We went fourteen thousand miles on that patrol.

Q: Did it ever happen during the course of the war that a submarine ran out of fuel?

Adm. B.: I don't--I never heard of it. But we were getting close to it. Fourteen thousand miles we went on that submarine during that patrol. We never had any means to refuel or get any more food or medical help. We were on our own. But, we did get to Midway and all is well. After we put some fuel in the submarine we went back to Midway and back to Pearl Harbor. There Admiral Nimitz presented me with a Navy Cross. That had to do with the patrol in which we'd laid the mines, etc.

Soon we started out on the fourth patrol of the TRIGGER under my command. We were assigned again the area containing the entrances to Tokyo Bay.

Q: This is the one that began on the twenty-second of May, I take it?

Adm. B.: Yes. The two weeks trip out was routine.

Perhaps this might be a good time to explain some of our periscope techniques. Maybe it is old hat; having been explained by everyone. Perhaps not. Anyhow--

If there were no enemy ships in sight we would put the periscope all the way up periodically and search slowly and carefully for initial evidence of a ship approaching. When we had enemy ships well in view we would expose less of the periscope for shorter periods of time. When we raised the periscope we did so with it set to the bearing (direction) on which the target is. From time to time a long, all-around look was essential. There were cases in which that look around was not done often enough and an enemy warship sneaked up and nearly sank the submarine. A glassy sea was good for the enemy but bad for us because it was easier for them to see the periscope.

We preferred at least ripples on the sea; better still, white caps. Many of us put the periscope up, when the enemy was close, about two feet below the limit switches. If the depth control was not perfect and the top of the periscope got ducked, raise the periscope up to the limit switches and see the target.

Enough school for a while.

We got out to our patrol area and had been out there for maybe a week when late one afternoon we saw in the distance the tops of some kind of a ship. As the ship got a little closer to us we dove and kept watching and we saw some more ships. We could identify now that they were warships. We were still watching and all at once we detected a cruiser. Pretty good size ship. This looked like a suitable target and we got ourselves inside the outer screen and set up the cruiser on the TDC (torpedo data computer) to fire at the cruiser. I was just about to shoot at this cruiser when, taking another look, I saw the tops of battleships and an aircraft carrier. I held my fire. I decided I wasn't going to shoot at the cruiser; maybe I could get a shot at one of the real big ones. So the cruiser went by and these ships, at least two battleships and a couple of aircraft carriers, were approaching. We were doing fine, but all at once they all zigged away, got away free, into Tokyo Bay they went.

Q: Now, let me ask you a question at this point. How skilled were you at ship silhouettes?

Adm. B.: We're pretty good if we could see enough.

Q: What kind of training did you have in this area?

Adm. B.: None really. No formal training. We had identification books to study. When we saw enemy ships we would try to find them in those books. I don't recall what these ships were. At the time I probably had some idea because as soon as they had gone by, as soon as it got dark, we got up on the surface and ran at high speed away from that region for a few hours. We then opened up on our radio and told the Admiral back in Pearl Harbor what we had seen. I must have said more than something like a couple of battleships and a couple of carriers plus escorts but I don't off-hand recall just exactly what it was.

Q: Wasn't it thought to have been a contingent of their ships coming back from the Aleutians?

Adm. B.: Could have been.

Q: I think this is what Blair calls it.

Adm. B.: But, anyhow, they escaped unscathed and we got out and ran fast for a few hours, opened up on the radio and explained exactly what we'd seen. That was of some value, but not as much value as if we'd sent something to the bottom. I should have taken the cruiser but—well it's understandable; to sink a cruiser would be great, but to put a fish in a battleship or a carrier would be greater.

But we got paid back to some extent. A little bit later on patrol, I would say that perhaps a week or some after this incident—

Q: Blair said two weeks later.

Adm. B.: We were still in that area when we got this message telling us that a new aircraft carrier was leaving Yokosuka, that was also in Tokyo Bay, was leaving Yokosuka and proceeding to Truk and she was going to leave on such-and-such a day, the very next day at just before sunset. She was going to be escorted by escort ships and aircraft and they had us lined up. We were going to be the first to bat, but they had something like half a dozen submarines along the way to Truk; in turn each one would come to bat unless the ship was destroyed.

Well, when it came to the exact time the ship was supposed to come out of Tokyo Bay, here she comes! And it was, I should say, maybe an hour or two before sunset and the sea was glassy and they had two escorts, if I remember correctly, and air cover. She was coming out at a pretty good clip.

You recall that from up on the surface we couldn't determine how far anyone was away? We could through the periscope; not accurately but much better than nothing.

It appeared she was making about twenty-five knots. She was zigzagging all over the place. We did get ourselves, however, into position, I guess about a thousand yards away and we were about, oh I'd say, fifty degrees on his bow.

We fired torpedoes. We got three explosions. We got a lot of attention from the escorts very quickly.

Q: You knew the carrier had been hit?

Adm. B.: Yes. But we didn't know--we knew he'd been damaged, but we didn't know if he'd sunk or the extent of the damage. We got a great deal of attention from the escorts, both the small ships and the aircraft. They appeared to have been augmented by other forces. They probably sent out more aircraft. We had an awful lot of depth charges dropping all around us all over the place.

Q: How deep were you?

Adm. B.: Oh, the water there was probably half a mile deep. There is deep water right up to the Japanese coast.

Q: How deep would you go for safety sake?

Adm. B.: Oh, our submarine test depth was three hundred feet. That three hundred feet is the length of the playing part of a football field. That's the maximum we were supposed to go. It was on this occasion that we caught her at four hundred and seventy. We were on the way down, something went wrong and we blew the ballast tanks at about four hundred and caught her at about four seventy. Then we had to fill the ballast tanks quickly or we'd been on the surface with the enemy all around us.

Q: That was an anxious moment.

Adm. B.: There were a lot of noises in our superstructure and when we got back to Pearl Harbor many of the welds of the superstructure hitched to the pressure hull had been sheared off.

Q: Was this by depth charges or--

Adm. B.: Apparently by going down to the excessive depth.

I don't remember other things that went on during that patrol. It wasn't very eventful except for these two things in which we let that task force go by and we hit the aircraft carrier.

I made a mistake when I sent my message back, I said, "We got him! Three hits on the flat top." This was a mistake as I was told when I got back. Too many people were able to read that message. A lot of people who were not supposed to know that we had some foreknowledge. When you read these words it sounds as if the person who got our message knew what we were talking about and he wasn't supposed to know. People weren't supposed to know that we had actually gotten a message, "We got him." That implies that the recipient of our message knew what we were talking about. So, we shouldn't have done that but--

Q: Yes, that opens up a question about ULTRA and its effectiveness in helping you--

Adm. B.: Tremendously effective.

Q: A question came to mind; you said that submarines had been told to be in certain positions along the route of this carrier as it was going to Truk. If the carrier had gone on and been approached all along the way, would not the Japanese had some idea that their secrets were known.

Adm. B.: I suppose so. I would think that it would finally be suspected.

So we proceeded home and we were greeted with many handshakes and hurrahs and so forth. Also, as usual, but more this time, there was a lot of interrogation. I didn't find out until a couple of years later. I don't know who told me. I believe that the war was still on. He shouldn't have really although I don't see anything wrong with it. He told me there had been three explosions; two premature explosions off the side of the carrier and one real good one at the stern. She had been rendered immobile and had been towed; she was brand new, and had been towed back into Yokosuka, Japan, where she had been built. They had tried to get her into dry dock but she drew so much water that she stuck on the sill and had to build a caisson around the stern and effect temporary repairs so they could get the stern of the aircraft carrier over the sill; it took them nearly a year to get that brand new aircraft carrier back out into the war zone.

Q: Well, the name of the aircraft carrier was the HIYO?

Adm. B.: That's right.

Q: HIYO, and she was actually Admiral Koga's flagship, was she not?

Adm. B.: Well, she was some admiral's flagship, because some years later I talked to the person who was his chief-of-staff. Subsequently, when she came out the next time, I understand, that she was present at the Marianas, at the "Marianas turkey shoot" and was sunk in that battle. I also found out a couple of years after this incident, that this was the patrol that caused Admiral Lockwood to make his decision that the magnetic exploders should be deactivated.

Q: Yes. I wonder if you'd talk about the whole area of the torpedoes, the defective exploders?

Adm. B.: I can talk about it. Early in the war we had great difficulties with our torpedoes and I'll describe them. The first difficulty we had was that just before World War II, before we got into World War II, they came out with something in which we had some very high top secret discussions. I remember I was the Executive Officer of the NAUTILUS and the Captain of the NAUTILUS and I went to a briefing. We were pledged to secrecy and not to tell anyone about this. "There is a Mark 6 magnetic exploder which we're going to have in our torpedoes."

Prior to the magnetic exploder we had a contact exploder. The torpedo would go out and hit the side of the ship and would set off the explosive. The explosion would be on the side of the ship. Well, it's pretty obvious that if you can send that torpedo just under the keel of the target and have it explode right under the ship, it would make a much bigger hole and it might sink faster. So, they devised this magnetic exploder and we were supposed to set them to go just under the keel of the target. So, we had to figure out approximately how much water the target drew and set torpedo depth about ten or fifteen feet below. We were all told to do this and so we started doing this. The only trouble was as we subsequently found out the torpedoes were running deeper than we were setting them. Therefore, a high percentage of these torpedoes were running so deep that the magnetic needle was not deflected and the torpedoes did not explode. In one case one of the submarine skippers fired nineteen torpedoes; apparently he fired and hit this tanker and the tanker was stopped and he fired nineteen more torpedoes at the side of this tanker and could not get a hit. Could not get anything to explode. These torpedoes were so made that the magnetic exploder could set them off or contact could set them off. Either way would do it. In other words, there was a dual ignition. In this particular case it was found later in the war that the trouble was that when the torpedo hit the side of the target the head would crush so fast that the firing pin was unable to move as it was supposed to move as set back from the torpedo having hit the side. Therefore, the firing pin was jammed and it wouldn't explode. They found this out by taking a torpedo over to the dry dock with an inert head on it, that is not explosive, and they dropped it; dropped it such that when she hit the bottom of the dry dock she would be going at the speed the torpedo would normally be going. This was forty-six knots, a little bit over fifty miles an hour. They took the torpedo, looked at it and found the firing pin had gotten caught because the head busted up too fast. So that was one of the things they needed to fix.

Q: When was this discovered?

Adm. B.: This was discovered, I would say, in maybe the end of 1943.

You recall it was in June of 1943 that I came back from having hit that carrier, when I said that I'd been told a couple of years later that that's when Admiral Lockwood--it was this attack convinced Admiral Lockwood that we've got to inactivate the magnetic exploders.

Q: Actually he was convinced long before that, was he not?

Adm. B.: I think so, but here was something that he could actually go and try to sell. Matter of fact, many of us, many of the early skippers followed the directions of setting the torpedoes to run about ten to twenty feet below the keel. Many of those early skippers produced nothing and were transferred out of the submarine service. The only reason they didn't produce anything was the magnetic exploder didn't let them--every time they fired at the target, nothing happened. They could watch through the periscope and see the bubbles coincide with the target and nothing happened. There were some people, I'm not going to say whether I was one of these or not, there were some people who had a routine on board the submarine in which when you ordered "make ready the torpedoes," the torpedo men would do several things, usually, but they would set the depth of the torpedoes at ten feet, automatically, and if you forgot to tell them to set it at forty, that's a mistake. We just overlooked it. I am sure that it actually happened. I'm fairly sure that if it did happen the culprit never told anybody, because the word was that you're supposed to set these torpedoes to run deep under the keel. But, at my level, we Lieutenant Commanders in command of submarines, we knew very well that setting them to run under the keel was not productive.

Q: And so to be productive you set it at ten.

Adm. B.: Some characters would engage in this.

Q: It was the more daring and astute ones did this.

Adm. B.: Well, anyhow, because--

Q: And had more success.

Adm. B.: Because if you brought the torpedo depth up and then if the torpedo did not explode because it came in the vicinity of that magnetic field, it would hit the target and bang. Now, what happened in this carrier incident? I'm sure that the torpedoes were set to explode on the side of the ship. But, two of the torpedoes exploded off the side because they detected the ship's magnetic field before they reached the target.

Q: Now, all well and good to have set them at that ten foot level rather than the forty; then in trying to present the case for defective torpedoes per se this data distorted them, distorted the data.

Adm. B.: Bound to.

Q: So, it was a deterrent in that sense, it delayed the real discovery of the defect.

Adm. B.: I'm sure that quite a few people knew that this sort of thing was going on, but they were still trying to sell the idea.

Q: It's quite clear, and I've known this for a long time, it's quite clear that Blair puts the onus in part on Admiral Christie who was so adamant that these torpedoes were good and it was the skippers who were in error.

Adm. B.: That's right. That's exactly why--

Benson #4 -250-

Q: Why was he so adamant; he'd been in BUORD and he'd designed this, had he not?

Adm B.: Well, I'm not sure whether he'd designed it, but he had a great deal to do with it, I understand, not only in the Bureau of Ordnance, but also out in the torpedo station in Newport. Obviously, there had been totally inadequate testing. They actually fired torpedoes, I think it was down in the South Pacific somewhere in which they set up a net to find out what depth they were running at. They were running at a depth greater than they were supposed to. So, some of the early torpedoes, even if the magnetic feature was perhaps no good, and even if you set them to run to make a contact, they were still running too deep and so these things had to be changed. This was a complicated scramble. I understand that the Germans had ran through this same thing.

The thing that astounds me is that how in the world the Japanese could have had aircraft dropping torpedoes. Most of the damage done in the attack on Pearl Harbor on the battleships was torpedoes dropped by aircraft in the shallow waters of Pearl Harbor. They were able to drop them from the aircraft and those torpedoes did not hit the bottom and they also did not come out of the water. The depth control was magnificent and went right over and hit the target.

About this time somewhere, oh I don't know when it was, I'd say in the spring of 1943 at Pearl Harbor, a mistake was made one day on board one of the submarines. A torpedo tube, loaded with a war shot, somehow by error was fired in Pearl Harbor. A mistake. That torpedo, if it had been as good as the Japanese torpedoes at the beginning of the war, would have gone over and it would have sunk some ship in the harbor. There were ships all over the place. But that torpedo went out of the torpedo tube and immediately went down, hit the bottom, and exploded and there were great chunks of unexploded explosive floating on the water. I don't know how to analyze what happened there. It was certainly not good; poor torpedoes.

When the torpedo leaves the torpedo tube there are two ways in which this depth is controlled. One of them is that there is a gadget that measures the pressure of the water above the torpedo. If the torpedo is set to run at twenty feet and it goes down to fifty feet the pressure is greater, therefore, it will cause you to get up flipper and bring you up. Also, if you're accelerating that would have a tendency to make the pendulum swing to the rear and therefore the torpedo thinks that the bow is up because the pendulum is to the rear. Therefore, it will have a tendency to go down. So, while you're accelerating from zero speed to forty-six knots there is a tendency for the torpedo to want to go down. But as it goes down and there is a tendency for it to come up for it's getting into water deeper than set. However, generally, it will go out, down and then come up and settle where it belongs. But the first tendency is to go down and this torpedo in Pearl Harbor did exactly that. It went down but hit the bottom. The Japanese torpedoes at the battle of Pearl Harbor did not hit the bottom. Maybe some of them did.

Q: And then you have the other instance where they were so successful sinking the PRINCE OF WALES and the REPULSE in Singapore at the outbreak of the war. Those were sunk by aerial torpedoes.

Adm. B.: Our destroyer, air and submarine torpedoes at that time were alike. They were all members of the same family. They all operated exactly the same way. There were some little differences. I suppose that dropping it from the aircraft takes a little more stress in some way and shooting it submerged another way, but it was essentially the same torpedo. When we went out on that patrol in which we hit the aircraft carrier, generally the torpedoes we had on board were Mark 13's, which were the aircraft torpedoes.

They must have been strengthened such that you could drop them from an aircraft because the explosive head didn't have as much explosive as our Mark 14's, or the destroyer Mark 15. They were all the same except that we had bigger explosives but the same torpedo.

Q: May I ask one more question about the torpedo? Was not one of the problems the fact that in the testing of the torpedoes prior to the war or shortly after they were available, that they didn't use warheads? Was that a problem, I mean, we didn't use actual warheads in testing?

Adm. B.: What we used was an exercise head. We used this for our peacetime practices. What occurred with the exercise heads, you fired the same torpedo except that when it exploded, instead of exploding it blew the water out. So, the torpedo then floated and you could pick it up and use it again.

Q: Was that as accurate a test?

Adm. B.: I wouldn't be surprised if the weight distribution with water in there was perhaps enough different that the hydrodynamics would be a little different. Obviously, they should have had a head on the torpedo that weighed exactly right and weight distribution the same. I'm not sure, but I've heard that the hydrodynamics were a little different. Remember the pieces of that explosive floating on the water; it looks like maybe the explosive didn't weigh as much as water. Maybe it was somehow different.

Q: In retrospect it seems almost impossible that these defects should have been permitted to continue for, what, over a year?

Adm. B.: Oh, yes. A year and a half.

Q: And why this was allowed?

Adm. B.: I know that the chief of staff, no, I know that the operations officer for the Admiral in January of 1943, this is before Admiral Lockwood arrived on the scene, the operations officer knew that people were setting torpedoes at a different depth than regulations required; he knew it.

What did I learn about ten or fifteen years later? Our friend Ned Beach and his wife invited us to a dinner party in Washington. Who did he have there? Why he had a retired Japanese admiral who had been chief of staff to the Admiral aboard the carrier that we hit in June 1943. He said that they saw the bubbles of three torpedoes. What happened to the fourth I don't know. I think we fired four.

Q: Actually you fired six according to the source I have.

Adm. B.: Is that right? I'm glad to hear that. I couldn't imagine my failing to unload the whole bow at the target; i.e., six torpedoes.

Q: But only three hits.

Adm. B.: If we didn't fire six, I can't understand it. We must have not had any more torpedoes left. We certainly would have fired six. But, there were three explosions. Two of them were off the side of the carrier. One of them, one of the three that exploded and damaged the ship was about one third of the way inside the stern. It busted the propulsion system completely. I think that's about all he told me. I had heard this information but I had his eyes tell me that it occurred. They were indeed making about twenty-five knots and indeed they were dragged back into the Yokosuka shipyard to rebuild.

Q: Actually it was a converted merchant ship to begin with, wasn't it?

Adm. B.: I hadn't heard that.

Q: Would you say something about Admiral Lockwood?

Adm. B.: Well, Admiral Lockwood came up from down around Australia about, I'd say, February of 1943. No, I believe he was up there by the time I came back from having laid the mines in late 1942. He was at Pearl Harbor then, that's when I first met him.

Q: Did he not replace English?

Adm. B.: He replaced Admiral English.

Q: Who died or was killed?

Adm. B.: He was on a trip to the West Coast in an airplane with half of his staff and they crashed. When I came back from laying the mines Admiral Lockwood was in Pearl Harbor, I think.

Whenever you went out on patrol Admiral Lockwood had you come up and see him and talk things over and then he proceeded down with you.

Q: To the ship?

Adm. B.: Down to the ship. When you left him, he was such an inspiring individual that you knew that if you go out and do your duty the war is over. You won it all alone. You know intellectually it's not true, but psychologically you knew that this was true and you're not going to let him down. What a tremendous guy. He was, I'm sure, beloved by everyone. It's hard for me to believe that he could be in controversy with anybody. He was very like Admiral Nimitz, also very much Admiral Spruance, I believe. I knew Admiral Spruance the least. But Admiral Nimitz was this type, a very kindly gentleman who had a great interest in all these people all the way down the line. He never turned his back on the subordinates. Tremendous leaders, just what you're supposed to do.

We have gotten far afield from the arrival of TRIGGER at Pearl Harbor in June 1943. May I tell something about our submarine repair system?

Q: Please do.

Adm. B.: At the end of each patrol of two months we had "Refit"; submarine base or submarine tender fix everything that needed fixing. Then a few days training. Then off.

Q: This was after every patrol?

Adm. B.: After every patrol. Sometimes you were in Midway and sometimes you were in Pearl Harbor. I'll tell you of one incident that happened when we were in Pearl Harbor. We went over to the shipyard, certain things to be done. In addition to the regular refit there was one specific thing they had to do and we had to get out of there by such-and-such a date because at the end of the refit we were supposed to have a day to load and a couple of days of training.

You know we lost approximately one-third or one-fourth of all of our officers and enlisted men after each patrol, went back to new construction. We got new people. So we wanted a couple days of training before we went out again.

Q: This is the cell theory?

Adm. B.: So this work was supposed to be done on the shipyard. It was promised that it was going to be done such-and-such a date. I checked on that date and they agreed "Fine." So I didn't say anything to anyone at the shipyard but I went up to the captain of the yard, of the shipyard, and got a pilot and a tugboat the next morning at eight o'clock to take my submarine over to the submarine base and put it alongside the submarine tender where we belonged. We had a tender over there in addition to the sub base. When it came to eight o'clock in the morning the shipyard people were still hammering on the submarine so we took in the lines and took the tugboat alongside and towed the submarine over to the submarine base. The shipyard people were still working. The people in the shipyard, were they irate! They called my squadron commander and he took my side, obviously. I was right in the first place and in the second place he was loyal, Admiral Styer. He gave them a blasting.

But, you know, they went to work on it. They finished that work post-haste. I wouldn't have dared to have done that when I was first skipper, but this time I was pretty well established myself. This happened after my third patrol in command of the TRIGGER in the spring of 1943.

Q: You had a few medals on your chest.

Adm. B.: It helps. Let's return to events in June 1943. Our submarine had been damaged. So they decided to give her a full shipyard overhaul. She was 1 1/2 years old; a thorough going over is needed; thirty days working in the shipyard. So they decided everybody in the crew, all the officers and crew, were going on thirty days' vacation. So, they broke out some airplanes flying boats (maybe Pan-Am) and flew us to Alameda on the West Coast. Then we had to report back within thirty days to the same place and they would fly us back to Pearl Harbor, Hawaii.

Q: That destroyed the possibility of the skipper overseeing what was going on the ship.

Adm. B.: Yes. I didn't know when I left that indeed I would never see my submarine, TRIGGER, winner of a Presidential Unit Citation, again. There were too many looking for submarines to command. Apparently I didn't have a prayer. I was giving up my position and somebody else would be there.

Q: Yes, but you had your share of adventures at sea as a skipper of a submarine, didn't you?

Adm. B.: Before departure I was presented my second Silver Star. I then proceeded, flew to Alameda, California, train to Concord, New Hampshire. I'd barely gotten there, my home town, when I got a message, "Cut your vacation short, report at the submarine base in New London, Connecticut. Thirty days temporary duty."

Q: They put you to work right away.

Adm. B.: So, I went there and what they wanted me to do--they had sent to Washington and said, "The next person you have that is coming around this area who's been a skipper out there we'd like to have him for thirty days. We'd like to have him go over what we're doing here at the submarine school at New London, Connecticut. Like to have him look over what we're doing and make suggestions." Gee, that sounded like a great idea.

Q: Well, that's putting your operational experience to work.

Adm. B.: They didn't have anyone around there who'd been a submarine skipper in the war. So, I reported in and the first day I came to work I found out I had made commander.

Q: And to put the date in this was July 1943.

Adm. B.: So, I came to work wearing my khaki uniform with my coat with Commander shoulder marks and I was all set. I reported to the executive officer of the submarine base and he said, "You know, you're not in uniform unless you wear your ribbons."

I said, "Well, Sir, I've never worn any ribbons so I'll have to correct that." The next day I came to work, this really had little to do with professional business, I came to work with my ribbons. I had the Navy Cross, a Silver Star, a Gold Star in lieu of second Silver Star and it happened that the NAUTILUS at that time had been awarded the Presidential Unit Citation for time including when I was executive officer. So I had that ribbon also. Subsequently the TRIGGER also got the same Presidential Unit Citation.

Q: Where did you get the ribbons so readily?

Adm. B.: Oh, they came with the medal. The Presidential Unit Citation ribbon was sent to me. So, I had those ribbons on when I came to work and the executive officer--no I didn't go to see him then, I went to see the officer-in-charge of the school. But, a few days later I ran into the executive officer and he said, "Listen, I don't think that that's very modest." He said, "You're supposed to wear all your ribbons. Not just the good ones."

I said, "What else am I supposed to wear?"

Well, I didn't know they'd invented one ribbon which we guys used to call "I'm alive." That's the one because you were in the armed services prior to Pearl Harbor Day. There was another one that had to do with American Theater, and Pacific Theater, and Atlantic Theater. I didn't know about these things and I didn't have any so I finally found some so I could put some more ribbons on and appease the individual who said I should be more modest.

Anyhow, I went to work; examined and looked over everything they did at the submarine school. Now, when we got into World War II, back in New London at the submarine school, the officer in charge of the school had set up what we called PCO school; prospective commanding officer school so that they could give a little bit of course of sprouts for a few weeks to a person who is just getting command of a submarine. That officer was experienced and "qualified for submarine command." For instance, a submarine is being built at New London, Connecticut, and he's going to be the skipper; bring him in and give him a little course of sprouts. Particularly based on what they read from the war patrols that are coming in. They had been doing this on a sort of ad hoc basis. The commanding officer of the submarine school was running this, it wasn't very well structured and so forth. I looked over what they were doing. It was certainly a good thing to do, but these people hadn't been to war yet and there were a lot of things that they were doing that were not quite necessary. There were also a lot of things they needed to do which they were not doing. Real adjustment; they were doing a good job, but we can do better. One of the things they decided was that unbeknownst to me while we were working at it, somebody, I'll bet, decided, "Hey, you know we ought to set this PCO school, not as just an ad hoc outfit which somebody does when he has time, let's formalize it and really set it up."

Then I made a very bad tactical error in that I prepared my report and submitted it several days before my thirty days were up. What I should have done is I should have gone to the railroad station and left it in the post office just before the train started and I was on the way to California. But, I submitted it a couple of days ahead of time whereupon some smart aleck got on the telephone and called up Washington and my return was cancelled. I was put in charge of PCO school. My report; apparently they considered it real good. I guess it's like when Eisenhower drew up the plans for how to attack Africa and Europe. They thought that he'd drawn them up so good that, "We'll let him show us how to do it." Anyhow, I found myself in charge of PCO school.

Q: That's an old technique, of course. People make suggestions and are put in charge of the implementation of them.

Adm. B.: Pretty good. Quite a few years later when I was in charge of all the submarines in the Pacific Fleet they had a small ceremony in which I was presented a certificate of being an honorary graduate of the PCO school. Obviously I hadn't been to PCO school. But, this was great.

So, I got to run the PCO school and they had a ceremony in which I got my second Navy Cross, for my last patrol of the TRIGGER.

Q: How long did you run it?

Adm. B.: I ran it for a year. What occurred at the end of the year was that one day I was downtown in New London. I ran into a good friend of mine by the name of R. L. Gross who was one year junior to me at the Naval Academy. He was a real good guy and a very fine submarine skipper. We exchanged pleasantries a little bit and he said, "Well, I came back from the war and I'm going right back again."

I said, "Why's that?"

"Oh," he said, "I was going to go to new construction and that would leave me here with my family for three to six months, and that would be pretty good. But I've got to go right now."

I said, "What are you going to do?"

"Well," he said, "didn't you hear about the RAZORBACK running aground off New London, here."

I said, "Yes, it seems to me I heard that."

The RAZORBACK was a brand new submarine built up at Portsmouth New Hampshire ran aground off New London coming from the shipyard. How in the world they managed to do that I don't know. But somebody was lacking in diligence. Well, she ran aground and the admiral became so irate that he detached both the skipper and the exec, detached them right now and they were looking for a new skipper and a new exec. They had decided that this friend of mine, Gross, would become the skipper. He had just barely arrived back going to new construction at New London and here he was going to get on board this ship that had run aground and depart almost immediately for the Pacific.

So, I said, "Say do you really feel that bad about getting on board the RAZORBACK?"

He said, "You bet I do."

I said, "Do you mind if I try to get command of her?" He did not mind.

So I called up the chief of staff to the Admiral. I said "I've got to command the RAZORBACK."

He said "Have you talked to the officer in charge of the submarine school?"

I said, "No, but I will right now."

I called him and he said fine. That was Captain Patterson who lives in Annapolis. I called him up and he said, "Fine." I called up the chief of staff and he said, "Okay, I'll mention it to the Admiral and we'll see what we can do."

So he talked to the Admiral and he talked to Washington and the very next day I took over the RAZORBACK. That's pretty good.

Interview No. 5 with Rear Admiral Roy S. Benson, U.S. Navy (Retire

Place: Arnold, Maryland

Date: April 1, 1980

Subject: Biography

By: John T. Mason, Jr.

Q: This morning I want to go back to the time you were operating submarines in the Pacific. There's one other type of difficulty you and other men experienced with torpedoes, the circular run, the rudder jammed. You want to talk about that?

Adm. B.: I'd be delighted. The way these torpedoes steer is there is a gyroscope and if you do not make a setting on it, when the torpedo goes out of the tube it will continue on the course that it was going when it went out of the tube. But, you could also, if you wanted to, set it such that it will turn a certain number of degrees. Matter of fact, the piece of equipment called the torpedo data computer, TDC for short, will generate continually through what angle the torpedo should turn after it's been launched to get on the track that the instrument thinks it ought to be on to hit. That instrument, of course, was up in the conning tower and was manipulated by the officer who was an expert at doing it.

When this torpedo went out of the tube it would normally have a setting in which it was supposed to turn a finite number of degrees and then go straight from then on under gyro control. The rudder, a little bit of a rudder, was either on the middle or it was full left or full right. In other words, it didn't come over a little bit. It went one way or the other or stayed in the center. Normally when the torpedo went out of the tube the rudder was over one side or the other because it's going to turn that certain number of degrees and then go straight. The rudder jammed. I'm not finding fault with anyone. I never heard of a circular run in the peace time operations. But, strangely enough, every so often the rudder does jam. If the rudder jams, obviously it's either on full left or full right and immediately it circles and there it is. Now--

Q: That's a danger to the submarine that sent it isn't it?

Adm. B.: Oh yes! If two submarines were operating in close vicinity, although that would not be very usual, but yes. So, that torpedo is circling and if you're up on the surface sometimes you might be able to see it. But, for you to try to outmaneuver it is very, very difficult. In other words, this is one way to throw the dice, practically.

Q: It's what you call a boomerang, isn't it?

Adm. B.: Yes. You can try, but to outmaneuver this thing you'd better have a rabbit's foot. If you're on the surface, however if you get tagged, some of the people on the ship, maybe two or three or four people are up on the bridge at the time, might be rescued. In the case of the submarine USS TULLIBEE, and in the case of the submarine USS TANG, they were indeed rescued and went to Japanese prison camps and came back from the camp after the war and told us that this was the reason that the submarine sank.

Q: Oh, really.

Adm. B.: Yes. If you're submerged you won't see it, of course, but you can hear it on the sound equipment and the operator will say, "Captain, torpedo circling!" He will notice that it hasn't gone on a steady course.

What do you do then? Well, you try to go a little deeper if you can. Of course, that might run you right into him. Again, you're throwing dice, practically. By good luck you don't get hit. In the event you do get hit, however, nobody is going to go to any prison camp. The whole submarine--

Q: There's no record.

Adm. B.: So, there is no record; no survivors. Now, on board the USS TRIGGER, and I should have mentioned this, while we were in the war in 1942 and 1943 we had on two of the patrols on each one of these two patrols we had a circular run while we were submerged. Fortunately we didn't get tagged. Now how many submarines got tagged while they were submerged or got tagged while they were on the surface but no one survived, we have no idea.

Q: Was any number suspected?

Adm. B.: I guess you could probably say, well let's see, of the submarines lost in which we got some people back from the prison camp—-so many and from two of them we actually got witness. So, if you lost ten and got somebody back and two of them had circular runs that might mean that twenty percent of the ones lost got tagged by their own torpedo. But that would just be sort of halfway guesswork. I don't think a mathematician would buy that very much. But certainly I would say, certainly at least a submarine, perhaps more, we don't know, got tagged by their own fish. "Fish" is a submarine torpedo.

Q: Now, isn't it surprising however, that there would be any survivors from a submarine even on the surface when it's tagged by its own fish?

Adm. B.: Well, they were and USS TANG was commanded by Dick O'Kane. He came back from prison camp and he finally wrote a book; his book is a magnificent book. I wrote the review for Shipmate magazine. What an outstanding performance! I'm absolutely dumbfounded when I read the book that he wrote. Why did he write it twenty years later? He said, "Because I couldn't stand writing it earlier. The memory was too vivid."

Q: Well, I think you feel that too, sometime, the memory is too vivid, it's too overwhelming.

Adm. B.: Now, we had two circular runs. I don't know how many torpedoes we launched, but say that we launched fifty. That would be that four percent of our torpedoes were circular runs. I don't have any idea how many others had, but every so often during the war we'd be talking to some other person and he'd say they had a circular run. We did have some circular runs. How many? We don't know. We had a very small number, but that's all you need is one, and you don't need it, either.

Q: The point I was trying to make a little bit before was if a torpedo hit a submarine the impact is so great that I think it would kill everybody on board.

Adm. B.: It sounds logical, but some people came back from prison camp. In the case of USS TULLIBEE the skipper did not come back. Maybe he wasn't on the bridge, I don't know. But, in the case of the USS TANG the skipper was on the bridge and he came back from prison camp.

Q: That's a very interesting note to have made to the recollections---

Adm. B.: Rudder jam had nothing to do with some exploder or it has nothing to do with firing pin jams when the head of the torpedo warhead crushed. It had nothing to do with this.

Q: No, actually the torpedo would be working well under those circumstances except that it was a circular run.

Adm. B.: Yes, and why didn't we hear about it in peacetime? I don't know. I never heard it during peacetime and I have no idea. I guess it's just---well I don't know. Without a warhead on it a submarine hull could very well take the impact of a torpedo.

Benson #5 -274-

Q: Yes, but this incident would have been reported wouldn't it?

Adm. B.: Surely, but--

Q: Did you ever have occasion to examine the records at the Bureau of Ordnance?

Adm. B.: No, I have not. I wouldn't be aware of it unless it was just sort of scuttlebutt among us submarine guys.

Q: Yes, but this is the sort of thing that would be scuttlebutt?

Adm. B.: I would think so. Maybe it wasn't that rare. Maybe it was such that after you mention these things for awhile everybody has had it and won't even mention it anymore. I didn't recall the two we had until you brought up the subject. That's the story of the circular run. It was dangerous but war is dangerous. Those things didn't bother me and, I guess I was typical.

Q: Thank you very much for adding that!

Adm. B.: You know the Germans had one tactic in which they would circle. They had a feature in their torpedoes in which they would set it for the distance to the group of ships. Set it for, say, two thousand yards and at two thousand yards an automatic rudder jam. In other words when it got over to where the target were if it didn't hit one immediately, instead of just continuing on and maybe hit somebody and maybe no one, it got a rudder jam and tagged somebody. Pretty clever idea.

Q: Yes. Yes. Now, shall we go back in July of 1943 to New London where you were called for thirty days of temporary duty in order to assist there at the prospective officers training School at the submarine base in New London? You told me last that you were there for thirty days, you wrote a report and as a result of that report you were made head of the school. Now, I wonder if you'd focus on that year that you served as head of the school and tell me some of the things you were able to contribute from your wartime experience in operating submarines. Some of the things you were able to teach these prospective commanding officers.

Adm. B. Yes. When I reported to the submarine school I reported to the officer-in-charge, a Captain George Patterson. This was in July 1943. What he wanted me to do was to look at not only the prospective commanding officers' school but also to look at all that they were doing in the submarine school and give them some recommendations for change. It didn't take me long to come to conclusions with regard to the many thousands of enlisted men going through the various schools around there. They were doing a fine job and I'd better not waste my time very much. They were doing all right. There was another school, the officers' basic school, in which they would have, oh, I think this was a three-month course. Six months in my day for submarine school in peacetime. But, now three months. I found that was a pretty good school except that they had certain things that they were doing that were quite unnecessary. They spent too much time on the attack teacher in which you could learn on land with a synthetic trainer. You could actually look through a periscope and the optics had been fixed up such that small ship models would look like they were big like at sea. You could practice "up periscope" and read off various things and you could operate that so called TDC, torpedo data computer, and make believe you were out there with some targets. We could learn how to do this and get good at it. Well, I found little reason, except for a couple of times for the fun of it, for these officers to act as if they were submarine captains.

I didn't think that that was at all necessary. Let him take a look at it once in a while just for the fun of it, but what he needed to do was to learn the basics of how a submarine is put together and what makes it tick. He needed that basically. But there were two things he really needed in addition: he needed a lot of drill on the diving training. There was a synthetic device in which you could practice diving the submarine and practice pumping the water from one end to the other, or pumping it out or flood it in and so forth. You could learn so you would have the fundamentals of diving and underwater control. You could practice at this until it was second nature to you. Similarly with the so-called torpedo data computer, the TDC, he could become an expert at the operation of that piece of equipment. This was really the heart of our torpedo fire control. They were doing fairly well, but they had too much of this periscope drill; no reason for it. A little bit, okay. Should put more TDC machines and practice on them. They couldn't get enough practice on them because the only TDCs there were at the attack teacher. Get more of them and have banks of them like slot machines and have them work on these things until it is absolutely second nature because it is the heart of our operation; the same for diving trainers.

Before we got this so called TDC we had some other gadgets. One was called the IS WAS, the other was called the "meat chopper," and there was something called the "banjo." We used to work at these and they were necessary. Just before we got into World War II the TDC came out and it was much better. These other things were really obsolete except to show them a little bit so they would know these things existed. That would suffice.

Q: The submarines were still equipped with them?

Adm. B.: Oh, some of them, but they were fairly simple to learn. Better concentrate on the TDC, get to be expert on that; get to be expert on the diving control.

Now this prospective officer school, this was really the heart of what we're talking about here and really the reason why I was there. It was set up early in 1942 and the students were people who were attached to submarines being built or about to be. They would come to New London if they were not already there. They'd come there for a couple of weeks and the officer-in-charge of the submarine school had taken it upon himself to set up this PCO school, as we call it. It was doing pretty well. But, he's got a big job being officer-in-charge of the submarine school. It didn't take me long to come to the conclusion that he needs someone with wartime experience as a skipper and preferably someone who had done pretty well out there. So, he needs to have this person have nothing else to do but run this PCO school and get with it. This was my first recommendation.

Q: Do you have any idea of the number of men who were being trained at this time?

Adm. B.: About six at a time and the course lasted about three or four weeks.

Now, the next point I want to bring up, I want to explain a little of the background for you. During our peacetime operations in the late 1930's and early 1940's we had learned that a submerged submarine, a submarine at periscope depth, can be so easily detected by an airplane that being submerged in the presence of airplanes is impossible. This we found to be fallacious! We found that we could indeed operate at periscope depth in the presence of aircraft. If we were careful as we should be, we could keep from being detected.

Q: At periscope depth, for the record, is what depth?

Adm. B.: About 64 feet from the keel to the surface of the water. If you put the periscope all the way up, four feet of periscope would be exposed. Take it from there. Depending on sea conditions and proximity of enemy ships you decide that you want more or less periscope exposed.

Now then, as a consequence of the belief that it was impossible to conduct periscope approaches close to the Japanese mainland or other places where there might be aircraft operating, it was believed that they wouldn't be able to get away with doing anything at periscope depth and they would have to be further submerged. Therefore, let's find a way and practice on it to be able to make an approach and attack without looking through the periscope. Depend upon the bearing, bearing is direction. Depend on the bearings that you would get from the underwater sound equipment. So, they devoted a great deal of time in that PCO school to working with this so people would be able to do it. Now, the only trouble with it was, in the first place it wasn't necessary; in the second place the equipment wasn't good enough to do it anyhow. What they did was they sort of guessed where they might be and on that TDC they would put in the various bearings and if it didn't quite fit he would change his course a little bit and fiddle around. Just before they got to the target they'd have the underwater sound man send out a single ping and they would bounce off the target and come back and tell them how far the target was away. One ping would never be detected, they thought. At least they wouldn't be detected as much as a raised periscope.

Well, the equipment wasn't good enough to do it and it was unnecessary, so my recommendation with respect to this was stop it. However, sometime when you're talking about new ideas or gadgetry you should mention this concept because they really ought to have it in their minds. Somewhere along the line perhaps we'll devise a way to do it. Maybe we can be ready with such an ability when needed. But stop putting all this time and effort on this project now for it wasn't necessary and not very good.

This first conclusion I came up with was they have a full time person running the PCO school and the second one to stop this bearings-only business. A great deal of time in the attack teacher, up periscope, working with TDC, and really this is what you want to concentrate on. Remember in the officers' basic course I said if you don't learn how to be a diving officer and running the TDC until it becomes second nature, no one can do it for you. Well, similarly, no one can do this for the skipper. He's the one that's got to put that periscope up, look at the target, and do what needs to be done. Night attack is slightly different, that's a motor torpedo boat, but the tactics are not very different. He needs to be an expert on this "up periscope." A great deal of that. Study and discuss previous war patrols. Strangely enough I found that apparently they weren't doing very much of that and we needed to do that. We had at the school a whole set of the past patrol reports of the submarines.

Q: They were all available there?

Adm. B.: They were all available. They had every one of them.

Q: But, they weren't using them?

Adm. B.: Yes, but they needed more. Issue them to the students. Issue one to each and have them come back to school the next day and let's spend an hour now and then; let's call on each one to get up and explain what happened on this patrol. What could we learn from it? Let's get into some real bull sessions with these people on this. They need to know in depth what happened and why.

Orientation on the equipment; there was new equipment coming out all along. Some new kind of a radar when we hadn't had a radar; other new equipments.

An important thing for them to understand, and I hadn't thought of this until it suddenly dawned on me so far back in the dark ages. A new equipment is designed and they build them and they put them on your submarine and the people on board go to school and learn how to operate them. Now we're ready to go on patrol; not yet! What are you going to do with the output from the equipment? In other words, if the equipment tells you certain things, you've got to do something with that. Otherwise you might as well leave the equipment on the beach. We should have related to this in Pearl Harbor, skippers coming in on submarines and they had not had a surface search radar on board, which we had not, but had we gotten one before we again went to sea. We should have been run through a course of sprouts to make sure that we knew exactly how to use the information which the new equipment would give us. It seems perfectly natural, often times overlooked.

Q: It seems like nothing but good sense.

Adm. B.: Yes. But, not quite that easy. Those were the only recommendations that I had, but they were quite crucial. Naturally when I put in my number one recommendation I was doomed.

Q: For someone with operational experience?

Adm. B.: Yes. So---

Q: Did you suspect that?

Adm. B.: No, no, I was naive.

That was quite a year. Students came and students went. I knew most of them before they even came because the submarine business was a very small outfit in the 1930's and 1940's. It was great to renew friendship with all of these smart and bright young guys.

Did I mention that while I was at New London I was given my second Navy Cross?

Q: Yes. Yes.

Adm. B.: Did I also say that when I arrived there in June 1943 that I made Commander?

Q: Yes, you did.

Adm. B.: Sometime during that year we received notice that the TRIGGER had been given a Presidential Unit Citation; the NAUTILUS had been given that before.

Q: So, you wore some additional ribbons?

Adm. B.: That's right. And we had some bad news. A Commander R. S. Rooney was in command of the USS CORVINA. She was lost on the first patrol in the Pacific. Rooney was a Naval Academy classmate of mine and relieved me as exec of the NAUTILUS when I left the NAUTILUS early in 1942. Also, my first executive officer of the USS TRIGGER came back to new construction and commanded the USS DORADO. She disappeared on the way from New London to the Panama Canal. So, somebody got her on the way.

Q: Well, there was speculation that the Germans had sunk her.

Adm. B.: Possibility. We also don't know how many submarines were lost during World War II as a -- just a simple operation matter. You get two or three things go wrong at the same time, and without an enemy helping you're lost. You can always lose one. We haven't lost very many, but you can lose one once in a while.

Q: What impact did this news have on the prospective commanding officers training in the school?

Adm. B.: I don't believe any. We were quite used to it-- really if you can get used to it. Because, well, it was something that went on regularly.

Q: It was the hazard of the service?

Adm. B.: Right. Well, very soon we departed for the Pacific. I was the only officer on board the submarine who had been to war yet.

Q: This is the USS RAZORBACK?

Adm. B.: I alone on board had been to war. So, we had a lot of things to learn.

Q: Now, the crew members were new recruits, were they?

Adm. B.: Many of them had been in submarine for from 2 to 10 years. We had on board also men who had been in the Navy for 6 months to 2 years, had been to the enlisted school, had asked for submarine duty, but before that been to recruit.

Q: How did you go about teaching them?

Adm. B.: You had "school of the boat," that's always been going on. There were senior enlisted men--hold school teaching the men all about these various things about a submarine.

Q: While you're enroute?

Adm. B.: Oh, yes. All the time in peace and in war. Finally we got to the Panama Canal and an interesting, humorous incident happened there. The laws and regulations of the Panama Canal are that any ship going through there must take a pilot. No ship can go through the Panama Canal without a pilot. When the pilot comes aboard he is totally in charge of the navigation of the ship. This is not true of the various ports of the world. Generally, if you take a pilot or don't take it is your business and even if he comes aboard, at least in our Navy regulations, the pilot is an advisor. Naturally, if the pilot runs aground or has any other kind of an accident it will sound good in the investigation held later, but according to our Navy practice the skipper is still responsible. But going through the Panama Canal, he has no choice.

Q: Then he's not responsible.

Adm. B. Correct. Well, he cannot take the conn away from the pilot. He can't say "Pilot, I'll take over." Can't take it away from him.

Q: Does it follow through then that he's not responsible if there is an accident?

Adm. B.: I would say that he's probably not responsible. Certainly they would never be able to prove that he was negligent when he was forbidden to take over.

Q: Have there been any examples of this?

Adm. B.: Well, I've not heard of one. Anyhow, we went through the Panama Canal and arrived on the Pacific side and we were to go alongside of a pier over there to stay a day or so and then continue on to the Pacific. He was coming in too fast and wide to put this submarine alongside the pier. Gee, I was standing there and I was not very happy; yet I knew that I was not supposed to take this over I could just see smashing up my submarine; what do I do? At that moment, almost the point of extremis, he turned to me and he said, "She's all yours, Captain."

Well, I was delighted. I wish he had given it to me a few minutes earlier, but I was delighted. I took over the conn, brought her alongside, and all is well. But this was a very interesting experience. Beautiful words: "She's all yours, Captain."

Q: These pilots in the Panama Canal, are they U.S. people?

Adm. B.: Oh, yes.

Q: Not Panamanians?

Adm. B.: They were not at that time. I'm not sure what they are now.

Most of the people though that you see, people handling the big mules, locomotives which pull the ships, handling lines, operating flooding valves, etc.; all Panamanians.

We went through the canal on a cruise ship last year. I felt that my good wife of all these years ought to go through the Panama Canal. Especially when it was so prominent in the newspapers.

We arrived on Pearl Harbor and had to get ready for Operation Zoo. Nine submarines in three groups, the whole outfit commanded by a Captain C. W. Wilkins, who had been my Captain on board the USS S-27 back in 1935. He was in command of the whole zoo of nine submarines. He also commanded one of the groups, "Wilkins' Bears" was his group. I had a group of three submarines and we were called the Dogs. Then a fellow by the name of Ike Holtz was in command of the third group. All well-experienced commanding officers. No neophytes in this outfit. What were we going to do? We were going to form a scouting line out in the middle of the ocean between the Philippine Islands and Palau.

I believe Admiral Halsey had asked there be such a thing. What were we there for? We were there for reconnaissance and to detect and report approach of enemy forces. We saw nothing--

Q: Were you to make attacks on them, too?

Adm. B.: I don't recall what instructions said about that. I don't think so. I think we were just supposed to observe and report. I don't believe we were permitted to make attacks at that time. But, we didn't see anyone. Didn't see anyone at all; several weeks of doing nothing out there, steaming back and forth looking. We didn't even see any aircraft that would make us dive. Like a painted ship on a painted ocean, there was nothing.

Oh, we were stationed something on the order of forty or fifty miles apart. I guess it was valuable because enemy forces might have come along. Anyhow, we did nothing and finally when we had about a week to go they disbanded these and we were given certain areas. My group of three got an area between Taiwan and the Philippines and north of the Philippines and we didn't see anything. The whole zoo, I believe, sank, observed, detected during the week the zoo business was over, detected maybe three or four very small coastal cargo ships that didn't amount of anything. I believe two or three of them were sunk, but they were inconsequential. My group of three never saw a target.

Q: Why the curious name assigned to the operation, zoo?

Adm. B.: I don't know.

Q: Now about this time was it not true that the Japanese were resupplying their island garrisons by submarine?

Adm. B.: Yes.

Q: Did you observe any submarines?

Adm. B.: No, didn't observe anything.

Q: And also were having submarines come from Germany with supplies for Japan.

Adm. B.: Yes. We never detected them either. You know this business of sending, in this case, three sets of three out to operate together was something we had been doing for about a year in the Pacific. We called them wolf packs.

Q: Well, the Germans did that, didn't they?

Adm. B.: The Germans did a great deal of that. They had many submarines so they operated in groups. The biggest mistake they made was constant radio traffic between submarines and back home. We didn't do this. We got messages from Pearl Harbor, but we didn't have to reply to them.

Our wolf packs were not really coordinated attacks, they were coordinated search. The idea was that the three of us being thirty miles apart, could be able to detect more targets. Once you've detected a target all you had to do was on your radio give about three letters of the alphabet in Morse Code Da Di Di Dit, Di Da, Da Da Da. The other two have picked it up and they know from that little combination of three little letters what you saw, which way they're going and how fast. You know where that submarine which sent the message is relative to you and so you find out where the target is, which way he's going, and how fast he's going, what he consists of and so forth. All three submarines then independently go in and try to get a shot.

Now, what did we have with regard to coordination so that we wouldn't run into one another? Well, we decided it wasn't worth it so we didn't pay any attention to that. It would be too difficult to do. It would require us to send a lot of messages over the radio. Therefore, we ignored the subject and when it came time for you to go ahead and shoot somebody you'd shoot them. Often times though the submarine which detected them a trailer, either in front or back. In other words, keep the target in sight and maybe open up on the radio and give a couple beeps. We did a lot of this before we went out with this zoo. We practiced all of this on the dance floor at the submarine base in Pearl Harbor.

We would be behind three screens and they would have some model targets out on the dance floor and all at once they would pull the screen and let one submarine's officers have a two second look at the target. They open up on radio and tell the rest of the people what you saw, where they are, and all about them. They would move some model ships to close the target.

Q: Now, one might observe that although the Japanese had large convoys from time to time I expect that the convoys in the Pacific didn't compare with the number in the Atlantic and was a lesser area of water, so the tactics of the German attack had to be somewhat different. They concentrated on a given convoy didn't they?

Adm. B.: Oh, yes. They had many more submarines than we had, also. Although, at the very beginning of the war they didn't have very many. If Hitler had waited a couple of years and built them up a little more it might have been a different war. Yes, they would have a dozen or more submarines go out there and operate on a big convoy. If their submarines and Goering's airplanes had worked together it would have been a disaster.

We were then finished with our zoo patrol and went back to Midway; that was around September 1944. I was then detached. I found out afterwards that after one patrol I was going to become a submarine division commander, which I did.

Q: Did the RAZORBACK show any signs of her accident right after she was commissioned?

Adm. B.: No, no difficulty at all. A submarine division commander had six submarines in his division, but it didn't work that way. You can imagine, many submarines came in from the West or East coast of the United States; brand new ones. The first place they would arrive was always Pearl Harbor. Then some of them might go on to Australia and be in a separate command. When you went out on patrol sometimes you came back to Pearl Harbor and sometimes you went to Midway. There were at Pearl Harbor four division commanders in one submarine squadron. The submarine squadron commander was in charge of the submarine base and the four division commanders under him. The four division commanders were a pool.

Q: What were his specific duties as a division commander?

Adm. B.: When a submarine arrived in Pearl Harbor, whether it was new construction or just come back from a war patrol, it was assigned to one of the division commanders. He was the boss over the submarine's Captain; told him what to do but also helped him to do what was supposed to be done. In the case of a new one coming out, there were going to be some training exercises for them before they went out to war. There was also going to be a mini-course in the various new equipments, new techniques and all this sort of thing. In spite of all the things they'd learned before they came there, there was a lot they needed to learn before they went out on patrol. The division commander is the person who schedules their training and sees that they do what they are supposed to do. If a submarine is coming in from war patrol he is the person who goes over the war patrol report with the commanding officer, discusses it all and submits it with an endorsement in which he comments on the various things that occurred during the patrol, send it on and it finally ends up in the Admiral's incoming basket. He acquaints the captain, officers and crew with new equipment and how to use it. The submarine coming in from patrol would always lose about two of its officers and something on the order of a quarter of its crew who would go back to new construction. Commanding officers would really be upset with this. Here they had come in from chasing Japanese and to their chagrin they would be told, "We need two of your officers and a fourth of your enlisted men. The ones we want are the ones who have been on board the longest, regardless of their seniority." Obviously their successful team was to be broken up. It was unfortunate but those people were needed to man new construction submarines.

Q: That was the rule of thumb?

Adm. B.: That's right.

Q: The men with the most experience would go on to the new submarine?

Adm. B.: That's right, particularly the enlisted men, with the officers it was also a question of what they needed in the new construction. If your executive officer has his command qualification, his commissioned service is about equal to those getting command of submarines, you have lost him right now. It's only fair to him. He's gone and that's what happened. I didn't lose any officers at the end of my first patrol, but at the end of the second patrol I lost my next two officers in seniority. That is my exec and my engineering/diving officer. I lost them and they gave me a couple of brand new officers right out of the submarine school to be among the officers on board.

The division commander is the guy who has to explain to the skipper and say to him: "Let me have your list of the people you're going to lose."

"But, Commodore, I can't spare these people!"

"Well, that's got nothing to do with it."

When a submarine comes in from patrol and we're going to send all the officers and crew to the Royal Hawaiian Hotel for two weeks, it's the division commander's relief crew that takes over the submarine and is responsible for the submarine, stand the watches, and fix things that can be fixed by ship's force.

Q: Now where are they derived from, the relief crews?

Adm. B.: Some of them came off the submarine and were attached to the relief crew. Otherwise they came out of submarine school and got on a relief crew. We had additional schooling, schools there on the beach in Pearl Harbor for training new people so that when we got them on the relief crew they would know their stuff.

Q: I take it that the division commander was shore based?

Adm. B.: He was shore based.

Q: Tell me how a division commander, how you kept abreast of the flow of new ordnance that was coming out so frequently at this stage of the war.

Adm. B.: Well, you just had to keep your nose to the grindstone. The squadron commander, the skipper of the submarine base, and the four division commanders, we took all our meals together. We worked seven days a week and we all, this group of six officers, the squadron commander, the skipper of the submarine base, and the four division commanders lived out there in the family quarters in Makalapa outside of the submarine base at Pearl Harbor. We lived together, we ate together, you can imagine we operated just about twenty-four hours a day. New pieces of equipment were explained to us and we discussed them at great length.

Q: Did you play horseshoes together also?

Adm. B.: No. Admiral Nimitz did that with Admiral Spruance but we--oh, naturally there was a tennis court there, there was a swimming pool, paddle tennis and so forth. We were together all the time and this was a very valuable source of news. New gadgets came out and you can imagine the discussions we would have on these new gadgets. Why, if we weren't working separately, we were working together. We were experienced and busy.

Q: Where would you lay eyes on a new gadget when it came?

Adm. B.: It arrived at the submarine base and they are going to start installing it on submarines coming in. Sometimes a new submarine would come in from the West Coast and there would be new equipments that were going to be installed right now, before they got out on the next patrol. Division commanders had been briefed, to know something about them, and then we had to make sure that this submarine gets it. We must make sure that it actually goes on board and the people on board need to go to school which we have set up for it. They must know how to operate and maintain the new equipment, and how to use its output.

Q: Did your group have direct communication with the Bureau of Ordnance? Did they supply you with data on these new bits of equipment?

Adm. B.: Oh yes, but not directly. The material people at the submarine base would give us briefings on these equipments. That's how we heard about the Mark VI exploder before we even got into World War II; the submarine base knew about it and briefed us.

Another thing that the four division commanders did was they formed Admiral Lockwood's awards board. That is, the Submarine Force Pacific Fleet awards board. In every one of our division commanders' offices there was a copy of every patrol report of every submarine. Obviously, one of the things we had to do was to read all of them as they came. Naturally we read the ones from the submarines that were assigned to us. We'd, however, read all of them. We'd pick up all kinds of information, but we'd also meet as an awards board and decide what we're going to recommend to Admiral Lockwood with regard to awards, decorations. Do we want to recommend that the skipper of the submarine get a Navy Cross or a Bronze Star, or the various others. Our recommendations would go up to Admiral Lockwood.

I think I've told you before that Admiral Lockwood never wanted the authority to issue any medal. He sent that up to the next level, which was Admiral Nimitz's.

So, when we, the division commanders, met and made up our recommendations they would go up to Admiral Lockwood and if he concurred with it, then one of those division commanders would present them before Admiral Nimitz's awards board, of which he was a member. He was Admiral Lockwood's member. Admiral Nimitz's awards board was made up of people from Marines, submarines, naval air, destroyers and various other parts of the Navy. He'd spend about half a day a week on nothing but being up at Admiral Nimitz's headquarters and also spent nearly half a day a week with the other division commanders with our own awards board. This was a time-consuming chore. I was Admiral Lockwood's member on Admiral Nimitz's awards board the first half of 1945 as relief to E. W. (Joe) Grenfell.

Q: I was meaning to ask you what was the prevailing philosophy on governing the issuing of awards?

Adm. B.: We didn't have any real standards; that is formally. It's bound to come up in our discussions because we'd look over this patrol report and see that they did this and this and that, and the difficulty of it, enemy action and all that sort of thing. Someone would ask: "Well, do we think that this skipper deserves to get a Navy Cross?"

Somebody says, "Oh, I don't think so." "We gave a lower medal than so-and-so." "We recommended him for the Silver Star--" etc., etc.

We would simply argue it out. It sort of percolates into your mind and you remember what happened on this particular patrol, so-and-so did so-and-so. We didn't have strict standards. There was a clerical force for our awards. There was some yeoman who wrote up citations and kept records and so forth. We would have those records with us when we came in, tabular records of what we did in this particular case. It's sort of like trying to hold mast on board ship for the punishment of people who have misbehaved. You keep track of what you're doing so you'll be-- you try to be consistent. So, we had those records and we'd refer to them.

Q: Back of my question was the thought that the Navy had the reputation of being far more conservative in issuing awards than did the military, the Army and especially the Air Force which was part of the Army.

Adm. B.: Yes, I'm sure that that was true. I think the Marine Corps was also, well, the Marine Corps is part of the Naval Service, more conservative than the Army or Air Force. But, I guess we can't help that. I think we are a pretty conservative outfit anyhow. Naval air and the Army Air Corps had a system by which everyone who made combat flights received the air medal for every five flights.

Q: Well, it brings one to think about the philosophy of awards. Is it well to hand them out very generously or make them have greater merit by giving fewer awards?

Adm. B.: It's hard to tell. I'm inclined to believe that, during a war, we should be fast and generous with medals. Then, when the war is over put them in the memory except for certain of highest which would continue to be worn. Napoleon said, "If you give me enough ribbon I can conquer the world."

There is something to this one, that if when people come in from battle and they are going again to face the enemy, if you can pat them on the back often enough and give them enough decorations, maybe they will go out and try harder. Maybe you can buoy them up. I believe medals should be awarded more frequently then we did in the Navy in World War II. But, as I said in the previous paragraph, I'm rather inclined to think that after the war is over most of them should go into the memory book and everybody get a ribbon saying that they did fine, a victory medal as we had. The remainder continue to be worn. I'm not sure that all these ribbons necessarily have to be on the uniform. To me it looks a little strange to see a person with ribbons all the way down his back. I don't think that makes a great deal of sense.

I'm inclined to feel that when it's over that the competition between people should be decreased. It's not quite necessary. But, anyhow, it's hard to tell.

In the spring of 1945 the TRIGGER was lost. Lost with all hands. The commanding officer was Commander D. R. Connole.

Q: What was the reason?

Adm. B.: Well, we don't know. She failed to come back. She was on her second patrol with Commander Connole in charge. An old friend. Fine, fine naval officer. Student of mine in PCO school.

Q: That was a blow to you, wasn't it?

Adm. B.: Yes, indeed; a particular one; loss of good friend, his officers and crew and my submarine, TRIGGER. In April 1945 I made Captain. Promotions go fast during war. On Pearl Harbor Day, I was a Lieutenant and three years and three months later I was a Captain.

Q: To me it's like the awards, I mean it gives you incentive.

Adm. B.: It does that. Early in August of 1945 I was detached and reported to the Navy Department.

Q: Now in the interim you had still been serving as the division commander.

Adm. B.: Oh yes, full time. A little less than a year.

Q: Would you talk about that, the accomplishments in that period? The submarines were being more effective, were they, in attacking the Japanese convoys?

Adm. B.: From the time I became a division commander in the fall of 1944 until I was detached in August of 1945, I would say that in the first half, the submarines were very, very effective. But, I believe in the last half their effectiveness was falling off. The reason was they were losing so much ocean. Admiral Nimitz's and General MacArthur's forces were gradually closing in on the Japanese. The oceans out there that had been ours early in the war were no longer ours. There were less and less areas where we could go and try to find some targets.

Q: These were more hazardous areas, were they not? The Sea of Japan and places like that where you were operating?

Adm. B.: That was certainly true. A very important part of what the submarine did during that period when the aircraft, both the Army Air Corps aircraft, and naval aircraft were attacking the Japanese main islands, a great deal of submarine effort, and I almost forget this, also engaged in rescue operations. When a big strike of air was going to be done anywhere, certain submarines would be assigned to the air-sea rescue job and the people in the planes would know where those submarines were going to be. They were going to be able to communicate by radio to the submarines. If they needed to tell a submarine something, the submarine would know what to do about it.

We assigned some of our most experienced wartime ex-skippers to the staffs of various aircraft outfits, both the Army Air Corps and naval aviation. We wanted the people on those staffs to understand submarine business. One of the fundamentals is airplanes were to go flying around and bomb Tokyo and we had some submarines located in various places along the Japanese coast. Maybe on one of those big strikes we'd have a dozen of them in individual locations out there. The aviators knew where the submarines are.

Q: This was a morale builder wasn't it?

Adm. B.: Yes, indeed, and also essential. They know where the submarines are. If one of the planes gets hit and he's coming down, it does no good for him to pass over the submarine position if he can avoid it. To pass over where the submarine is supposed to be and still be at 5,000 feet he might land fifty miles away. These numbers are just pulled out of my hat. It's going to take that submarine hours to get there. It will get there, but it will be hours and the plane probably sank. If they can land closer to the submarine, particularly if they can land within five miles or so, the people on the submarine will be able to see the splash and they would know where to go and get there sooner. If somebody lands fifty miles away you can very easily miss them completely. You can't see very far from the submarine. It's pretty close down on the water. So, we used to try to indoctrinate them, these air people, so that they would do the best they could to help themselves. So that we would also help them.

If they landed within the five-mile circle around the submarine there would be many people who would be rescued. Submarines did a tremendous job of this.

Q: Now, what is the capacity of a given submarine to rescue-- how many can you rescue?

Adm. B.: Oh, let me give you an example. I lost a submarine over in the Barents Sea up off the tip of Norway in 1949; we lost seven people. So, we had almost two crews on board the submarine and we went all the way from Tromso, Norway, to New London, Connecticut, non-stop with two crews on one submarine.

Q: That being approximately how many people?

Adm. B.: Oh, if we had seventy-five on each we had a hundred and fifty on board.

Q: Did that hinder your diving ability?

Adm. B.: No. No problem at all. We didn't have any problem; you can see that the submarines would have the capacity to pick up an awful lot of people.

Q: You were crowded?

Adm. B.: Well, it's crowded before you start, but you just get more crowded.

Q: How do you compensate in terms of ballast?

Adm. B.: Oh, you can do that, no problem at all. For each additional person, pump out about 150 pounds of water. If we could get the aviators on board we had a pretty good chance of surviving.

Q: During this period at the end of World War II approximately how many rescues were made?

Adm. B.: I'd say several hundred. It seemed to me there at Pearl Harbor that almost every time a submarine came in they had some people on board that had been rescued. That was quite an operation. We also did a few other things; there were times when we had a submarine carry supplies to some place that was under attack. Acted as a cargo ship. Very early in World War II one of our submarines carried tremendous quantities of gold out of the Philippines.

Q: Yes, that was Fritz Harlfinger's outfit.

Adm. B.: Yes, he was on board. The submarine captain was Mike Fenno.

Q: That was the treasury of the Philippines which they carried.

Adm. B.: That's right.

Q: What about minelaying operations at this stage of the war?

Adm. B.: No, as far as I recall we didn't do any after we laid mines in the fall of 1942. I think practically all the submarine mines that were going to be laid were laid about that time. I think they were laid by a total of not over ten submarines.

But, a tremendous amount of minelaying was done, however, by Army Air Corps aircraft in the Inland Sea, the harbors of Japan and so forth. It took quite a toll.

Q: I recall at this time you did send submarines on very dangerous missions through the Straits of Tsushima up into the Japan Sea.

Adm. B.: Oh yes! In the spring of 1945.

Q: To get Japanese shipping?

Adm. B.: That's right. We sent a group on the order of nine or ten in together. They had a special piece of sound equipment which had been especially designed such that when they picked up a moored mine it made a tinkling sound. We used to call it "hell's bells." A submarine officer by the name of Barney Sieglaff, a bit junior to me, was boss of this whole outfit and they all went into the Sea of Japan. They all held their fire until a certain moment and then they started shooting. They took quite a toll. One of our submarines failed to come back from there.

Q: Yes, this was a really dangerous operation.

Adm. B.: Yes, they went through the minefields between the Japanese Islands and Korea. When they were done they went out north of Honshu.

Q: Were any of these submarines in your division?

Adm. B.: No. Well, but we really didn't operate by divisions at all. We division commanders were hardly aware of what submarines were in their divisions. We didn't see those submarines any more than we saw the others.

Q: How were these submarines selected that went into the inner sea area?

Adm. B.: I don't know.

Q: Volunteers, were they?

Adm. B.: Oh, no. We didn't do that in submarines. They were simply assigned and I'm sure they assigned very experienced people, particularly submarine captains.

Benson #5 -313-

There were some other submarines later in war that individually went through minefields with "hell's bells" saving them. It's amazing how we can learn to operate and depend on a gadget to help you do your work.

Q: Who's responsible for the development of so many of these gadgets?

Adm. B.: The scientific community. When we got into World War II, oh, great numbers of scientists were hired by the various services to work on all sorts of things; and on operations analysis which was need, logic and mathematics. Scientists and mathematicians can look at what you're trying to do and say, "The probability is that you really ought to put nine tenths of your efforts on this because you're already doing about as well as you can here." They tell you where you can concentrate. These mathematicians can really figure it out. Scientists came out with all sorts of equipment. They had a tremendous organization, NDRC, I guess, National Development Research Committee. They thought up all kinds of gadgets. Not all of them feasible. They were very alert.

One of the bad things we had on our submarines, all during World War II, aided somewhat near the end, was underwater sound equipment. We had the same underwater sound equipment that a destroyer would have. Except that the destroyers' use of the sound equipment was different from ours. They wanted to send out a supersonic ping and have it echo on the target and come back. It would not only tell the direction of the target but by the length of time it took to measure the distance to the target. We in the submarine business did not want to make noise; we wanted to listen. We had a piece of equipment that also sent out these pings, but it was especially adapted to listening to that ping that you sent out and would come back. That was not in the frequency range in which we needed to listen. We did not learn this until after World War II. We needed to have equipment designed to listen at much lower frequency. What we wanted to listen to were the screws of enemy ships. We generally did not want to make noise; we were trying to be the silent service. The destroyer knows that he's been detected, so it doesn't hurt him at all to send out a ping and get a ping back. Not us.

Q: A ping that hits the side of a ship?

Adm. B.: And echoes back off the side. So the underwater equipment we had wasn't really suited for submarine use. Strangely enough, back in the middle 1930's we had on board the submarine S-42 some microphones, about a dozen of them on each side of the bow. There was a piece of equipment by binaural audition you could detect the direction from which the sound is coming. We actually had it about that submarine then and perhaps many of them had it. The principle is the same as our two ears can tell from what direction a sound is coming.

We had it on destroyers out in China in the early 1930's. By that time, apparently, people had decided listening sound gear would also be useful in surface ships, so they put it on destroyers, too. That was practically useless because they make too much noise. The submarine, however, very quiet and very slow, could listen on this equipment. That would have been fine except that it didn't work very good. Instead of improving it, they abandoned it and gave us this other type of sound gear. I hasten to add that correction has been made. This was an example of: "We tried that several years and it was no good. Forget it." This goes on all the time on all subjects.

Q: Did your submarines have any encounters with the kamikaze; they were so very strong towards the end of the war.

Adm. B.: No. No encounters.

Q: Submarines were not targets for kamikaze?

Adm. B.: Not that I'm aware of. I don't recall anything of that kind.

Q: Having talked about submarine warfare in the latter half of World War II, we come to the abrupt ending of the war. Do you want to tell me about that?

Adm. B.: Early in August 1945 I was detached. It appeared that Japan would certainly be defeated and it was only a matter of time. Indeed it was. I don't believe there will ever be total agreement as to whether or not Japan would have surrendered without atomic bombs. There are people who believe that they are unnecessary, there are others who believe that they were essential. I don't suppose we'll ever solve that one.

Q: Yes, I might ask you this question. The planned operation for landing on the main islands of Japan, Operation Olympic, was there any provision in that plan for the use of submarines?

Adm. B.: Not that I ever heard. But, at my level, being a division commander, I perhaps would not have known about it.

During the spring of 1945 Admiral Nimitz and part of his staff and the Submarine Force Commander and part of his staff moved to Guam. So, even if there had been something, we wouldn't have heard of it. We became sort of a rear guard. Anyhow, I left out there in Hawaii early in August 1945. I was going to duty with the Navy Department in Washington.

The first atomic bomb took off while I was visiting an uncle of mine in Chicago. Japan surrendered while I was visiting my father's brothers, etc. in Concord, New Hampshire, my home town. So when I reported to the Navy Department, Japan had just surrendered. I was assigned to the headquarters of Fleet Admiral King. He really had two hats. One was called COMINCH. It meant commander in chief of all our Navy's operating forces. With his other hat, he was Chief of Naval Operations. Chief of Naval Operations sounds like he was in charge of operations but I don't know why that word is in there because, under the other hat, he was in charge of naval operations. The Chief of Naval Operations job was really the backup for the operations.

Q: Well, since 1958, it's that.

Adm. B.: Yes. On Fleet Admiral King's staff of the operating side I had cognizance, well, staff responsibilities, for everything having to do with the submarines.

Q: Well, what does this mean?

Adm. B.: The way a big staff like this works is that when something comes in, either a message or letter, that has to do with the submarines business, it would find itself in my in-basket. I was startled. I'd never served at that kind of level before in anything. I was startled to realize that with regard to that letter which was in my in-coming basket, nobody else had seen it around there. I have it and I'm supposed to do something with it. Now, if there's nothing to do we can put it in the files, but usually there is something to do with it, action to take, reply to it, research the subject, etc. But, if there is something to do about it, then staff-wise, you proceed to do all of the necessary research work and come up with a course of action. You have now prepared what you think is appropriate and then you go around the corridors of the headquarters and get various people to make comments on it or initialling it and saying that they agree. Then it works its way up. It gets approved and out it goes or it comes back for some sort of change signed by some higher authority. I was startled to realize on incoming letters or messages pertaining to submarines, no one was going to do anything about it if I didn't. There were lots of people like me who were at the bottom of the totem pole with cognizance over various subjects. The organization was not made up by operating types. With the exception of naval air, no other operating type held a high position in the organization, i.e., an admiral. In other words, there was personnel, operations, logistics, and then when the atomic business came that was initially a separate entity. But, there was no high admiral in the front corridor in charge of submarines, in charge of destroyers, cruisers, amphibious, or anything. This is not intended as a complaint. There are a number of ways to organize a large organization; none of them perfect.

Q: Under whom were you, Edwards or Cook or--

Adm. B.: Well, I was under both of them, but there were about three or four levels of people between me and them. My first immediate boss turned out to be a submarine officer who had been one of the division commanders out in Pearl Harbor while I was one, an officer by the name of Captain David C. White. He was my immediate boss and he was in charge of undersea warfare. In other words, he had cognizance of both submarine and anti-submarines. Then he had a subordinate on the anti-submarine side and I had the submarine side. He worked for a Captain by the name of France. I don't know what his title was. It was a very strange experience, and bewildering, to arrive in this organization in which you wonder where to start. Well, it doesn't take you long to find out where to start, but for some time, what's next. I found to my astonishment there was a post-war plan.

Q: I was going to ask you about that.

Adm. B.: It actually existed. I was startled at this and I was surprised that I was startled. I said, "Why in the world didn't I think about that before?" Of course, there would be a post-war plan. I'm sure it had never crossed my mind; during that last year out in Hawaii and now in the Navy Department. I don't think it had ever crossed my mind that there would be a need for a post-war plan. All at once all of the enemies quit and now what do you do? That is the reason why there must be a planning section on the staff. Operators are too busy to see beyond their noses.

Q: I think, if I'm not mistaken, that George Dyer, a submariner, worked on that plan.

Adm. B.: I wouldn't be surprised 'cause he's a very, very capable gentleman. I don't know if they had various alternatives post-war or not, but they did have a plan.

Q: For every part of the Navy they did, yes.

Adm. B.: I understand they didn't have one at the end of World War I. All at once the enemy quit and now what do we do?

Q: I think that's why they had it at the end of World War II.

Adm. B.: It's strange, but it never crossed my mind. I've often wondered what percentage of Admirals had even given a thought, or Generals had even given a thought to a post-war plan. Maybe they all had but we, at the next lower level, had not.

Q: Well, quite a considerable staff was in on this for quite a long time.

Adm. B.: Oh yes! That's what I found out that-- I had been there a few days, when my boss, Dave White said, "I'm going to take you over to meet so-and-so and he's going to brief you on the post-war plan." That was great! They had figured out a tremendous number of things.

Q: The only thing they didn't really figure out adequately was demobilization.

Adm. B.: Well, of course that should be part of the plan. That was an extremely difficult thing. What in the world are we going to do because we've got all these ships and people; what do with them? Actually I didn't get into it a great deal, but here suddenly was a new experience.

It's very difficult to describe how a big staff works. I already explained briefly how you do staff work on letters and messages that came to our headquarters from: White House, commander of chief of fleets, bureaus (for personnel or material matters), quasi-official from submarine admirals or their staffs. Obviously you should also use your own imagination; dream up things that ought to be done or try to keep something from happening which you think is no good. Of course, there being no top-side admiral in charge of the submarine business you find the persons in the various bureaus and other parts of the Navy Department who correspond to your job. You find people who are engaged in doing something which has to do with submarines and you establish real good rapport with them because you need to be crossing back and forth with them. For example, you find the person over in the Bureau of Ships who has nothing to do but submarines. He has to do with the development, building and repairing and all of this sort of thing that has to do with submarines. This was an officer by the name of Buck Weaver at that time. There is no use of my sitting on my cubicle and him sitting on his cubicle and address one another by official letters via our respective chains of command. Let's get together and talk things over for the general benefit of the Navy and specifically for the submarine part of it. Similarly you want to find the people who have to do with the submarine business in personnel; in the Bureau of Ordnance and over in the Research and Development Office. Make contact with all of the different outfits so that you can work together.

On this matter of there not being a submarine admiral in Washington, I don't want to sound as if submarines ought to be a separate service. That would not be good. I can see why the top of the Navy Department is organized like it is. That's the way the other services are also organized and that's the way business is organized. It's organized by functions, rather than every little subject coming all the way to the top.

To meet this particular problem such that submariners can get together, back in 1926 they set up something called the "submarine conference." They met from time to time and, oh I don't know how often. They got together and talked over things so that they would be able to reach some sort of agreement. One of the specific things they came to agreement on, in the middle of 1930's, was a big argument between submarine officers as to what the characteristics of new submarines ought to be. There were people who believed that we should have many small submarines, there were others who thought we should have fewer but bigger. What we called "big" then would now be called "small."

Q: No comparison?

Adm. B.: No way of comparing it; today when everything is a giant. Everyone agreed that we should not build a submarine bigger than it has to be, but we needed to have long legs. We need for it to be able to go across the Pacific Ocean and come back without refueling. If it had been possible to have foreseen exactly the type of submarine you would need for World War II, back in the middle thirties, some bright people came up with a design which couldn't have been better. Considering what we had to work with it could not possibly have been better. That submarine had the flexibility, had four fifteen-hundred horsepower engines. They were air conditioned. That was the new submarine that came out in the early 1940's, air conditioned. Without air conditioning in the submarine during that war it would have been extremely difficult. So these people were ahead of their time. They were designed perfectly. Couldn't have been better for the war that we were in.

Had the faction that wanted to build the smaller ones, had they been able to sway the opinion to their side we would have had submarines that could barely go from the West Coast to Hawaii without having to refuel. That would have certainly been too bad because we couldn't have done what we did.

"Submarine Conference" had gone on from time to time. During the war it sort of subsided. We started it up again after the war.

Q: Wasn't there a big one right after the war on the Pacific coast? A submarine get-together for a conference?

Adm. B.: I recall such a conference somewhere on the West Coast but believe it was just before the war's end. During the time that I was in charge of the Submarines Pacific Fleet we had them twice a year. We usually had them on the West Coast; about half-way. About a fourth of my staff and I would come. About the same from the Atlantic. Also some from Washington.

In addition, the submarine conferences in Washington resumed. I think they probably go on every two or three months. These are mostly informative rather than to try to make decisions. They sort of grew into lectures.

Q: Going on my recollections, it seems to me that there was a big one on the Pacific Coast immediately after the war to absorb, discuss and absorb the lessons of the war.

Adm. B.: Now I recall it. I think there was. But, it wasn't only submarines, it was the whole Navy involvement. Yes.

I just remembered another facet on how to get my job done. I remember when Dave White, my boss, told me once, when I was going to make a trip to New London, "Don't take a paper and pencil with you, because you go up there, they are going to give you more ideas than a dog has fleas." Then he said, "Tell them to write you a letter. It's much easier to negotiate with a piece of paper than it is negotiate something which came off the top of somebody's head." "If a letter is prepared, even if it is personal, the subject will have been thought through better."

They had a staff duty officer system in which, outside of ordinary working hours, there would always be one of the Captains in the organization there. You slept there overnight and you get a lot of telephone calls in the middle of the night from somebody who's been drinking (or not been drinking) but wants to talk to Admiral King or the President or someone else. You are the one who gets up to answer the telephone; handle it in a friendly manner.

When you had that duty you took your meals in the dining room of Fleet Admiral King. That's where his top people had their meals also. When they weren't around or doing something else, then you had the duty. This is where you took your meals and in that space also you slept over night until the telephone rang.

I remember one Sunday when I was in the midst of eating lunch in this dining room when all at once the door opened and here was Fleet Admiral Leahy followed by Fleet Admiral King followed by Fleet Admiral Nimitz and Fleet Admiral Halsey and two or three four star, and all of the top people like Vice Admirals Arthur Radford, Forrest Sherman, Conolly and Denfeld. Naturally I was standing at attention. It was interesting to observe they all looked at me with a pleasant look on their faces, but they kept going. The only one who actually came--

Q: The tape ran out when you said there was only one in this contingent of top brass who came over and spoke and you have yet to identify him to me.

Adm. B.: Well, they didn't have any sort of mean looks about them, they all looked at little me in a friendly manner. I recall distinctly Admiral Nimitz smiling at me. I was way down at the far end and they all sat up at the other end. One of the group came over and introduced himself to me and asked me to come up and join them. So I went up and sat next to him and he engaged me in very fine conversation. During the meal I learned that he was Admiral Arthur Radford.

Q: Oh, really? That surprises me too.

Adm. B.: It was great. I would have been very ill at ease during that meal had it not been for Admiral Radford.

It didn't take us long in Washington to find plenty to do because we had captured various German submarines. We had gone into their various characteristics. Certain things that Germans had done during the end of World War II, we were very fortunate that they started as late as they did. One of the things they did was to invent the snorkel. Actually it was invented in the Netherlands, I believe, but first really used by the Germans.

On the surface our submarine was about the same length as the playing part of a football field. That's a considerable target to put up on the surface. Now, if you put up the periscope it's like putting up a broom handle. But, when you've got the periscope up you are totally submerged and you cannot run your diesel engines because they require oxygen and they also have to be able to exhaust. So, the Germans developed the snorkel. Instead of putting up on the surface something the length of a football field, the snorkel was the size of a garbage can. It's sticking up, oh, three feet and it's maybe a foot and a half in diameter. It has an intake for the air to get to the engine to support the combustion in the engines. Also, the exhaust gas goes out of the snorkel. Therefore, they could operate almost submerged. Naturally, they had to keep a good lookout because this garbage can was something on top, but it was much better than having the whole submarine.

The Germans also had devised a way to streamline the hull of the submarine and to take away a lot of the top hamper which slows you down. They had also developed batteries which had a higher capacity. Therefore, instead of being limited to a speed of say, eight knots for only an hour they could go, say, fifteen knots and last for two or three hours. They had made great improvements here. They also worked on the hydrogen-peroxide engine. The idea here was that they would have the hydrogen-peroxide (H_2O_2) in great big tanks. This hydrogen-peroxide is not the stuff you bleach your hair with. It's a much higher content of hydrogen peroxide, very little dilution.

Q: That's only three percent.

Adm. B.: Yes, and this is very close to a hundred percent. If you have that hydrogen peroxide in a container it has to be in some kind of plastic polyethylene container. It doesn't take much of a catalytic action for the hydrogen peroxide to break down. When it breaks down into water and oxygen it is accompanied by a lot of heat. So, they would have this come into a, sort of a boiler burning fuel supported by the oxygen and the heat turning the water into steam. Then the steam would turn the turbines and propel the ship. They actually built one small one called the METEORITE, a research vehicle, and they made twenty-six knots totally submerged. They made it for twenty-four hours. This was a tremendous improvement and they were beginning to build submarines which would have this type of propulsion. That certainly would have been a bad one. Had they come up with any of these new developments it would have been very difficult for them to have been defeated.

Naturally, over in our Bureau of Ships they were studying all of these things to try to come up with what we should do.

Q: Our intelligence knew that they were doing this, or did we capture them?

Adm. B.: We found it out afterwards.

We were about to start building two new post-World War II submarines. The proposed design for the post-war submarines were nothing; they looked to me like they were nothing more than maybe twenty feet longer, a foot wider and the torpedo tubes bigger and so forth. In other words, not very much imagination. They came up with a better design. The two first submarines laid down after World War II, the post-war ones, were the TANG and the TRIGGER. The TRIGGER was the first one launched of the new ones. Unfortunately the two of them had some very poor engines and after they'd been running for about a year they had to be re-engined because they were not much good.

Q: How did they differ from the classes that were operating in World War II?

Adm. B.: They were streamlined, that is, the hull didn't have great big guns on it and projections and all that sort of thing. They were, well they followed some of the German ideas. Streamline the hull, snorkel, high capacity batteries.

Well, I got into debates on the subject of these new submarine. There was a question at one of our meetings; some of us submarine people with the people over the bureau of ships. The question was whether we should have six torpedoes forward and four aft and someone asked the question, "If we cut it down to two aft would we be able to go faster?"

The person from over at BUSHIPS said, "Why, certainly!"

I said, "Let's not have any aft. Let's go faster." I said, "What we ought to do is to try to learn how to run fast in the submarine. To build a submarine so it will go as fast as we can submerged and the greatest endurance submerged. If in order to do that we have to turn out completely a research vehicle rather than a warship, let's do it. Let's try to find out how to go fast, while submerged."

I couldn't sell the idea, so while the TANG and the TRIGGER came out far better in this respect than it would have been with that other design which was nothing but a World War II one with a little longer and wider. But, we didn't do as much as we should have. A few years later we did. But, there were six members of the family, the TANG-class submarines, not as good as they could have been.

Q: What was their speed?

Adm. B.: Oh, I think they could probably make 20 knots submerged for about 10 hours; some improvements. Ned Beach commanded the TRIGGER. He had started on the old TRIGGER, remember, and he got command of this new one.

My wife hit this on the bow with the champagne bottle at launching in 1950.

He said it was the first submarine that was able to run faster submerged that it could on the surface. But, one of the reasons he could say that was that she wasn't quite as fast on the surface as the ones we had in World War II. In other words, she could run about twenty knots submerged and about seventeen or eighteen on the surface. It was a great advance. It was a fine class of submarine. The ALBACORE came out about 1955 instead of coming out in 1950. If we had done what I wanted to do, we would have come out with one shaped like a whale; we'd come out with that one in 1950 instead of 1955. It didn't do any harm; but one can say that about any new development.

Q: Was there any particular person who was your nemesis when you presented this idea?

Adm. B.: No, no, just a difference of opinion. Still good friends and everything fine, but I do recall one meeting of the Ship Characteristics Board when there was such a thing as a Ship Characteristics Board. That had to do with the whole Navy. All kinds of ship types. You kick around the subject. What are you going to put in? What are you going to take out? For every benefit there is a cost; trade-offs.

Q: In that respect a very valuable board, I think.

Adm. B.: When you're going to build a ship you have to repel boarders or the ship will have everybody's pet. It will be too big; too costly. Also, everybody has his pet idea on it.

Q: It turns out to be top heavy?

Adm. B.: It turns out that it's full of equipment that are all in the development stage and it won't work. You need to get the bugs out of equipment before installation. So, this Ship Characteristics Board really kicks this subject around. There are trade-offs. Something you leave off so you can put something else on. Or maybe you can make it a little smaller. In other words, it's at that stage of the game, before the design has been decided.

I remember at one meeting of the Ship Characteristics Board when I was still on my soap box about a high speed submerged and members of the Ship Characteristics Board were no more interested in submarines than they were in destroyers and aircraft carriers and cruisers and everything. In other words, don't think they are going to just sit there and talk submarines all the time. I will, but not most of the members. On this TANG and TRIGGER business, I had already lost a debate among the submarine guys. But, I thought I'd bring it up again.

Rear Admiral Styer, my squadron commander while C.O. TRIGGER, had arrived on the scene in Washington and became Assistant Deputy Chief of Naval Operations for Operations and Plans. He wasn't present at the meeting. The chairman of the Ship Characteristics Board when I started getting on my soap box said, "I have talked to Admiral Styer about this and he doesn't agree with you."

I said, I thought I said it under my breath; talking to myself but everybody else got quiet at that time and out came the words, "I wish he were here so we could hear him say it!"

This Vice Admiral presiding wasn't very happy. He adjourned the meeting. He said, "Meeting is adjourned." He walked out and to his office.

Q: Insubordination?

Adm. B.: So, I followed him. Went down to his office and told him that I didn't really mean it.

He said, "You know damn well you did mean it!" But he said "What you didn't mean was that we should all hear it."

But, it's one of these things where there is a lot of noise going on and you're going to say something to the fellow standing next to you and the moment you say it everybody gets quiet. Anyhow I blurted it out. That's what happened on this occasion.

About that time "Mom" Chung came on the scene. This is a new subject. "Mom" Chung had been a great friend of the Americans who were flying to help the Chinese. I forget what they called them. Flying Tigers! Yes.

She came into town and she had been a good friend, not only of all aviators, and had formed a club that she called the

"Kiwis". These were her friends who did not fly. Then she started one in the submarine business and I became one of her "Golden Dolphins." Golden Dolphin number 168. While she was here on the East Coast she also came down to the Naval Academy and presented a replica of the TRIGGER's battle flag. The flag we used to fly from the periscope when we came into port, with Japanese flags all over it. She had made up a replica which was maybe three or four feet long and a foot and a half wide. A replica all in silk and satin and she presented it to the Naval Academy Museum. It's on display down there right now. Mrs. Connole was present at this ceremony. I had met her when her husband was a student of mine at PCO School in 1943. She had written to me after World War II because she had become widowed in the spring of 1945. She was the widow of Commander David R. Connole who was commanding officer of the Submarine TRIGGER lost in the spring of 1945; my command 1942-1943. She had not gotten one cent from anywhere and she was supposed to get something from the Veterans Administration. He was still missing rather than having been proclaimed dead. So, his accounts were frozen. She worked in the library here in Annapolis. She wrote me a letter and I got hold of someone in the Veterans Administration and very soon she had a check coming. So, that was a victory.

Interview No. 6 with Rear Admiral Roy S. Benson, U.S. Navy (Retire

Place: Arnold, Maryland

April 8, 1980

Subject: Biography

By: John T. Mason, Jr.

Q: Well, Sir, we're going to resume the story of your two years in the Operations Readiness Section of the CNO. We came back there in 1945 and remained until 1947.

Adm. B.: For those who know that the rank of Captain in the Navy is fairly high, it would be strange for them to understand that a person who has been a Captain in the Navy for about three months and suddenly finds himself at the headquarters of the Navy, the whole Navy, he is quite a junior officer. It is a very bewildering experience to arrive there and try to find out what you're going to do.

I would like to mention there were several subjects new to me.

One was, and this surprised me, there was a good deal of talk going on about unification.

Q: You had not heard this?

Adm. B.: No, I had not heard any such talk at all, but apparently it was going at real good speed. Even before the war was terminated.

Q: Yes. The Air Force, part of the Army, was very adamant about this.

Adm. B.: The three services had differing ideas. The Air Force one was to separate from the Army. What the Army wanted to do was to set up a single service with a single Chief of Staff and a single Secretary of Defense. They thought that this would be a good idea because they had been through this in the Army a few generations before when they set up their general staff system. So, they knew that this was a good idea. But, this is what they wanted to do.

The Air Force was perfectly sincere. The Army was perfectly sincere. But the Naval Service, the Navy and Marine Corps was also perfectly sincere in that they thought things had gone along pretty well.

As one of the top people in the Navy said, "Just imagine the difficulties we would be in if we had lost the war."

It happened at this time that the President was in favor of the unification of the services that the Army was in favor of.

Apparently the top people in the Navy and Marine Corps knew that they would be barking up the wrong tree if they simply opposed the whole business. What they were hoping that they could do was salvage something from it rather than to go the whole way.

Q: Make the strategic approach.

Adm. B.: Yes. Now the post-war plan, we had mentioned, envisioned a very large naval service spread all over the world with all kinds of bases here and there. For example, in the submarine business, if I recall correctly, we would have a submarine base somewhere on the West Coast. We'd have, certainly, Pearl Harbor. There would be one on Guam. Probably another in the Philippines. Certainly one in Yokosuka, Japan. We'd have one in Bermuda; where else in the Atlantic I don't know. Of course, we would continue to have a base at New London. We'd have one at Key West and Norfolk. I don't recall the details.

It didn't take long, certainly within the first year, after the war was over, it was completely clear that we weren't going to have armed services of the size that the armed services had envisioned.

Q: This was punctured somewhat, wasn't it, by the rapid demobilization?

Adm. B.: Rapid demobilization and also the cutting of the budget. Apparently it was very fashionable not to give the services very much money because the country had other things to do. So they were being cut and cut and cut. I remember that we were rather shocked when we saw a setup in which we would have considerably less than a hundred submarines on active duty.

In the post-war plan also, naturally, I knew more about the submarine side than I did anything else. But, I wasn't in on it really. It was an entirely different organization that dealt with this. I recall that we were going to have quite a few submarines that would be in reserve and would be school rooms for Naval Reserves who are not on active duty. We would also have a considerable number of them in what we called "mothballs."

I remember there was a big discussion on the subject of, what are we going to do with the submarines that are in the process of being built. Well, of course, you draw a line and those beyond a certain line go ahead and continue to build them and below you scrap them. I don't recall exactly where the line was.

Q: Admiral, this vast and fast reduction in the immediate post-war period was influenced somewhat, was it not, by the fact that there was no potential enemy on the horizon?

Adm. B.: That's right.

Q: There was no real need to have this tremendous Navy?

Adm. B.: No. That's right.

Another thing I hadn't thought very much about, but the top of the Navy apparently was of the opinion, and I'm inclined to agree with them now, that it wasn't necessary to drop atomic bombs in order to get the Japanese to surrender. In other words, I found out, I guess mostly by gossip coming down because I didn't hear the top people in the Navy explain this. They were not in favor of the invasion of the main Japanese Islands at all. It wasn't necessary. That they (Japan) were going to quit anyhow.

Now, one of the reasons that it was so bewildering to arrive there in my job in the Navy Department, I found out soon they were in the process of doing away with Fleet Admiral King's hat of COMINCH. They were going to merge that into the Office of the Chief of Naval Operations.

Q: Well, that was merely a wartime billet anyway, wasn't it?

Adm. B.: I suppose so. Anyhow, they were going to do away with it. It happened in the fall of 1945 and this Captain White that I worked for, our little triumvirate, got into the part headed up by Admiral Cook. He was the Deputy Chief of Naval Operations (for Operations.) The OP-03 billet. Admiral Edwards became the Vice Chief of Naval Operations. Not really a change but in title because that's what his title had been under the previous set up. He had been in charge of the Office of Naval Operations side. Admiral Denfeld was in there. Admiral Bieri, Admiral Farber was logistics. Admiral Mitscher, Admiral Horne, they were all in that organization.

I think I mentioned once that in the Office of the Chief of Naval Operations side there was a submarine officer by the name of Karl Hensel, a aptain. He got into the logistics side. We were in the operating side.

In December 1945 Fleet Admiral Nimitz relieved Fleet Admiral King and became the Chief of Naval Operations. He never had that hat of COMINCH. His immediate subordinates--it seemed like a big change--people who had been in these jobs under Admiral King were soon not there. I suppose most of them retired the same time Admiral King did.

Q: King was over retirement age by far.

Adm. B.: Yes. During the middle of the war he had already reached the retirement age, I believe. But, they kept him on. We got a new set of faces up in the front corridor.

Admiral Nimitz, Chief of Naval Operations. An aviator by the name of Ramsey became the Vice Chief of Naval Operations. Forrest Sherman relieved Admiral Cook. Radford became the air deputy. Blandy got atomic and nuclear matters. A new job. Admiral Lockwood soon came back to Washington. He had been Submarine Force Commander in the Pacific. He came back and became the Inspector General, which was a job he didn't relish at all. He didn't want to find fault with people. He wanted to get on with the operations. He was not a person who would find fault with anyone. He was a real leader; no one would let him down.

I heard at that time Vice Admiral Sherman was the Navy's action officer having to do with the discussions with respect to unification. There was a three-star general of the Army Air Corps, I don't remember his name, who became his counterpart. They and their small special staffs for the unification kicked this around for quite a long time.

Now this is not a criticism but a fact. In this organization of ours you notice that I had a submarine job, full time. Captain Hensel on the logistics side also had it. Going up the chain of command toward the top, the first flag officer we got to was a rear admiral by the name of Jerauld Wright. It was at least fifteen years after World War II was over before we had a flag officer in Washington who had nothing to do but submarines. It is only about the last two, three, or four years that we now have a three-star admiral in charge of the submarine business.

This is not a criticism, it is simply the way things were put together. Prior to recent years the only part of the Navy which had a tight setup was the naval aviation: OP-05, Deputy Chief of Naval Operations for Air. The rest of the setup of the Chief of Naval Operations was not by type of vehicle. It was operations, logistics, intelligence, communications and these were functional rather than by type.

Q: Isn't it true that as a result of the war effort in the Pacific, the air arm of the Navy was so dominant that you had in that post-war period the dominance of the aviator?

Adm. B.: Yes. But, it's probably a good thing we did it too. It certainly was a very important part of our organization.

Another hot potato flying around Washington at that time was universal military training. Again in this case the President was in favor of it. This was President Truman. There were a lot of people against it. This was not drafting the youth that you need in the armed forces. This was everyone. Every male when he became---

Q: Women were not included, were they?

Adm. B.: Not included in those days. Every male when he reached the age of eighteen was to enter universal military training. The reason that the services generally were against this is this would be their full occupation. There would be so many millions of these youth coming in that the armed forces would have no time to do anything but give a little training to all of these youth.

Q: And what period of time was involved in their enforced service?

Adm. B.: I don't recall. I don't know if they ever got that far. But it was a hot one around there.

New subjects: One day a Captain by the name of Dan Gallery came in to see me. We recall that around 1944 he was in command of a jeep carrier operating near Iceland and he had some other ships along with him beginning of the hunter-killer group. They captured the German submarine U-505. Well, what Dan Gallery's coming in to see me about was, he wanted to have that submarine brought to Chicago and there it would be a museum. I told him that I didn't think that this was very feasible.

I said, "Why don't you do as we did with the SQUALUS. The conning tower of the SQUALUS is sitting on top of a large block of concrete, but not the submarine itself. This is something they can look at and why don't you--or, if you insist on having this submarine, why don't you take it down to Pensacola? It could be down there."

"Oh, no," he said, "Chicago is my home town. That's where I want the submarine."

Q: That's where he got it.

Adm. B.: Well, he wasn't very happy with me when he left and I hadn't given him any encouragement. I said, "It's impossible."

Well, I visited in Chicago some years later and went through his museum. I understand that he got it up just the way we moved, oh, a dozen and a half new submarines built in Manitowoc, Wisconsin, during World War II. They would take them down the Mississippi

River. I suppose he brought it up the same way.

Anyhow, I understand that when they got it to Chicago, it was necessary for them to take this submarine across a super-highway. It had at least eight lanes of traffic.

Q: This is Michigan Boulevard.

Adm. B.: Full of automobiles all the time. But, they succeeded in bringing it across the boulevard.

Q: They did it after midnight when they blocked traffic.

Adm. B.: Just imagine what a plan that must have been, to be all set and ready to go and here she goes. And there she is! Pretty good. I thought it was impossible.

Another item that rather startled me was that I was convinced that not only all through the Navy and the public were very commendatory of what the submarines had done against the Japanese. I didn't realize that the rest of the Navy and certainly the public was not, but certainly the Navy was aware that our submarine force, which was smaller than one Marine division, or four aircraft carriers, had sunk more Japanese ships than everyone else put together. I didn't realize that that was not known.

Also not known were the great limitations under which we had operated; we needed more submerged speed and submerged endurance. But, in the public media there seemed great interest in getting the submarine story out to the public. Well, this was a Navy group, don't know what they called them but this group was engaged in going through the action reports of all the battles, etc. during World War II in which our Navy was involved. They were trying to declassify, to the extent possible, these reports so that they would be available to the public as they should. There is no use in keeping a bunch of secrets which are no longer secrets. Well, hardly a day went by at work that I didn't have a pile of papers on my desk. This group didn't have a submarine guy on it so they would bring me a whole pile of these action reports for me to look through to see what can be declassified and what must be kept classified. I got a little tired of this because this was all in the submarine patrol reports. So, I decided: let's do all the submarine war patrol reports. There had been about fifteen hundred submarine war patrols and, when I counted around Washington, I found there had been something on the order of about a hundred and fifty submarine officers in various jobs, all through the naval establishment there. Only two of us, you recall, actually were in submarine jobs. They were in all kinds of jobs. All of these 150 had actually been in command of a submarine at some time during the war.

Now, we had, in my office in a safe, a complete set of the patrol reports. Naturally, I'm going to get permission to do it before I do it. If I could issue about ten of these to each one of these individuals and issue them a suitable statement of guidance, we could really do something. So, we got some rolls of opaque tape, sort of like Scotch tape, but it was opaque and they would go through the reports and they would cover over the things which had to remain classified. When we finished with all of these, this was about a hundred and fifty officers, one did approximately ten.

Q: Did you get the Admiral's cooperation?

Adm. B.: Yes.

Q: They did it on their office time?

Adm. B.: Yes, or took them home with them. When we finished then we microfilmed the whole business and destroyed the originals. These patrol reports were still classified because all you had to do was pull off the tape and you could see what was said.

Sometimes it would be a whole page that would be blocked out. So, we burned them up. We didn't need them because there were other places in Washington that had the classified patrol reports not mutilated. We had the microfilm of all fifteen hundred war patrols. They were unclassified. They are still in several places in Washington, Norfolk, and San Francisco. The public media thought that was a real good idea. It is basic to anyone who is going to write something about submarines in World War II.

January 1946: Admiral Lockwood came to Washington. Also Admiral C. W. Styer also arrived. Admiral Styer had, when I was first a skipper early in the war, he was my squadron commander. He was a Captain. Toward the end of the war he was in command of the submarines of the Atlantic Fleet. He came to Washington and became Admiral Forrest Sherman's assistant. He was the Assistant Deputy Chief of Naval Operations. It will be noted that I have covered matters in the order in which they occurred. Not serious.

There was another thing going on in Washington, and these do tie together. You recall that I mentioned that with the exception of naval air no other type was recognized as such. The organization wasn't set up that way. Admiral Nimitz brought this matter up once and said, "Let's look at it. Let's see what we really ought to do. Should we have some top admiral in charge of amphibious, and another one in charge of gunfire support, of all these various kinds of things? Submarines, anti-submarines mining all kinds."

It's endless. And he asked his Deputy Chiefs of Naval Operations to give him their recommendations. Out of this came the setting up of Rear Admiral Styer with an extra hat. He was still the Assistant Vice Admiral for Sherman. He was assistant for DCNO Operations. But he got another hat known as the Co-ordinator of Undersea Warfare. This was quite a step. I'm still rather at a loss to figure out why they gave him, who was purely a submariner, also to do with anti-submarine warfare. I didn't quite understand that.

Q: What was accomplished by the conferences in this immediate post-war period?

Adm. B.: I thought it would be a very nice idea to have a submarine party to welcome the Lockwood's, Fife's, and the Styer's back to Washington, though they had been here for some time. The few people that I called up and tested the water thought it was a great idea. But, I didn't hear any ideas on who should be chairman so obviously I became the chairman. We had a real nice party at the downtown Hilton Hotel. I had two members of my committee help me. When the party was over we made a little profit, I believe, but anyhow we made a reservation at the Army-Navy Country Club for the following fall and nominated someone to be chairman of the committee. That person accepted in and in the fall we had a submarine party. We still have them in Washington.

Q: Annual affairs?

Adm. B.: Yes, and sometimes twice during a year. I was slightly shocked last year. A year ago April 10th we went to the submarine party in Washington. When they were going to cut the birthday cake, they decided to have it cut by the youngest and the oldest who'd qualified as submarine officers. I was wondering who--I knew that I'd be chosen the youngest. I wondered who would be chosen as the oldest. They chose me as the oldest. That was a little shock to my system.

Q: Well, it just shows that the gathering is keeping up with times by including the younger element, too. No longer confined to World War II.

Adm. B.: Oh, no. Early in 1946 the Naval Research Laboratory made a study and came in with a recommendation that the Navy build a nuclear-powered submarine. There was a great deal of action over in our bureau of ships. I mentioned about the snorkel, the high submerged speed and the hydrogen peroxide. But they were also very busy in kicking around the subject of nuclear power.

The Chief of the Bureau of Ships at that time, Admiral Cochrane, sent a group, I don't know how many, maybe a half a dozen to a dozen, engineering officers somewhere to study nuclear matters. Among them was a Captain by the name of Rickover who has come far since then.

There were a lot of things going on, as you can imagine. In the absence of having anything directly to do with the demobilization, the scrapping of ships and many other things, I found myself in on the edges a little bit. In the absence of other things to interest myself, I interested myself in new developments I tried, instead of looking back on World War II, I was interested in what are we doing to make our performance even better.

Q: Then you must have been highly interested in the atomic submari

Adm. B.: I was very interested in it also, but I didn't know very much about it. I came down here to the Engineering Experiment Station and observed some test work having to do with the hydrogen peroxide engine. But, we didn't hear very much about the nuclear power. But, at least it was grinding away a bit.

In the spring -- oh another thing I failed to mention, the fact that I tried to interest myself in the new things made me get acquainted with quite a few scientists who had been in, I think they called it the NRDC, National Research and Development Committee during World War II. Many of them had obviously been in the armed forces during World War II.

Q: And many of them stayed on during this early period, didn't they, in government service.

Adm. B.: Oh, yes. They were at naval research laboratories, National Academy of Science was a very important one. The Underwater Sound Laboratory in New London. These are full of people who had come in during World War II and stayed there. Even if they were back at their universities and colleges, they came in to serve on various kinds of committees to study this and that. I guess they could get a grant from the government to study something that was worthwhile.

I became acquainted with a few of them because I went to the various conferences that I was permitted to, dealing with new developments. That resulted in my next tour of duty. We had now gotten to the spring of 1947 and I was ordered to go to the Naval War College. Our friend Admiral Fife had come back to Washington during the same time that Admiral Lockwood and Admiral Styer were there. Admiral Fife got on what we called the General Board. Then, in the spring of 1947, he got orders to go to New London and become Commander Submarine Force, U.S. Atlantic Fleet. He called me on the phone and asked:

"Would you like to come with me?"

I said, "Well, I'm going to the Naval War College."

He said, "Would you rather come to New London with me?"

I said, "Yes, Admiral."

And he fixed it up so I proceeded to New London to be on his staff. I found myself in charge of new developments. I guess that assignment stemmed from having taken so much interest in that particular line of endeavor.

Q: Had you thought of getting sent to the Atomic Energy School to learn about that subject?

Adm. B.: No, I hadn't even thought about it. In the first place, I'm not an engineering officer. I'm sure they wouldn't have sent anyone who wasn't. So, I found myself in New London, Connecticut, on the staff and was the new developments officer.

Q: This was what, this was in March 1947?

Adm. B.: 1947.

Q: You were there for exactly a year so tell me about that year.

Adm. B.: Now, having come up to New London to be the new developments officer on the staff, I became very well acquainted with people at the Navy's Sound Laboratory, Underwater Sound Laboratory there in New London. We called it USNUSL.

I became very interested in what they were doing and naturally they were kicking around the subject of underwater sound equipments and this was great. I then became acquainted with people at the Wood's Hole Undersea Oceanographic Institution. They had, looking over their backs, some people from a part of Columbia University.

Q: How extensive was the work at Wood's Hole at that point?

Adm. B.: Well, as far as we could see, there was a lot going on there. But, it was general oceanographic studies. Of course, submarine and anti-submarine warfare are both interested in underwater sound; oceanography and underwater sound are very close to one another.

During the time that I had this particular job, I recall making one trip to England. There were about a dozen of us who went over as a team and was headed up by Captain E. W. Grenfell. Joe Grenfell, I don't know if you've run into him or not.

Q: No. He just died.

Adm. B.: That's right. He had relieved Captain White and was still in that job. We went to Portsmouth, England, to meet with the British submarine people and up to the Admiralty. We went up to Londonderry, North Ireland where they, the British, have their Joint Anti-submarine Warfare School. It was a very strange arrangement there. This particular school for anti-submarine warfare had two commanding officers. One was a Captain from the Royal Navy and the other was a Group Captain from the Royal Air Force. Each had a deputy. Then they had a naval aviator as the executive officer. This was a very strange operation. I asked, "How can you run it with two commanding officers? Who is the umpire?"

"Well," he said, "the only meeting place of our chains of command is the top person having to do with defense matters in the British government, the Defense Minister; we can't bring our problems up to him, so we solve them here."

But, that was quite a school. We spent some time up there trying to learn as much as we could from them.

We learned more about how they use their underwater sound equipment. They were ahead of us apparently in the listening part of underwater sound.

You recall that I said some time ago that we originally had some listening hydrophones which listened across the whole spectrum of sound while the ones that we had on board the submarines in World War II were especially tuned to a higher frequency for the purpose of sending out a "ping" and getting an echo come back.

We hadn't done much in the listening part across the whole spectrum and so we learned something from them.

Q: They had the ASDIC?

Adm. B.: Well, yes, but the ASDIC was a pinger.

Q: Then they had the echo sounding gear?

Adm. B.: Yes. This group also made a trip down to a place called Barrow-in-Furness and there they had a Type-26 German submarine. Type-26 German submarine was a small prototype, a small model, propelled by hydrogen peroxide.

Q: They got this as an aftermath to the war?

Adm. B.: Yes. You know we, the British and the French each got a certain number of submarines that we could look over very, very carefully. The Germans were way ahead in the listening sonar. They were way ahead of the British and the British were, in turn, ahead of us. But, the German underwater sound equipment for their submarines, naturally, was studied very carefully in our various laboratories including USNUSL at New London. This fascinated me greatly because, obviously, this is the way we had to go somewhere along the line.

In about March of 1948 Admiral Fife was on a trip somewhere in the middle of the night. A fire broke out and burned down his headquarters. Now, the curious thing was that the day before the fire we had a big scientific conference there at the submarine base. Naturally, again, the theme really at this point was my association with the scientific world relating to do with things having to do with submarines. We had a great big pow-wow there at the submarine base in New London. I had walked back to my office and the Captain in charge of the Underwater Sound Laboratory had come along with me to have a little final discussion. My incoming basket was about a foot deep with papers because I had been at this confab for a few days and there was a lot of work here. I said to this fellow, Bill Pryor, "You know somebody ought to burn down this place sometime and burn up all the papers and then we could get to work," or words to that effect.

You know that night the place burned down. Bill Pryor called me on the phone and said, "I won't squeal on you."

It's quite a sensation to be on a staff when you have a fire. I guess we had about a dozen officers and two or three dozen enlisted men, clerical mostly. Every paper you're working on yesterday with rare exceptions is gone. It doesn't exist. Well, there was a safe in my office and in that safe I had classified material and a few other items. Some of it came out all right and some of it didn't. But there were items there which will be of interest. There was a company by the name of Exide Storage Battery Company. When they put batteries in a brand new submarine they gave the ship a cigarette box with the name of the ship on it. We had one on board the TRIGGER. We didn't usually have it out. We put it out on the dining room table when we had some guests. Otherwise, it was kept in the captain's cabin.

You recall, in the summer of 1943 I was going to go back on thirty days' leave and I never came back to the submarine. Well, I had left for the thirty days' leave and the ship had gone to the shipyard for the overhaul. Things had been all locked up in my state room. No one was going to touch them. When I wasn't coming back they packed all of the stuff and sent it back to New London to me. And, the cigarette box was with it. Well, I don't know what my thoughts were, but anyhow, the cigarette box was in the safe. That was a magnificent safe.

Q: Heat resistant?

Adm. B.: Because here is the cigarette box.

Q: That is the cigarette box intact. That is a beauty.

Adm. B.: Do you know what I did? I was a very magnanimous sort of an individual. I gave this to the widow of the last commanding officer, Commander Connole. I gave it to his widow. Wasn't that nice? But I didn't give it to her until a few days before we got married, April 1948.

In April 1948 I married Vida Connole who had been the widow of the last commanding officer of the TRIGGER. We have a son living in Massachusetts who is Rick Connole and has a couple of Connole sons. One of them is David R. Connole, just like his grandfather.

Q: I take it that Mrs. Connole gave it to you as a wedding present.

Adm. B.: No. Mrs. Benson could have.

During that time I was in New London, Connecticut, I used to go to Portsmouth, New Hampshire, where they build submarines. Up at Portsmouth I went out for a ride on the first snorkel equipped submarine that we had. I also was up there to make a ride on the first, what we called a Guppy. I don't know why we gave them that name, but anyhow, this submarine had all the top hamper taken off so it was as streamlined as it could be. It had a newer design of batteries and various kinds of things so that it actually could run much faster submerged and for a longer time.

Q: It was a post-war development?

Adm. B.: Well, it was a conversion of a World War II submarine.

In July 1948 I changed jobs from new developments to plans.

Q: Now before you do, tell me a little about Admiral Jimmy Fife, having worked under him for a year.

Adm. B.: Well, I'd known Jimmy Fife for some time and he was a very kindly gentlemen and also a very tough one. He--there is one story about him when he was in command of the submarine NAUTILUS. They had been out for a week's operations. They'd been too busy for him to do all of his routine studying so he did not go home over the weekend 'cause he had to study. He always was trying to learn a great deal. He was like a sponge trying to pick up information. He really had it at his fingertips all the time. One of the first things that happened when I came to New London to be on his staff was when he was going to make a speech. He had worked on it very, very hard. So, he got all of his staff over in the movie theater and he got up on the stage and went through his speech. Well, he talked a long time. Just before I had left Washington to go to New London I had taken a public speaking course at night at George Washington University. I had just finished that course of two nights a week, an hour each for a couple of months. So, I sat there and was listening to Admiral Fife give his speech, and, well, what he did didn't quite conform to what I had just been taught. So, when he--when I was a young fellow I always had my hand in the air. If anyone wanted expressions of opinion they could get them straight from the shoulder.

When he finished his speech he said, "Any suggestions?"

I said, "Admiral, I've got a couple of suggestions."

"Well, go ahead. Give them to me, Roy."

I said, "Well, you started your speech and you spent the first two or three minutes explaining who was there. You named the mayor and the governor and everybody. You named all these people, dozens of them. Then you spent the next few minutes explaining how glad you were to be there. Then you spent the next few minutes on what your previous association had been in that particular part of the world and the particular organization you're addressing. "A period of at least ten minutes had gone by and you hadn't started your speech yet. I'm afraid that you're going to lose a lot of your audience."

There was quietness. Admiral Fife said, "Is there another recommendation or suggestion?"

Nobody said a word.

Walking back to the office the chief of staff said to me, "Boy, you have really done yourself in. You've had it!"

Well, the strange thing is that Admiral Fife accepted some of them. He wasn't quick to accept somebody's suggestion, but often times you'd see the evidence. He'd do it anyhow. In his speeches from then on he didn't do these things. He still talked too long, but that's all right. He did not do the other things. We'd been taught at school that you say to the person who introduced you, "Thank you," and then you go into your speech. Right then. If you want to come back sometime and recognize some of the celebrities or say why you're there, that's all right. First get their attention.

Admiral Fife was so thorough, so learned and so experienced that if a subject came up--some message or letter -- if we didn't get a look at it first, he would already have decided what to do and that's the end of it. He'd call a staff meeting and tell us what to do. Most of us would have preferred if he gave us a chance. Give us the first crack at it. That's the way you really ought to run a staff. Let the staff kick it around a little bit. You don't have to do what the staff says to do. At least you ought to recognize that they exist. If you wanted a crack at the problems, you almost had to hijack the mail in order to get your two bits in. Otherwise the admiral has already decided.

He was very amicable socially and very amicable in the office unless someone did something that teed him off. One of the things that would tee him off was a failure to do something that was supposed to have been done and all you did was forget. He didn't have very much patience for that. He also didn't have very much patience for lack of knowledge. He--for you to be responsible for some particular thing on that staff and he asked a question and you don't know, that's not very good. So, if you lasted it out with Admiral Fife, you must have done your homework. Of course, he chose us. There was that psychological point also. If a person chooses you for a job you must perform terribly to convince him that your performance is poor. He had good reason to choose the people he chose. At least he thought so. It was a real pleasure to work with a tough taskmaster, who was not lazy, knew his stuff, takes care of his people. If something came up that he could help you with in some way, he was right there. A tremendous individual.

Q: He was endowed with a great deal of common sense.

Adm. B.: Yes, tremendous common sense.

Q: And a certain, as you indicate, a certain degree of conceit.

Adm. B.: Well, he was a smart one. He was confident. Where is the boundary between confident and conceit? He was a smart guy and everybody recognized that he was a tough taskmaster. But he didn't require anything of his subordinates that he didn't require of himself. That's pretty good.

In about July of 1948 I changed jobs on the staff. I relinquished my new developments job and became the head of the plans department. I still didn't have anyone working for me. Plans had to do with planning for various fleet exercises and so forth. But, it also had to do with war plans and other contingency plans. We had a whole book full of all kinds of plans for various kinds of contingencies. They were, of course, general, because they were not pointing in a particular wa

Q: Now, in the case of war plans, did they have to be coordinated with submarine operations elsewhere, say in the Pacific?

Adm. B.: No, they had to be coordinated with the plans of the other types in the Atlantic Fleet, but not having to do with the Pacific. But, they were still in very general terms and nothing very specific. Well, based on my previous experience when we laid mines, when I had command of the TRIGGER, I proceeded to make a study and finally came up with a plan how our Marines would lay mines across the neck of the entrance of the White Sea up near Murmansk and also down in the Black Sea. We got these war plans all set and everything was ready so that we could do it. Naturally, we did not do it. The Berlin blockade was on at that time. I'm not sure just exactly when it started, but that was the general period I remember that I made a trip over to England to discuss plans with them and when I came back that time, Admiral Blandy, who was then in command of the Atlantic Fleet, wanted to see me. I went down and we talked about the things that I had picked up over in Great Britain. Also, he broke out my mining plans and seemed to be very pleased with them.

One day, I don't know how it happened, but I said to myself, "You know, if we should get ourselves into a limited war at sea with the Russians, and it's possible to have such a thing. Maybe it isn't, but it's a contingency. We might all at once be told by the Commander in Chief of the Atlantic Fleet to get our submarines into the anti-submarine warfare business. Russian submarines might be causing so much damage that everything we had would have to help in ASW; throw the submarine in too. In addition to the mining business. So, I said to myself, "What in the world would we do then?"

So, I wrote up a proposed directive which Admiral Fife signed. It was addressed to the four submarine squadron commanders in the Atlantic and to all members of their staffs and the Captain of the submarine base at New London. They were supposed to reply in a period of about two weeks, if I remember correctly. It gave the background, in the event of any war limited or otherwise, we might be told to get our submarines into the anti-submarine warfare business. If we received that order now, what would we do? What should we do?

Next one, what if we received six months' warning?

Next one, what about if we got a year's warning?

And the other one, what if we got five years' warning?

I think those were the increments.

When we received our replies we had all kinds of suggestions. It was tremendous. Many of them not feasible. Some of them not much good. I was going to say "stupid," but they weren't quite that bad.

Q: Were these staff replies?

Adm. B.: Also the squadron commanders. I know very well that the squadron commanders when they prepared theirs, used the division commanders' ideas also; maybe also the ideas of the commanding officers.

Q: So it was a composite?

Adm. B.: We had all kinds. It was a good way to get a cross section of opinion. I don't know whether one of these--what we did, what we specifically did came out of this or not. But, I prepared a piece of paper that I sent around the staff and to Admiral Fife that suggested that we should set up a small group of submarines who should be given the job of finding out how to use our submarines in anti-submarine warfare other than mine fields. Find out what we can do and how we can do it for the short interval and the future.

When Admiral Fife approved this I said to him, "Well, now I would like to go down to Washington and Norfolk where the commander in chief was. I would like to go down and touch base and talk with various people in those two places. Sort of prepare the ground so that when your proposal arrives, this idea might be acceptable and maybe also get some good ideas."

So, I went down to Norfolk and talked to various people there. Everything seemed to be all right. I went down to Washington and it was accepted so well there that in lieu of Admiral Fife requesting it officially the Chief of Naval Operations issued a naval directive for us to do it.

Q: Was this still Nimitz?

Adm. B.: Yes, but I don't think he signed it. I don't remember if it was Sherman signed it or who. But, anyhow, we got a directive and it said for us to form such a group. Admiral Fife asked me if I wanted to head it up. Of course, I said yes. He told that, at first, I could have one other officer on my staff and I could have up to two enlisted men. That was meager. Naturally, I didn't have such a big staff that we got lost in our own paper shuffling.

I then went around and talked to various people at the submarine base on the various staffs and tried to get their ideas of what we should do. I also talked to the people down at the Undersea Sound Laboratory and other scientists before we really started down the road. The reason that I did this was that the first person that I went to to confer with to get some advice was Captain H. C. Bruton. He had been the chief of staff to Admiral Fife but was now in command of one of the submarine squadrons in New London. I wanted to talk to him. He gave me some very sage advice.

The first piece of advice he gave me was start slowly. He said, "If you're driving an automobile and you're driving down the road and come to a 'Y' in the road and you're not sure which way to go you'd better stop and figure it out. Because by the time you're ten miles down the road you're sort of hesitant to go back and start it over. Therefore, you'll go wandering around all over the place trying to find the road you should have gotten on in the first place." He said, "So start slowly. Don't head down the road until you're sure that you've got the road ahead of you that you want."

And he said, "The next bit of advice is you're going to have to depend very heavily on underwater sound equipment. You are going to have to listen to these enemy submarines. You must detect them at long distance with underwater sound equipment. The sound equipment on board these submarines is not equal to the task. They can be made equal to the task if we will give them the kind of loving care that's necessary and, if we try that, we might be able to get something." "Loving care for underwater sound gear."

Then he had another bit of advice. He said, "You know, you're going to have to get some kind of positive results very soon, otherwise it's all over. They'll cancel it." He said, "Someone is looking over your shoulder and if he doesn't see something that looks pretty good you'll no longer be useful. So, don't drag your feet and finally a year from now come up with some kind of results. You've got to come up with some results soon." He said that with regard to the equipment--

Q: But, was it a project that would permit you to come out with something tangible in a short time?

Adm. B.: Well, I'm not sure. We didn't know, but he certainly advised, "Try to come up with something that looks like you're making some real progress; that there really is some light which will come through the tunnel."

He suggested that the first thing I should do is go down to the Underwater Sound Laboratory where there are a lot of scientist and experts in underwater sound. Get them to tune up the underwater sound equipment of your submarines and do everything else they possibly can in noise reduction of the submarine so that you can start doing something with the underwater sound equipment.

He said, "We've never come anywhere close to getting these underwater sound equipments to operate the way they should."

So, I did exactly that. I went down and got the underwater sound equipment experts at the Underwater Sound Lab to go over our underwater sound equipment. It was in terrible shape. They really were poor. In three cases of the four it was as if you did not connect your radio or television to the antenna. Not even connected. The hydrophone that's supposed to pick up sound was in three out of the four not connected to the receiver in the ship. Lack of--this is personnel again.

When I first got up to New London in 1947 one of the first things I learned was we do not have enough skilled people to really man these submarines. We can't man them with the kind of skilled people we're accustomed to. This underwater sound equipment was a part of it.

Well, when I found out down at the Underwater Sound Laboratory how poor the equipments were on our four ships, naturally I told Admiral Fife and I told everyone else, "Now, we've got a job ahead of us because we want to get these underwater sound equipments to work."

Once we got those to work we went out there to--

Q: How did you achieve it?

Adm. B.: The Underwater Sound Laboratory overhauled our equipments and overhauled the hydrophones that were supposed to pick up the noise and the connecting link between them. They simply put them in the kind of condition they should have been all the time.

Q: Yes, but how did you get the proper personnel to operate them?

Adm. B.: They learned down there at the same time.

Q: Oh, I see.

Adm. B.: They—

Q: They taught the personnel of the submarine?

Adm. B.: Yes. They were scientists and technicians at the Underwater Sound Laboratory. They fixed our equipment and taught our people.

Then we went out and practiced. One submarine listened and one submarine was making noise, turning over its screws. We got much better results than we ever had before.

Then a fleet exercise came along and we took a chance. Our submarines weren't supposed to be in the fleet exercise, but we asked to try it a little bit. You know, we did very well. We actually detected our own submarines at distances that were most unusual. So, we had already come up with some positive results. These were not the early World War II pingers. They were the new listeners developed by scientists during World War II.

Q: That was within what time frame?

Adm. B.: Oh, that was in a matter of less than two months. We had come out with a great increase in the ability of these people to use the underwater sound equipment.

These four submarines that I had been issued were the USS COCHINO, the USS TUSK, the USS TORO, and the USS CORSAIR. The COCHINO and the TUSK were guppies, that is they were the snorkelers and the high submerged speed. The TORO and the CORSAIR were as they were originally built in World War II.

Q: What was their speed underwater?

Adm. B.: Oh, eight knots for one hour and then the battery was completely gone; any combination between that and about 1 1/2 knots for twenty-four hours. When the battery was all gone, the submarine had to surface and charge them.

Q: The others were capable of twenty-six?

Adm. B.: No, that was the German; using hydrogen peroxide.

Q: Oh, I see.

Adm. B.: The COCHINO and TUSK would make maybe twelve knots submerged. But, they could make it for about three hours. A lot of the top hamper and projections had been removed, anything sticking out slows you down. During World War II, when we ran on the surface most of the time, to have a gun up there or anything else that messes things up didn't do any harm really. You didn't even think about it. We ran on the surface. Now, if you're going to run submerged, you take all that stuff off, take off the lifelines and anything that causes--it will all slow you down. Just like in an airplane; so you smooth it out, the entire profile of the submarine. We actually got permission also to take the lifelines, the guns and other things off the TORO and the CORSAIR which were not supposed to be going faster and longer, but when we took that top hamper, guns and so forth, they went faster, too. They couldn't go as fast as the other ones because they didn't have the new style battery.

I could have one officer. I immediately wanted a commander by the name of R. B. Lynch (Ozzie Lynch). He's the one I wanted for this job.

Q: Why?

Adm. B.: Well, he and I had been shipmates on the submarine USS NAUTILUS and you recall the story about our taking pictures through the periscope. He was the photographer. He had gone to school. One of the first also to go to school learning something about radar. He was an electronics hobbyist. He was the fellow that could make your car work. He's the guy that can make your radio work. He's the fellow who takes apart your television and puts it together again and it works. He was very good at all of these things and very, very smart. Also, a good guy. I knew that he would have certain capabilities that I needed. I knew that if I asked him his opinion of something I would get it straight from the shoulder but I also knew that when I decided what we're going to do he'd jump in there and help me do it exactly that way. He wouldn't get all grumpy because I didn't accept his advice. But, his advice was good. We were very close friends. He was working for someone down in the Navy Department in Washington. So, I proceeded to Washington. Went in to see his boss and succeeded in getting him sprung. For office we had a corner of this Captain Bruton's squadron office.

Q: Was this a result of the fire earlier that you didn't have space?

Adm. B.: We didn't have an office because this was a new organization and space was all taken up. But, it didn't take us long to get a part of the BOQ up there and get it all squared away. As a matter of fact, that organization is still running with the same title. It doesn't have the same mission. Its mission is broader. That organization is still running and its office is exactly where we set it up there in 1949.

Q: A monument.

Adm. B.: Then someone in Washington thought of a real bright idea. That's what he thought. We had barely gotten started when this directive came in that the four of us were to go over across the Atlantic to Londonderry, North Ireland, to operate with the British anti-submarine forces. Then we were going on reconnaissance mission up in the Greenland Sea, the Barents Sea, up to the north of Norway. This reconnaissance mission was top secret.

So, early in August in 1949 we started across the Atlantic. We did operate with the British forces; the British anti-submarine flotilla. Than we proceeded to go up and do some reconnoitering. I divided the submarines into two parts. The two that did not have the snorkel and high submerged speed I put under Commander Lynch. They were not to get to east of the line up the center of Norway. They were supposed to stay out of, perhaps, the more dangerous areas. The other two, the TUSK and the COCHINO, they wou go into the areas closer to the USSR. I went on board the COCHINO-- no the COCHINO was my flagship but I went on board the TUSK. The reason I did not go on board the COCHINO was the TUSK had not been doing very well paperwork wise. There were certain reports that I required from my people and theirs were always slow. So, I was giving the captain of the TUSK a bad time and he said, "Well, you know we don't have a yeoman on board at all."

I said, "That's no problem."

They had allowed me two enlisted men. I had only one and that was this Chief Yeoman that I got to work for me. I had him along, so I said, "I'll bring my Chief Yeoman over and he can help you out with the paperwork." So, I moved to the TUSK. That's the reason I didn't have to be rescued from the COCHINO.

We split into two parts and started up the coast. We were snooping, taking down the characteristics of the radar up in that region. Why that was so necessary I have no idea.

Q: You mean the installations they had or the actions of radar?

Adm. B.: What came out of the radar. The frequencies. The pulse repetition rate of the radars. The frequencies, the pulse repetition rate and that sort of thing. The strength of them and all that business. I don't know why we had to send submarines over there to find out.

Q: Was it different from what it would be elsewhere in the ocean?

Adm. B.: The idea was not only to determine the characteristics of radars but to tie those to locations ashore.

Q: Was any of the water up there mined?

Adm. B.: Not that I know of. I did find out that there were mines in another place. For example, when we left Londonderry, North Ireland, I got permission to go down to Portsmouth, England, for a few days, that being the home port of British submarines. Then we'd go up to the North Cape. I was planning to go up through the English Channel, but the British said, "No, there are a lot of mines in there. Don't go that way."

So, we went up between Ireland and Scotland. Even then, in 1949, apparently, the English Channel had a lot of mines in it.

We got up there around the North Cape of Norway and, in addition to getting the frequency and the pulse repetition rate etc. on the shore radar, we also practiced with our underwater sound equipment. Practicing to listen, and listen and listen. Or course, we were under strict radio silence. No one was suppose to know where we were. When we left England we disappeared.

This particular morning, the twenty-fifth of August 1949, the COCHINO and the TUSK had both submerged.

Oh, there's one important item that I need to explain before we continue. I was acquainted with a scientist from some scientif organization on the West Coast and he had been visiting the Underwater Sound Laboratory. He told me that they were developing underwater telephones. They were underwater sound equipment, but they were voice modulated. You could talk on the telephone back and forth from one submarine to another through the water.

So, when I got this outfit, the Submarine Development Group Two, I wrote to that gentleman at his scientific organization on the West Coast and told him that I'd appreciate very much if they would send four sets of that equipment. "We'd like to install it right now; help with development. If you work on your end, we'll start work on this end and we'll see what we can do." It didn't take long before they had four pieces of equipment there in New London and installed them in our submarines. Hey; the name of the company, I think, was BENDIX.

Q: Is this the outfit in San Diego?

Adm. B.: I'm not sure, but it was California. We installed them and they worked. So we had them with us. Now we go back to August 25, 1949.

The COCHINO and the TUSK were up to the north of the North Cape of Norway. We both submerged. What were we going to do? One of them is going to try to listen to and detect the noises the other one is making. Type of noise had meaning. Naturally, that other one, the target, is going to stop and they're going to start. They're going to turn around and do all kinds of things which they can and record what they're doing, and times. Suddenly, over the underwater telephone came a message from the COCHINO, "We're having a fire! We've got to surface."

What had happened? Both submarines surfaced. What had happened on the COCHINO was --. Oh! In order for someone to understand the COCHINO's trouble, I need to explain submarine storage batteries as they relate. In our automobiles we have lead acid storage batteries. Most of them are twelve volts. They have six cells. Each one of those cells is not very big; about the size of an old ordinary toaster, not even that big. How big is one of the cells at that time in the submarines? They stood, oh, three and a half to four feet high and they were something like three feet wide and maybe a foot and a half thick. Each one weighed a ton. We had on board the submarine something on the order of two hundred and fifty of these. So we had about two hundred and fifty tons of nothing but lead-acid storage batteries.

Q: How was this compensated for?

Adm. B.: That was simply the way the ship was built.

Q: Yes, but what did they remove in the way of weight to compensate for that?

Adm. B.: Well, you had these great big ballast tanks and when the water was pushed out they held the submarine up, and when you opened the flood valves and the vents they filled up with water, down went the submarine. Of course, they had to take into consideration this two hundred and fifty tons of lead acid storage batteries.

When they converted-- oh, those storage batteries were in two groups. Forward battery and aft battery; batteries below; living spaces about them. When they converted them to the high submerged speed they had installed higher capacity cells and they divided them into two parts. The forward battery was in two parts and the after one was in two parts.

Well, what happened on the COCHINO was that one half of the after battery started charging the other half of the battery. One of them had gotten a little bit low on voltage and the other started charging it. When you charge a lead-acid storage battery you generate hydrogen gas. Hydrogen gas plus a certain amount of air, oxygen really; when you get the proper proportions of the two of them, you don't even have to have anything to set it off. It will turn into steam and fire, explosion. Generating hydrogen gas is very, very dangerous. We had hydrogen detectors on our submarines long before my time. We old-timers all experienced hydrogen flashes.

The first indication they had on board the COCHINO that anything was wrong with the hydrogen detectors in the after battery showed hydrogen going up and then they had an explosion. Then they had fire. The whole compartment, living space above the after battery, bedding, everything was ablaze. So, they shut off that compartment and the people came topside. They couldn't stay down below because the fumes. But, they had isolated that battery compartment. If they had been able to separate the two halves of "after battery" they might have won the battle. (This is going to be a brief account. As an indication of how long it could be, there is a book about it.)* It was cold, of course; it was in August, but at the same time you were up off the North Cape of Norway, north of the Arctic Circle; and even in August it not very warm up there. The ocean was probably a temperature of forty or something like that. They're all up topside on this submarine. Some of them with hardly anything on, well, most of them with hardly anything on. Only the people who were on watch on the bridge at the time of the incident were properly clad. The rest of them were not. There were some people who were slightly burned. The COCHINO skipper sent word over that unfortunately there was no "remote disconnect." In other words, there was no way in which you could flip a switch outside this compartment

―――――――――――
*See William J. Lederer, The Last Voyage (New York: Henry Holt and Co., 1950).

and take those parts of the battery away from one another. So, it would continue to feed on itself. This half was charging that half and this was generating hydrogen. The hydrogen burned because it burns real good, and that caused the voltage on this side to be even less than it was in the first place so it was charging it more and more. It was a continuous operation making it worse all the time.

On the COCHINO they broke out a rubber boat and sent one of the ship's officers over to explain to me exactly what the situation was. Also, unfortunately, the ship's medical equipment was all in that burning compartment. The Pharmacist's mate, an enlisted man, couldn't get to it and they needed to bring over certain of these things from the TUSK to the COCHINO to treat burns.

Q: How far were you offshore?

Adm. B.: Oh, I should say a hundred miles maybe.

The rubber boat arrived and they got the medical equipment and then went back to the COCHINO so they could have some medical supplies. But, about that time a big wave came along, and why there were so many people up on the topside I have no idea at all, but about twelve men were in the water.

Q: From the TUSK?

Adm. B.: Yes. From the TUSK.

Q: The survivability at that temperature is very limited, isn't it

Adm. B.: That's right, and that became quite an emergency. The strange thing was that no--oh, six of them were never recovered. No one, not one of those rescued, came aboard under his own power. The people who came aboard did so because their shipmates either jumped into the water and pulled them over or they were close to the submarine and someone was able to help them.

Q: Where were you at this time?

Adm. B.: I was on the bridge of the TUSK. About that time the executive officer of the COCHINO decided that we've got to stop this fire and so he put on a rescue breathing apparatus that firemen wear. He was down in the forward engine room; he decided to open the engine room door and go in. He knew exactly where the disconnect switch was. It was near that door that he would open. All he would have to do is to open the door and flip the switch, shut the door again and the fire would subside as soon as the hydrogen there would burn up.

When he opened the door, however, of course, he was overwhelmed by the fire and so forth. He was very badly burned on his arms which were not covered appropriately. He was not in very good shape.

One of the engines was running slowly at that time and hydrogen came out of the compartment and into the intake of the engine and the engine burned hydrogen instead of diesel oil and it speeded up and burst all to pieces.

Q: Was the door closed again?

Adm. B.: The door was closed, but he never got to that disconnect switch and so it's still going. When the fire and flames came out of that aft torpedo room into the engine room, there were several other people there who also had burns, but they weren't anywhere near as bad as the executive officer.

Q: That wasn't a very intelligent action, was it?

Adm. B.: Well, if he had succeeded in doing it, it would have been a miracle. Let me return to the TUSK. We actually lost seven people. There were six enlisted men and one officer; no five enlisted men, one officer and one civilian. We had one civilian from the Philco Corporation who had been with us all the time. He was an underwater sound expert. He had been issued to us by the Philco Corporation so he could help us keep our equipment in good shape.

Q: Was he from the COCHINO?

Adm. B.: Yes, from the COCHINO. The one officer and this civilian expert were in the rubber boat that came over to get medical supplies and to inform me of the situation. They tried to get on board the TUSK. The officer got aboard and returned with the medical supplies. The civilian slipped as he came aboard, banged his head, was back in the water. Efforts to rescue him failed.

About that time I got a message from the COCHINO that he has two of his engines running, the after engines are now running. So I said, "Okay, let's go."

Hammerfest is about, maybe a hundred miles away, something like that. You remember we had been on radio silence all the time. We now broke radio silence. I had written up message and it was addressed to the Chief of Naval Operations with information copies to various people. We had it all set and naturally it was enciphered and secret. Anyhow, we opened up on our radio, sent it out and we got a receipt from the Naval Station, Guam. It went over the North Pole, apparently, and landed on Guam and they receipted for it. It was really amazing; it said we were on the way to Hammerfest and we needed medical help. We gave the names of the people who had been lost. We explained very little. By the way, of course, the midnight sun was in vogue so it's a little hard to know whether you're doing something in the day time or the night time. Anyhow, when we were on the way to Hammerfest all at once there was a tremendous explosion on the COCHINO. Now, the COCHINO people are still up top side with hardly anything on and this is very bad, but it's better than succumbing to the fumes down below. Still got a fire going down there. A great big tremendous explosion.

The skipper of the COCHINO sent a message over saying, this by semaphore or flashing light, said that he thinks we'd better start getting some of these people off here. So --

Q: Of her crew, how many did she have?

Adm. B.: Oh, she had about six officers and seventy crew. I told the skipper of the TUSK that I wanted him to prepare-- we had certain number of warhead torpedoes on board. I think we had two fore and two aft. I told him to get them ready because while we were trying to rescue them if anybody would like to interfere, they were going to have a fight on their hands. So we got two fish ready.

Q: Did you actually expect that you might be interfered with?

Adm. B.: No, but I'm going to be ready anyhow. Murmansk was about 300 miles away. I also said to the captain of the TUSK: "Now we are going to go alongside the COCHINO; our bow is going to be by his stern." In other words we're going alongside the wrong way. The reason is we've got one disabled ship. We're not going to have two. You put the two of them right together and maybe---

Q: Another explosion and you'd be damaged, too.

Adm. B.: That's right, and also you might get your propellers damaged. So, we have to make sure. They are only going to be alongside about half of the length.

Someone found a board to use as gangplank. It was about a foot wide. Naturally, no hand-rail or any stuff like that. We got alongside and it was rough. Oh, it was rough. The wind was blowing and it was terrible. We started taking people off. We got everybody off.

Q: Did they have to crawl across on the plank?

Adm. B.: No, they would be ready to go and they sort of ran on this plank and people on the other side would catch them. Then the next guy.

Q: How far was that, how far did they run?

Adm. B.: Here to that wall, maybe.

Q: About six feet or so?

Adm. B.: Something like that. Just start going and the other people sort of catch them on the other side. Next one, next one and finally the captain, Benitez, he came across.

Q: Were they abandoning ship?

Adm. B.: They were abandoning ship because she was sinking. You could see that she was sinking all the time. She sank only about two or three minutes after the skipper came on board. By the time the captain left the submarine the waterline was on the deck up to the conning tower. In other words, approximately two-thirds of the length of the submarine was underwater.

Q: Did that increase the danger of another explosion? The fact that she was sinking?

Adm. B.: I don't know. I don't recall any other explosion. Anyhow, we got the skipper off; we got everybody off. We had lost seven people, which was too bad. But, we had rescued the others. Then we put on full speed ahead.

Q: Headed for Hammerfest?

Adm. B.: Yes.

Q: Were you able to notify the authorities at Hammerfest that you were coming?

Adm. B.: No. In our message that was picked up in Guam, we asked for that to happen.

Q: Did they do that?

Adm. B.: Yes, indeed. Guam, of course, would have sent this message to Washington and they would get going.

Q: Was Hammerfest a Norwegian naval base?

Adm. B.: No, no. It was just a fishing village. I believe when we were there, it had inhabitants of about four thousand people. The Germans during World War II flattened it completely. Most Northern permanent abode in the world, I believe.

Q: It's near Abo isn't it?

Adm. B.: I don't recall. It's near Tromso.

    The executive officer, you recall, had been badly burned getting from the engine room into the battery compartment to flip the disconnect which would have saved the submarine. How in the world he got up the ladder? But he did. He was in terrible shape. He got down the ladder on the TUSK. You know the ladders on submarines are vertical. Up the ladder he came and he came across the gangplank and then down the ladder on the TUSK.

Q: He came up the ladder from the COCHINO and down the ladder into the TUSK? Isn't is almost impossible to help someone up or down a ladder?

Adm. B.: Yes. He actually--it was amazing that he could actually get across that gangplank, up one ladder and down the other. He was very, very badly burned.

Q: The opportunity for salvation is a potent force.

Adm. B.: I should say so. So, there he had at least some medical help. We headed for Hammerfest and we arrived, came up the entrance to the harbor and here's the harbor master in a boat. He came aboard; the city was all lighted up. A little town. When we arrived there the doctor, only one doctor in the village, he came aboard and was able to do some things to deaden the pain of the burns.

Then a very interesting thing happened. I had asked the harbor master, "Who should I call on?"

We didn't have any idea how long we'd stay in Hammerfest. I don't know now how long we did stay in Hammerfest because it was daylight twenty-four hours a day.

I asked the harbor master, "Who should I call on? Should I call on the mayor or somebody?"

"No, no", he says, "don't bother with that."

Oh, the Norwegians sent up a small escort ship which was waiting for us.

Q: From Tromso?

Adm. B.: From Tromso and had brought an additional doctor. A little bit later in the afternoon I overheard, I can understand their language, I overheard a discussion between the harbor master and the Chief of police. I think the harbor master was making sure that I heard it. They were talking loudly.

Q: Did he know that you understood Norwegian?

Adm. B.: The harbor master knew. The harbor master said to him, "Please don't feel excited or insulted because the American Commodore hasn't been to call on you. You know he's been very busy."

The chief of police was really upset. So, I waited a little while until the chief of police had gone away and said to the harbor master, "You know, why don't you and I go up and call on the chief of police?"

"Oh well, if you'd like to, sure."

So we went up to his office. We came in and the secretary let us into his office. As soon as we opened the door this chief of police was really eating the harbor master out. "It's about time you got up here!" Stuff like that in Norwegian. The harbor master was trying to shut him up. He finally stopped saying anything and the harbor master said in Norwegian: "I just want to inform you that the American Commodore understands everything you said." The poor guy was crestfallen. When we left we parted good friends, but he was a crestfallen-looking individual. He had been caught.

Q: That was rather ridiculous that he should expect amenities to be observed in the face of a disaster wasn't it?

Adm. B.: Of course it was. We parted friends. A couple hours later I was over in the harbor master's office and the telephone rang and--oh, by the way, by this time it had been decided that we would leave at such-and-such time and go down to Tromso because we really needed more medical help than we could get there. We needed a hospital. A proper hospital and so forth. But, I was over in the harbor master's office a couple hours later and the telephone rang. The harbor master had turned his back to me and said in Norwegian, "What are you saying? You're saying that an American submarine sunk. Sunk out here? And all the people have been transferred to the submarine that just came in? You've heard all of this?" He said, "The American commodore is right here and I will ask him if there is anything to this story."

So, he turned to me and he said, "This is a newspaperman from down in Oslo who is inquiring about this story."

I hadn't heard anything at all from our naval authorities and never did. Normally, if they put out a press release they would inform the person in charge at the scene. But the story was so complete that obviously they couldn't have gotten it any other way. So I said, "You may tell him that that's correct."

Now this harbor master was quite a guy, wasn't he?

Q: Protecting you.

Adm. B.: And he said -- he told me later on--"I knew that there was something going on, but it was up to you to tell me when you could. You had twice as many people on board the submarine as you'd ever have." He also said, "You hadn't gotten those burns on board the TUSK submarine. There was nothing wrong with that submarine at all. If they had had a fire on board bad enough for all these people to get burned, you would smell it in the submarine. But, we didn't smell it in the submarine."

Of course, in addition to burned people, we had a lot of people who had been exposed in the water.

Q: Well then, looking back on the chief of police, he didn't understand why the submarine was there and that was his reason for insisting on the amenities.

Adm. B.: Apparently he didn't understand anything that was going on. But, we parted good friends.

Away we went. We and the Norwegian ship headed out for Tromso. When we got there we proceeded to the Grand Hotel. I had my two skippers with me. We went to a press conference. They asked me if that would be all right. I said, "Sure."

By that time in Tromso was the U. S. naval attaché. We went to the press conference and that was an interesting one. The person who introduced me and asked for questions didn't mention to them that I understood their language. There were people from Oslo, London, etc. I don't know what other countries, if any. I think there were some other foreign people. It was quite a story.

Q: Russians?

Adm. B.: I don't know. It was just after NATO had been set up. I don't recall that exact date. NATO just barely had been set up or was just about to. Suddenly in the middle of the press conference I heard this one Norwegian say in Norwegian to the other guy, "Ask him such-and-such."

Before he had a chance to ask it I answered it in Swedish. Greatest thing they had ever heard. They were delighted. Then one of the things I explained to them was that--oh, we had a couple of Philippine stewards on board and the newspaper guys were very interested in the nationality. Were they Chinese or something? They didn't know what they were. We told them. Then I told them the names of my four skippers. I said my chief of staff is Lynch, that's Irish. Then we had Schwab and we had Worthington, and we had Marcy, and we had Benitez. There was a German name, a British name, a French name, and a Spanish name in addition to the Irish chief of staff, and I was 100% Swedish.

They were very much interested in how the families of the deceased would fare. They were very interested in that. One of the newspaper guys explained to me that, "We Norwegians live close to the sea. We're always thinking of those things."

Well, we had barely gotten to Tromso -- oh, the Norwegians put us up. I believe it was at a Norwegian Air Force barracks that extra members of our crew stayed in. I believe the officers were put up, I think, at the Grand Hotel there in Tromso.

An American destroyer came up from Plymouth, England with another doctor. The offer was, if we wanted to, this destroyer would take the extra members of the crew.

I had sent a message to Admiral R. L. Conolly in London. He had been an old shipmate of mine when I was teaching school here at the Naval Academy. So, I sent him a personal message in which I said, "When we are finished with Norway we want to go directly to New London." I had also given this desire to Admiral Fife.

In other words, I didn't want us to go to, for example, England and have some bright character decide this is the time to have a board of investigation here. In other words, let's go home first.

It's also nice to have that destroyer with the doctor on board the destroyer. But, no, thank you, if they want us to go to Plymouth, England, or anywhere else. We'll head for New London, Connecticut. Besides, going by air or destroyer is dangerous. I don't think there is anything else to say about the Tromso business. There was--

Q: Did you need to refuel before you could go back?

Adm. B.: Oh, yes. We took on diesel fuel there in Tromso. We were assured that it was fine. That Norwegian ship that had come up to Hammerfest and had come to Tromso with us, the engines were built in the United States. They used the same fuel as we did. This was one of the things we were supposed to check on anywhere we went; was diesel fuel appropriate for use in our engines? There was no strain at all so we were all filled up. We headed across the North Atlantic and--

Q: How did you accommodate all these extra men?

Adm. B.: Well, someone said, "Isn't it too crowded?"

I said, "Well, you know a submarine is crowded anyhow, so we'll just be a little more crowded."

What we did was every person in the TUSK crew when he went on watch took a COCHINO guy with him. Of course, we had hot bunk system going on great.

Q: You had enough food?

Adm. B.: Oh, yes.

Q: Did you travel on the surface?

Adm. B.: Sure. Straight---and all of these people, you've never seen so many people in all your life. Naturally, they didn't have clothing, but the TUSK people would lend clothing. We were all set once we were on board. Everything is fine.

We arrived at New London---

Q: How long a journey was this?

Adm. B.: Oh, gee, I wonder how far? It must have been about 4000 miles. Well, let's see, say we traveled about at fifteen knots. That's about three hundred and sixty nautical miles per day. I would imagine it took about ten days. We probably went a little faster than that, I'm not sure. But something on the order of ten days. I don't think it would be sooner than that. Naturally, before we got there we sent a message to Admiral Fife as to exactly when we would come alongside. We were outside the harbor for several hours because we were going to arrive at the time we're supposed to arrive. People will be there to meet us.

There was quite a welcome. That evening, Vida and I went down to the Lighthouse Inn in New London to have dinner, In one of the dining rooms of that hotel was a group of scientists having a meeting with the underwater sound people and I found myself making my first speech. Captain Bill Pryor, head of the Underwater Sound Lab, saw us and said, "I would like to introduce you. Come to our meeting."

It wasn't long before someone said, "Would you tell us something about it?" Pretty good, so I had a rehearsal before the sun had set.

Q: And you could do that prior to the inquiry?

Adm. B.: Sure. I was careful as to what I said. The investigation was, of course, conducted. There were several lessons learned which caused changes in our submarines. You go on board a submarine today, or even surface ships, you will find that on deck is a sort of an indentation, a track. People who are out on deck in bad weather have a life belt around them with some chain on it. They can plug into this track. That came out of this COCHINO incident.

Q: So you can't be washed overboard?

Adm. B.: Yes. So you can't be washed overboard. That was one of the several changes made. Of course, it didn't take long for the submarine to get a remote disconnect to the storage batteries. There were quite a few other things.

One of the things we learned was that everyone who operates in cold waters must remember that no one is going to be rescued out of that water by his own efforts. He is going to have to be manhandled. You have got to get a raft, or a boat, or a person to him as soon as possible; grab on to him. He can't do it himself.

Q: He's virtually paralyzed the moment he hits the water?

Adm. B.: That's right. Therefore, on board ships, if you're operating in any kind of cold water you really ought to have some underwater demolition team suits, the wet suits. People can put them on immediately to jump in the water to help people on board, because they're not going to get on board on their own power.

Q: Well, we should have known that from World War II.

Adm. B.: Of course, but you've got to make sure that it gets down far enough. Make it such that it is routine. Don't trust memories.

Q: But the underwater telephone helped a great deal, didn't it?

Adm. B.: Yes, it certainly did. Had we not had the underwater telephone, the COCHINO would have been on the surface and the TUSK would have been submerged. The people on the TUSK, including me, wouldn't have known that anything was wrong. I think maybe for three or four hours we wouldn't have known anything about it. As it was we knew about it right now. We might have lost the submarine and the whole works. Might have lost all hands.

Q: Well, that certainly was a dramatic story. A dramatic incident.

Adm. B.: It was a dramatic incident, all right. Of course, then it was time for us to get back to work and in the place of the COCHINO we got the submarine USS HALFBEAK.

Q: HALFBEAK?

Adm. B.: HALFBEAK. We used to call her the "Semi-Snoot".

Interview No. 7 with Rear Admiral Roy S. Benson, U.S. Navy (Retired)

Place: Arnold, Maryland

Date: April 16, 1980

Subject: Biography

By: John T. Mason, Jr.

Q: This chapter is a continuation of the story of Submarine Development Group Two. You had just returned to New London in the TUSK after having lost the other submarine, the COCHINO, in northern waters. That was in 1949.

Adm. B.: Before we leave that incident I'd like to, sort of, tie it up in a bow. Naturally there was a board of investigation on the subject. This disaster wasn't a total loss. We did learn some things from it. But, also, I would like to mention that it was a saga of heroism and capability on the part of the people on board the submarines.

Q: A fitting place for a saga?

Adm. B.: Yes, yes, indeed. Also, I would like to mention some of the people who helped us a great deal in this whole matter. There is the company, the company on the West Coast that produced the underwater telephone. You recall that it wasn't in production yet. My knowing a scientist who was working on this underwater telephone was why we had them in our four submarines. Had the COCHINO not been able to tell us by underwater telephone immediately that they had a fire and explosion, it might have been hours before we knew that there was anything amiss.

Q: It must have put the underwater telephone in production immediately.

Adm. B.: It did indeed. Also, helping us a great deal was the radio operator in Guam who got the message and then did what he was supposed to do with it. That is, send it on and get it to the proper people in that entire communication chain. It was encoded; addressed to the Chief of Naval Operations, Washington, D.C. The information on our plight got various places including a village in northern Norway. Hammerfest knew about it in a very few hours and the inhabitants were there to help us. Our first helper was Hammerfest's harbor master.

The Norwegian government sent a destroyer escort up to Hammerfest from Tromso. The U.S. Navy Headquarters in London sent a destroyer from Plymouth, England, with a doctor on board. The Norwegian ship also had a doctor on board. Many others helped us with this whole situation. There was great interest in the world press; newspaper reporters from outside of Norway came to Tromso, Norway.

We had not been happy with being assigned to this cruise because it interfered with the work we were trying to do.

We were trying to find out how we can best use submarines in antisubmarine warfare. We thought that this trip was a waste of time. But, as it turned out, it wasn't really a waste of time. It gave us an opportunity to really think, argue, and so forth about what we were trying to do and how to do it.

We had given the underwater sound equipment on our ships tender loving care. If you want to accomplish something, whether it's long-range, high-caliber naval gunnery, naval aviation, ballet dancing or whatever it is, if you really want to get somewhere you must give the subject tender loving care and lots of priority. This is what we did with the underwater sound equipment. The reason we had the civilian from Philco Corporation on board was because our underwater sound equipment had been produced by Philco Corporation. He was on board to help us give this equipment tender loving care.

We also had a chance to scoop out of "the bottom of the barrel" our friend from World War II PCO School: the bearings-only approach and attack. Perhaps you recall that when they started that PCO school (prospective commanding officer school) in 1942, they tried to develop a system of solving the fire control when limited to the direction of the target. With listening sonar we did not have the distance to the target. You recall that it was ahead of its time. The equipment in 1942 wasn't adequate to do that job. Now, in 1949 our equipment was getting better. We were moving in the direction of having adequate equipment. We did it! And we demonstrated a little bit of the progress even before we went on the trip to Norway. We had also a period of a couple of months when we were on the Norway cruise in which all of our people discussed, argued, drew pictures; they did all kinds of things as to "How can we better use this equipment?" Obviously we wanted to limit ourselves to listening because if we made sounds the target would be alerted. We had direction of the target and a little bit of the nature of the sound, but no distance. We, indeed, developed a way to take care of that.

Soon after we'd gotten back to New London we went out and demonstrated it again. People were amazed. We were amazed, too.

From the very beginning when we set up this Submarine Development Group we got a tremendous amount of help. Lots of people were interested. Scientists particularly. The Underwater Sound Laboratory in New London, I understand was set up during World War II, but not as a naval activity. It was set up by scientists who were working on underwater acoustics. A doctor by the name of Frederick Hunt, who we will hear of a little later, was the director of it during World War II. Also there was a Naval Academy classmate of mine, John Knight.

After World War II was over it was turned into a naval establishment. The commanding officer at the time we are now in was Captain William Pryor. He was the boss man of what we called the USNUSL, the Underwater Sound Laboratory of New London, Connecticut.

Q: How does it happen that it was not related to the Navy in 1942 and that period when the subject was being investigated was Navy almost exclusively, wasn't it?

Adm. B.: Yes, but the U.S. Government had established a committee--I think it was called the NDRC, National Defense Research Committee, and there was an underwater sound section of it. They were working very closely in connection with the Navy, but I understand it was not really Navy property after the U.S. Government had taken it over, but it was in underwater sound totally.

We had help from many other organizations. Captain L. R. Daspit in the Navy Department was essential. He was of tremendous help. He happened to have electronics as a hobby; our electronics and underwater sound particularly appealed to him.

There was also a gentleman by the name of John Coleman. He was attached to the National Academy of Science on Constitution Avenue opposite the Main Navy Building in Washington. John Coleman was the executive director or secretary of the Undersea Warfare Committee of the National Academy of Science. For many of the top scientific physicists and others who had an interest in undersea warfare, this was sort of their home base. This is where they, from their various colleges and universities, sort of focused in on the U.S. Government. The U.S. Government got so much out of them. They were probably on some sort of ad hoc contract. Whatever the arrangement, it was magnificent.

Q: They certainly had chosen a very handsome headquarters, the white marble building.

Adm. B.: Oh, yes, a very nice building. I got acquainted with quite a few of them when in 1947 I had that first job up in New London, the new developments job on the staff of the submarine Admiral, James Fife.

Also Woods Hole Oceanographic Institution. Their mission was "study the ocean and not make any money." Scientists from Woods Hole were essential to our progress.

Q: Are they tax exempt? Is that why they can't make any money?

Adm. B.: Oh, yes. They are a "not-for-profit" organization.

A fellow by the name of Allyn Vine and a fellow by the name of Bill Shevill were among my most valuable contacts.

Q: At Woods Hole?

Adm. B.: Yes. They spent more time, I'm sure, at New London with us than they ever spent anywhere else--Woods Hole or anywhere else.

Here is a change of tempo but a part of the picture. Soon after we got back from Norway Admiral Fife, who was my boss there at New London, got hold of me on the squawk box and said, "Say, I'd like to have you come with me. I've got an invitation to give a speech at the Rotary Club here in New London."

I said, "Yes, Sir, I'll be right there."

So I went with him and when they called on him he said, "Well, I'm not going to make a speech, but I know who is." And he introduced me and had me tell them about our adventures up on the north coast of Norway.

Q: Bosses have that kind of authority, don't they?

Adm. B.: Yes, but it had a preface. Earlier I got a request to make a speech on this matter and some of the members of the staff said, "Well, we don't think this is a very good idea because it was a disaster. People were lost and so forth." But, Admiral Fife said, "Let's find out. After lunch tomorrow, Roy, I want you to make a speech and tell us what happened up there and you make believe you're talking to the Rotary Club. Let's hear what you've got to say so we can judge whether this is a good thing to do or not."

It was a good thing to do and, of course, very soon thereafter he gave me a chance to do it to the Rotary Club.

The strength of our setup, our organizational setup, was the tremendous flexibility. Generally if a scientist wanted to try out some new idea, there really wasn't anywhere where he could go, present it and test it immediately. Large organizations are ponderous. Someone comes in with a proposal and it gets kicked around and it goes up the channel and down and all that sort of thing. Sometimes you forget what the subject was before you get to try it. Here was a case where various scientists and organizations and technical people could come and say, "Hey, I have an idea. Let's try this and see if it will work." We tried it at once.

One item was called the "dunking sonar." Normally a sonar hydrophone would be attached to the ship somewhere. The trouble with having it attached to the ship is that it is interfered with by the ship's own noise and the noise the ship is making running through water. So, you put it on a long line and put it down a hundred or two hundred feet and you are now away from the surface noise, which is considerable, the noise of the ship itself going through the water, and its own self noise. You tether this sound head and you can listen with it. We experimented with that. We experimented also with one sonar antenna up on the bow of the ship and another one on the stern of the ship. We then have a baseline and we can try triangulation to obtain distance. Another one: we have two submarines and we know the distance between them; we use that as a base line for triangulation. We tried all of these things to see what we could get out of them. Sometimes we got something, sometimes we didn't. But, we really got to be awfully good at being able to detect and not only detect something, but we could have a nice narrow beam. We became very proficient.

Now then, here is our star example of this flexibility. One morning, I'll never forget it. Allyn Vine and Bill Shevill were there. They were there all the time, it seemed like. Allyn Vine would say sometimes to Bill, "Now, Bill, when you're going to explain something, would you please differentiate between the things that you know and the things you're only thinking about."

That morning they said to me:

"We want to take your four submarines off to Bermuda for at least a week. We'll probably be gone from here for two weeks."

I said, "What in the world do you want to do, it's a nice place, but what will we accomplish?"

They said:

"Well, at the northeast corner of Bermuda, St. George's, we have an instrument called geophone that is sitting on the bottom. That geophone will detect underwater sound and it will detect it across the entire spectrum. In other words, it will detect what we call white noise."

Across the whole spectrum? Refer this to the rainbow. The rainbow is made up of all kinds of colors. You put them all together and you have white light.

This geophone listens real good to all frequencies of sound and at long distances.

Q: It gets fish sounds and everything?

Adm. B.: It will pick up any kind of sound that is out there. I'm glad you mentioned fish because the sound of the fish are a part of the ambient noise.

They also told me: "With this geophone there at Bermuda we can hear grenade explosions off the Azores.

Q: That's quite a distance.

Adm. B.: Yes. They added: "We want to take your four submarines over there and find out how far the geophone can hear the noise of the screws or any other noises that your submarines are putting out. When you're on the surface, when you're at snorkel depth, when you're at periscope depth, at deep depth. Also when the propellers' noises are heard directly and when the submarine is shielding some of the noise. All of these things we want to find out. Find out how far we can detect these various noises and tell the nature of the sounds. In order to design underwater sound equipment to listen, we need first to know what kind of sound do we want to listen for. We hope to find out off Bermuda."

Q: Did you at anytime see this geophone? How big was it?

Adm. B.: It was a great big thing. I never saw one, but they described it.

Strangely enough, if you've ever seen a piece of sound equipment on board a more modern ship you find that it takes up the whole bow. Tremendous great big thing.

One of these strange phenomena that they explained to me at that time was that this sound coming from the Azores to Bermuda went in something called a deep channel. It seems that if the sound is going through the water the consistency of the water changes. It changes in temperature. It changes in viscosity, another name for salinity. I guess depth also. But, it somehow finds the best path to go. So, when getting a little deep, it will curve itself up and vice versa. There is a deep channel down there, maybe a couple thousand feet--

Q: You mean off Bermuda?

Adm. B.: Anywhere in the seas where the water is deep enough this sound will move itself up and down, sort of undulating, so that it has the most favorable path to follow.

When we got out to Bermuda they had their confederates in the Azores set off an explosion. We could listen to it coming in and some of the parts came in a little bit sooner than the others. It sounded, really, sort of like a person playing the kettle drums. It sort of rumbled-rumbled-rumbled-bang!

Q: It travels underwater faster than sound above water?

Adm. B.: Yes; the speed of the sound in water is something on the order of five or six times as fast as it does through air. But, it also varies. The temperature of the water, the salinity of the water affect the speed.

Q: Now, does it follow that a detonation off the Azores sending sound to Bermuda would also send the same sound to the coast of Spain?

Adm. B.: Yes, yes. They would be able to pick it up anywhere around. This probably was going in all directions. Omni-directional I believe they would call it.

I hope no acoustics and underwater physicist is going to read this because he will probably be in hysterics after listening to my non-professional explanation of this thing. But, I'm doing the best I can.

I had heard from Allyn Vine, Bill Shevill and the other people that it isn't only a question of finding what the sound is, but we also want to measure the ambient noises. Now, maybe ambient noise means only the noise the ocean is making of itself and maybe it includes also the noises made by fish and dolphins and all that sort of thing. Vine and Shevill explained that generally in the acoustics society it is believed that the noise of the ambient in the ocean is concentrated in the same levels of frequency which are projected by ships and submarines. If true we will not be able to detect at long distances.

But, Allyn Vine and Bill Shevill, I say them together because they were inseparable. They said, "Well, you take a thousand full grown pigs and get them stuck in a fence. The pigs make a lot of racket. Not being a farm boy I'm not aware of that. But, take a thousand of them and in some way get them to make as much noise as they can. Maybe tweak their tails. They're making all the noise they can. We believe if we remove one of them or bring another one in there the noise will change and if you've got sensitive enough instruments you will detect that the noise has changed because one has been pulled out.

Q: It has reduced in volume?

Adm. B.: That's right. It has reduced not only the volume but the tenor of the sound.

Q: Why don't you use the Biblical example rather than the manufactured one, the Gadarene swine?

Adm. B.: I don't think I know that one, what is it? The Gadarene swine?

They also said, "So, we're listening to all of these thousand pigs and all this racket and you take a small pig and let him get caught in the fence and he will turn out some noise also. We believe that you would be able, with the proper instruments, you'd be able to detect this little pig through the noise of the 1,000 grown pigs because he's different.

Q: His volume would be almost as large as the group actually.

Adm. B.: Might be. Then some suggested that if you walked into a room where there were a lot of people, say a cocktail party, and your wife or some close friend is over at the other side of the room, if your ears are good enough you can probably detect that particular specific noise coming through the multitude. If you concentrate and try to listen, you can probably do that.

Q: Well, that's something that we do from experience.

Adm. B.: They wanted us to find out. So, we went out there and we found out. We found out a lot of stuff. We had a great time. We found out that the noise of submarines generally were concentrated around a hundred cycles. The submarines were quiet. The ambient also was concentrated in the one hundred cycle, but we would listen to the ambient and then have the submarine out in the distance there turn on its engines and propeller starting: we could detect even though their spectrum looked almost the same. We could detect that different sound coming through the ambient. So, what they believed was true. I think they knew, but they wanted to demonstrate. It really stood out in the ambient.

Q: Wasn't that demonstrated in effect in the Pacific War in the breaking of codes? They could begin to identify the Japanese sender of messages by his particular emphasis which was different from the next guy?

Adm. B.: Yes. Back in the dark ages when as a junior officer I was in the communication business aboard ship, the radio operators could identify one another. They would call it "by his fist." That's what they called the particular spectrum analysis of what he did. His dashes and dots would be a little different.

Q: Isn't that related to what you've been telling me about?

Adm. B.: I wouldn't be surprised. It's the same idea.

Well, what we'd found out was we could detect at much greater distances. What if we had some equipment that was specifically made to listen at those particular frequencies? Just what could we do, and of course, we've done it.

You know, out of this came the fixed installations that we have. The fixed installations with receivers.

You recall Dr. Hunt, whom I referred to as the first boss of the Underwater Sound Lab when it wasn't a naval organization during World War II. He was a physicist and acoustical expert from Harvard. When he heard of what we had been doing he said, "We've hit upon a way to have a search rate of one ocean per hour."

A search rate in the underwater sound business is the rate at which you can search all around three hundred and sixty degrees and pick up anything. This is particularly talking about sending out a supersonic ping and having the echo come back. The rate at which you can go through three hundred and sixty degrees and get any targets that are within the receiving distance is called the search rate. They'll put the sonar on a certain direction, send out a ping, get an answer, turn it a little bit and do it again.

Now if we can work on this one, why, we could get a search rate of an ocean an hour because all we do is we send out this great big noise in all directions and it goes out and comes back with all of these echoes and all we have to do is have the equipment to sort it out.

Q: You mean the entire ocean?

Adm. B.: Well, that's what he said. I think he was exaggerating a slight bit. But, certainly he meant we now can really get some distance. We can really track people down. Of course, submarines would not want to put out sound, but listening would also benefit.

Soon after return to New London I had an invitation to come down to Washington. They wanted me to get up on the stage of the auditorium and cover two subjects. They wanted me to talk about what we'd learned out in Bermuda and they also wanted me to talk about the disaster off the North Cape.

I took my chief of staff with me, that being Commander R. B. Lynch (Ozzie Lynch). I had him get up and explain what we'd learned in Bermuda and then I explained what we'd been doing up off the North Cape of Norway. That auditorium was really full of people. We had two tremendous subjects that a lot of people were interested in. That, of course, spread this information out pretty well in the Navy Department.

Sometime after that a group of scientists came to New London. Our speeches in Washington may have been why they came there. This group had been put together by the Secretary of the Navy, and were sent out to various naval activities that had anything to do with antisubmarine warfare. They would find out what people were doing, thinking, etc., in antisubmarine matters.

When they came to New London they first had a session in the forenoon at the Underwater Sound Laboratory. After lunch they came up to the submarine base. Admiral Fife had then been relieved and he had gone on to Washington. He had been relieved by Rear Admiral S. S. Murray.

Q: Sunshine Murray?

Adm. B.: Sunshine Murray. Well named.

So, we all gathered in the conference room and we had an agenda of various people. I was the last one--no, not the last one, I was about the middle.

We had barely started the briefing--Admiral Sunshine Murray was not presiding. Someone on his staff was presiding. We had barely started when one of the scientists said, "Say, I'd like to ask you a question."

The presiding officer said, "May I suggest that we hold the question until after each presentation? The matter you want to ask about might be covered in the presentation."

This scientist said, "Well, I'll tell you, when I want to ask a question I want to ask a question and all I need is the answer."

So Sunshine Murray then laughed as he would and said, Please, doctor, would you please ask your question?"

Of course, he did get an answer.

I said to myself, "Well, these are some tough cookies and they might be just the people I need."

It came time for me to get up there and I had barely started when this scientist said, "Now, we've been to a lot of places and we haven't found very much enthusiasm for this idea you're coming up with. What do you suggest? Why are you so optimistic?"

I said, "Well, the people you've been talking to were not with us in Bermuda. I can only suggest there are three options; one of these options is that you believe everything I tell you and start from there, the second option is, don't believe anything I tell you, and the third one is let me prove it."

This physicist said, "Of course, we'll choose the third one."

I said, "Well, it might take a little time, but we're ready."

Q: This had to do with the sound identification?

Adm. B.: Yes. This new thought. So, I said, "I would suggest that I stop what I'm doing here now and we proceed with the rest of the agenda. When the rest of the agenda is over, put me back on the stage and then my time is your time."

So, we did that and we did take out about thirty minutes or so to have a little supper. We adjourned, I believe it was was ten p.m. But, we adjourned and they had been convinced.

Q: Was this all classified?

Adm. B.: Oh, yes. Yes.

The results have been fixed installations, better sound equipment, better everything.

Q: The results were accomplished then over a period of time?

Adm. B.: Oh, it took quite a few years. I would say that certainly some items came up in a year or so, but let's say five years before most of it had been done.

Now we have in a movie something called a flashback where a middle aged man goes back to his grammar school. This time I'd like to have a flash-ahead if there is such a thing.

Q: Well, that's being clairvoyant, isn't it?

Adm. B.: I'd like to jump from 1950 to 1953. In 1953 I was a student at the National War College. We had a great succession of speakers from cabinet members, members of the Joint Chiefs of Staff, physicists, everybody. One of the speakers was a Doctor Vannevar Bush. You recall that I said there was a government organization of scientists just before World War II and then they changed the title. Well, he was the chairman of the National Defense Research Committee of 1940 to 1941. Then, as I understand it, they changed the name and he became the director of the Office of Scientific Research and Development of the U.S. Government.

In his speech to us at the National War College, among many other statements, he said, "If you have read a book of mine by the name of Modern Arms and Free Men, you'll find that I predicted that we, in antisubmarine warfare, are going to make slow progress but it's going to be in the directions we have already investigated. All we have to do is be better." "I am very optimistic about it." "I said, also, we do not envision any breakthrough."

Then he said, "There has been one." He then explained what we did in New London. It was amazing.

Q: With that experimental group?

Adm. B.: Yes. He explained all about this sonar business that we found out. So, the people from Woods Hole had done quite a job.

In the spring of 1950 I got orders to the Industrial War College of the Armed Forces. That's in Washington, D.C.; to be a student for ten months.

The Army had had that Industrial College for many years in order that Colonel level of the Army through the years would learn something of industrial processes and how the industrial part of the United States is put together.

After World War II was over they made it into an all-service Industrial College of the Armed Forces.

Q: This was intended to enhance your knowledge?

Adm. B.: Yes, so that you'd understand the industrial world.

Q: So they did tie in with your experience in the experimental field, didn't it?

Adm. B.: It sure did. I thought this was really going to be great.

Q: Well, that must have been a very logical assignment for you from BUPERS.

Adm. B.: You recall, that I had been ordered to the Naval War College for the three previous years, but I'd never gotten there. But, I got to this one. I was going to be a student for ten months and went down to Washington in June of 1950, house-hunting and finally bought a house being built in Arlington, Virginia.

On June the twenty-fifth, about the same time we were house-hunting (1950) the Korean War started. Early in August I was relieved by a Captain W. B. Sieglaff as Commander of Submarine Development Group 2. And, sometime in August on a Friday I reported to what was called ICAF (Industrial College of the Armed Forces). We spent that Friday getting our committee assignments. What room we'd be in. Who would have what desk. Draw all the books; you've never seen so many books before. How in the world are we ever going to read all those?

We started school on Monday. On Monday morning we all trooped into the auditorium, all one hundred and twenty-five students from all services. Colonels and Navy and Coast Guard Captains. I believe there was one Coast Guard Captain. The Commandant of the College made his welcoming speech.

Q: Who was he at that time?

Adm. B.: He was a Lieutenant General in the Air Force. I went to the welcoming speech and, when I was leaving the lecture hall, here stood a Navy Petty Officer and he said, "Captain Benson, here are your orders."

I thought that was the reporting endorsement. But it wasn't. It was my orders to the Pentagon.

What had happened was about like this. On Friday I had gone to ICAF; drew my books and so forth. About that same time the Chief of Naval Operations, Admiral Forrest P. Sherman, met our old friend Rear Admiral Jimmy Fife. He said, "Jimmy," we need one of your submarine Captains in the public information business."

Jimmy Fife said, "Well, I'll tell you, Roy Benson is right now reporting in to the Industrial College and certainly he is the guy you need for this PIO job."

Forrest Sherman said, "Thank you, Jimmy." He went back to his office and told his aide, "Roy Benson is over at ICAF. I want him transferred to the Pentagon. I want him to come over here immediately."

So I followed the Lieutenant General right down to his office and congratulated him on a magnificent welcoming speech and bid him goodbye. I went to my committee room and bid my classmates goodbye.

I arrived in the Pentagon that Monday afternoon and became the relief for Captain Harry E. Sears. His title was Director of Public Information.

He had a very small staff. I think two officers and one civil service stenographer. I was rather amazed at that and shaken. I had lost a year of study of industrial America --for what?

What had happened was the Secretary of Defense, Louie Johnson, when he became Secretary of Defense, decided that for the services to have public information offices was nonsense and therefore he set up the Public Information Organization of the Armed Forces and put it up in the office of the Secretary of Defense. That was where the public information office for all the services were. Then he did permit each of the services, Army, Air Force, Navy and Marine Corps, each one to have a small outfit headed by the Colonel, Navy Captain rank with a very small staff. Their function would be when members of the press asked questions down in the office of the Secretary of Defense these people in the individual services would help chase down the answers. That was the purpose of the organization.

Q: This was in keeping with the idea of the unification of the services?

Adm. B.: That's right. When the Korean War started they started having daily briefings by the public information officers; daily briefings of the press. Regular members of the press who actually had desks in the Pentagon. That was their job. That was their beat.

The Captain or Colonel of the individual service always went to those sessions and explained what his particular service had done during the last twenty-four hours; also answered questions. Occasionally they would have some celebrity at a press conference.

Q: Let me ask, why did Forrest Sherman want a submariner in this job at that point when submarines were not very prominent in the Korean War?

Adm. B.: I don't know the reason. The Korean War was new. Harry Sears was an aviator and maybe that was the reason. We've had an aviator, now let's have some other kind of a person. Spread it around. Certainly in the Korean War the submarines didn't do much. The enemy did not depend on the oceans.

When the Korean War started they started augmenting the service PIO organizations. They started ordering people in to build up the organization. I found that Rear Admiral Robert F. Hickey had already reported to the Navy Department, but had not taken over anything. There were people coming in almost every day. They were setting up a different organization. I received additional people gradually. Rear Admiral Hickey's title became the Chief of Information. That was the title of the corresponding general which was being set up in the Army headquarters. In addition to serving the public media this office would also service the people in the service and also the public itself.

Q: Now this was the nullification of Louie Johnson's scheme, was it not, but he had left the scene by this time?

Adm. B.: I'm not sure. This, you see, is only August and the war has been going on for only two months. Maybe he'd already gone; General Marshall relieved him.

One of the first helpers that I became acquainted with, some kind of special assistant to the Secretary of the Navy, was a historian by the name of Walter Karig. A very, very knowledgeable individual. He was of tremendous help to me. Apparently he'd been around the Navy off and on for years. I don't know what his history was at all. With this new organization being set up under Admiral Hickey I still kept my old title, Director of Public Information. I continued to have what Harry Sears had turned over to me in his relations to the public media. Suddenly, I had in my employ four reserve officers who had come to active duty. The senior one was a commander by the name of J. Burke Wilkinson. He was an author and magazine article writer. He became in charge of the magazine and book branch. Then a Lieutenant Commander by the name of Alan Brown came from Hollywood. He's still in the motion picture business, in the production side. This was in the days when newsreels were important. Television, of course, had not gotten to be anywhere near the importance it is today. Alan Brown had "still and motion pictures."

Then there was Dusty Rhodes; Lieutenant Commander Dusty Rhodes came in from being in charge of a small radio and (beginning) television station. He got "radio and television."

Then the fourth one, Lieutenant Commander Bob Barracks. He came directly from a St. Louis newspaper. He became in charge of my press department. They were all a great help, as can be imagined.

They all taught me a lot of things. I guess they had someone who was willing to listen. I took what they said and sopped it up like a sponge. I had to learn a lot.

One of the first things Bob Barracks said to me, "When a member of the press, or any other public media, asks you a question, he wants you to give an answer because he wants to put it in the paper." He said, "The first thing you do is write down the question he asked and read it back to him to make sure that you're going to go hunt the answer for a question that he wants answered. You don't want your interpretation of what he says; you want his interpretation of what he says. So you have it clearly in mind before you go and chase down an answer. Otherwise you'll wear yourself out and come back with an answer to a question which the fellow wasn't interested in." He said, "Don't try to fool the media. If they ask you a question, don't take it off the top of your head unless you put a great big flag on it saying this is guesswork. But, don't give them an answer till you are absolutely sure of the answer! Because it will come back and bite you."

"Don't play favorites. There will be newspaper people that, when you meet them, you will think are great guys, and you'll find that you have some that give you a lot of trouble. They are not your favorites. When they ask questions don't let this have anything to do with it. Don't play favorites!" He said, "They notice everything. You'll be in trouble if you play favorites or if you try to fool them or tell them stuff that isn't true."

There was a slight difficulty up at West Point. This is part of the same subject. Suddenly we had a question.

Q: You mean at the Military Academy?

Adm. B.: Yes. Some slight difficulty and it had come out in the newspaper. A question came in, "How do you do it at the Naval Academy?"

Bob Barracks said, "Hold on now, don't jump at it." He said, "You want to find out just exactly and be sure you tell whoever you're talking to at the Naval Academy that no fooling, no guesswork. Any question that gets asked you want to get them a straight answer and an answer you can prove." He said, "Because if you give them an answer which sounds too favorable, sounds as if you're covering up something, they will find it. So, tell the people down at the Naval Academy to be very, very sure." He said, "This can really ruin you."

Of course, Bob Barracks knew this was exactly the way he would do it when working for his newspaper. He would chase one down.

Q: Yes, now let me ask you this question: if that is laid upon you as the Director of Public Information, why isn't the same responsibility laid upon the reporter to report accurately and without bias?

Adm. B.: I would think so.

Q: It isn't.

Adm. B.: Well, I guess not. I recall an excellent responsible newspaper reporter. He reported something and I noticed that the story was fine, but the headlines were wrong. When you read the headlines they gave you the wrong picture. When you read the story, the story was great. I took it up with him.

He said, "Yes, those headlines aren't very good, are they?"

I said, "How does this come about?"

He said, "Well, did you like the story?"

I said, "The story was magnificent, great. Just like you would do it."

He said, "I don't write the headlines."

I said, "You mean that you write the story and you let somebody get away with putting out headlines that don't follow the story at all and get away with it?"

"Well," he said, "this is the real world."

Well, I guess it is a real world, and this happens. He was a fine gentleman. I remember a press conference at the Pentagon and the person on the stage was asked a question and he gave an answer. This same newspaper reporter said, "Now, General [or Mr. Secretary], are you sure that what you just told us in the answer is free for us to print? Are you sure it's not classified or a secret matter?"

The speaker said, "No, I checked on it and it's perfectly all right." This newspaper reporter wanted to make sure that this General hadn't slipped and given them stuff that he was not supposed to. So, this was the other side.

Q: That's not always the case. Some of them would relish something that is classified.

Adm. B.: There are all kinds. I found generally that they were very fine people. They were--they don't give up easily. They ask you a question and they like to have an answer at once. They will keep after you and when you come back and answer them they have another question. This goes on forever, it seems like.

I did not find, at least initially, that I was treated very well by my friends in the Navy Department. The person who was in the public relations business bridges a gap between the public media and the organization that he is working in. In other words, I was sort of a bridge between the public media and the Navy Department. Naturally, every Navy Bureau in and around Washington and everywhere else has a PIO office. They couldn't call it that in that particular day. But, there was a place. Newspaper people didn't have to ask all their questions in our office or in the Office of the Secretary of Defense. They knew the number to call over in the Bureau of Personnel, for example, or of Medicine and Surgery and so forth. There was someone over there that they could call and get answers also.

Q: Was it not true also that at the time you were there at the PIO Office there was still a residue of feeling in the Navy, as such, that it was a silent service? It did not relish giving out information to the press.

Adm. B.: Correct, that's correct.

It was difficult to get people to give you the answers to questions. They were not quite sure which are classified and which are not classified. So they hesitate, they would prefer to forget about the whole thing.

There was one incident that was sort of funny; really absurd. Roll with the punch. There was a flag officer out in the Far East in charge of antisubmarine matters. An American newspaperman asked for an interview with this particular flag officer in the Far East. This flag officer, in my belief, did the wrong thing. The thing to do if an American newspaper reporter wants to interview you, why, "Welcome aboard." Saying no or asking for guidance from higher levels doesn't do any good. But this flag officer did. He sent a message. Naturally, we now had it and we had to send out an answer to grant or not grant the interview.

I wrote up a message that simply said, "Grant the interview." The recipient did not even need that guidance. I took the proposed reply to the flag officer with responsibility for antisubmarine matters. He looked at it and thought it was terrible.

He said: "You tell him yes. Grant the interview. Be careful not to disclose any classified information."

I replied, "We shouldn't have to say the rest of it because he should know that you don't give away secrets."

Q: But obviously this officer felt very insecure.

Adm. B.: I guess so. Anyhow, he said, "Let me think about it."

I said: "He'd like to interview him now. He doesn't want to interview him next month." That didn't make this Pentagon flag officer very happy with me.

A couple of hours or so later this rear admiral in the antisubmarine warfare business had pondered this matter and decided that he'd better settle it some way. So, he went up to see Jimmy Fife--Jimmy Fife was then Assistant to the Deputy Chief of Naval Operations. In the midst of their conversation he accused me of trying to give away the country's secrets.

Jimmy Fife let him have it, because Jimmy Fife knew me very well and knew very well that I wasn't trying to give away the country's secrets. Anyhow, Admiral Fife released my simple message. Then he jokingly called me and asked: "You don't want to give away secrets, do you?"

People were distrustful of the work of the information business.

You recall the very interesting story I told you about in the Pentagon corridor I ran into my old friend Vice Admiral Denebrink and he asked me what I was doing?

"I'm in the public information business."

And he said, "Why, that's distressing." He said, "The only thing worse would be if you told me that you were either in personnel procurement or in the amphibious business."

He said, "You've got a pretty good record, but I don't think the public information business will do you any good."

Of course, it turned out that the next thing I did after I'd finished the PIO and after I went to the National War College, I did go into the amphibious business and then I went into the personnel procurement business; while in that position chosen to be a flag officer.

New subject: Drew Pearson was living at that time. Jack Anderson used to come in to see me quite often.

Q: He worked for Drew Pearson, didn't he?

Adm. B.: Yes. He had come in to see me quite often, I'd say certainly once a month. He'd come in and I would try to detect what he was interested in. It was very difficult because he would jump into various subjects. I'm sure that he was trying to find out things; perfectly all right with me. I was in the public info business.

He never really asked any questions. He just talked about things.

Q: He, of course, or Drew Pearson in that time, had their own sources, did they not, who handed over documents?

Adm. B.: I'm sure they did. But anyhow, I got along quite well with him. No problem.

We did have one interesting facet, as I remember it. I think it was in New York there was a man who I recall worked for a newspaper, and when one of the columnists was going to say something that was not very pleasant for the Navy the newspapers would have the story for that column a few days ahead before it got published. This fellow used to call up Bob Barracks and tell him that, "Hey, we've got an article coming up."

Q: Was there any action you could have taken?

Adm. B.: We could find out some information; have some facts available.

Q: You mean in order to defuse it.

Adm. B.: I doubt it. All we could really do at that time was get information and maybe we'd be ready when something comes out we can give an answer. It's certainly better to know about it.

Secretary of Defense Marshall had put out a directive soon after he became the Secretary of Defense which said, in effect, "Whenever in the public media anything is said derogatory to the Department of Defense or any of the services, I want on my desk by noon a piece of paper. First paragraph, where did this item appear? Quote the item which was deorgatory. Paragraph two, what are the facts?" This report could be unclassified or classified, whatever was necessary. Paragraph two are the facts, regardless of whether it is top secret or what it is, what are the facts? "Number three, if we are interrogated by the press, what are we going to say?"

That had to be on his desk by noon. Well, of course, these would mostly be in newspapers because if it came out in a movie or a magazine article or so forth there would be no tremendous urgency. But, it would still have to go in.

So, okay, in the morning <u>Washington Post</u> here is something derogatory about the Navy. I've got to have on Secretary Marshall's desk by noon, what was the criticism, what are the facts, interrogated by the press what are we going to say?

Now, this is very easy to say, "Sure, there is nothing to it. All you have to do is write it up. Except I don't know what the facts are yet."

Q: And you have very little time to find out?

Adm. B.: Indeed, I have very little time to find out. You know very well that I'm not going to run up to Secretary of Defense Marshall's office. I've got to take that through the Secretary of the Navy. I'll probably have to take it through the Chief of Naval Operations. Just how many various levels; naturally I have to find out the facts and then I have to figure out what we can tell the press and I have to get some agreement. I have to get some agreement within the Navy to take up to the Secretary of Defense's Office. You don't take it directly to him. He had a civilian public information and that's where it goes and he puts his chop on it and it goes--I don't know--you can imagine what a madhouse it was around there sometimes.

But, it was certainly a good thing to do. It made it such that we really knew what we were doing.

New subject: One day when Forrest Sherman was the Chief of Naval Operations I got a question: "What is the mission of the Sixth Fleet?" The Sixth Fleet is the one over in the Mediterranean. Forrest Sherman had been the Commander of the Sixth Fleet before he became the Chief of Naval Operations.

"What is the mission of the Sixth Fleet?" So, I decided, it's no use wandering around and try to find it out. Maybe I can find it out directly from someone who served as Commander, Sixth Fleet. He ought to know. So, I went up to see the flag secretary of the Chief of Naval Operations. He was a Captain by the name of Ira Nunn. I went in to see him and

I said, "Here is a question. What do you think would be the answer?"

He said, "Let's go and see the boss."

So we went in to see Admiral Forrest Sherman. He looked at it and he said, "Have you got your pad and paper together?" He said, "I'll give you the answer."

I knew that Forrest Sherman, I had seen him in press conference where a newspaperman would ask a question and he would immediately come out with an answer. Then the newspaperman might say, "Admiral, did you mean so-and-so, and so-and-so?"

And Forrest Sherman would say, "I'll tell you what I meant. I mean precisely what I said."

Well, he was very capable of coming down with exactly what he meant.

Q: He was a very bright man, wasn't he?

Adm. B.: Very bright.

"What is the mission of the Sixth Fleet? Do you have your pad and paper ready?"

So, he dictated and I wrote down the mission of the Sixth Fleet. I was amazed. "The mission of the Sixth Fleet is to operate in support of the land warfare in Europe." I was amazed at this and thought this was very strange. I said, "Admiral, are you sure?"

I thought he was going to fall out of his chair. He laughed! The only time I ever saw him really laugh. He said,

"Yes, young man, I am sure."

I said, "Thank you very much, Admiral."

That was great. This was a fascinating job.

About that time Captain H. Page Smith, who later on in years was four-star Commander of the Atlantic Fleet, arrived and became chief of staff to Robert Hickey, Rear Admiral who was the Chief of Information.

Here's another typical incident that is interesting. A little bit humorous. The Secretary of the Navy was going to appear on <u>Meet the Press</u>. So, naturally, it was scheduled, oh, say, a few weeks ahead. So, we formed a little task force to make up probable questions so that we would try to get Admiral Dan Kimball, I mean Secretary of the Navy Dan Kimball, to hold a practice session. We made up questions. Sticky ones--

Q: Tough questions?

Adm. B.: Tough questions. I hadn't been shipmates with this phenomenon before. I must have been new in the office because I had not done this one. But, we got the questions all set and went in to see the Secretary of the Navy, Kimball. He looked at the questions and he said, "Well, are we ready now? Who is going to read the questions?"

I said, "I will read them, Sir."

"Well, why don't you have someone else read them because you're going to answer them."

I said, "Well, thank you very much."

He laughed and so away we went. I guess Bob Barracks probably read it and I did the best I could with answering them. We had made up what we thought was a suitable answer.

Q: But Kimball didn't attempt to answer them?

Adm. B.: No. He listened and he commented on it. He talked about it. It was pretty good. It was a good way to do it.

Q: It was kind of unorthodox, wasn't it?

Adm. B.: I don't know.

Q: It isn't really done that way very often, is it?

Adm. B.: Well, I'm not sure. We were not involved often. I do know that when you have one of these press conferences at length in U.S. News and World Report, it was worked up, questions and answers, by the staff of U.S. News and World Report and the staff of the individual being interviewed.

Q: Yes, and consequently I find them very dull myself.

Adm. B.: Yes, nothing spontaneous. They don't ask any sticky ones like that fellow used to on Meet the Press. He could ask them. That lends a little flavor. Of course, we were trying to get Secretary of the Navy Dan Kimball to not get astonished by something that they asked. But, I found that he was quite capable of handling the thing. No problem at all there. It really wasn't necessary for us to have gone through all this thing.

Here is an incident which is interesting. These are incidents to indicate the trials and tribulations of the PIO. Especially perhaps if that is not his specialty.

Up at Philadelphia Naval Shipyard there was an aircraft carrier being converted. You recall that during the Korean War they soon found out that if we didn't do something we were going to run out of airplanes. The carrier deck, flight deck, was in the same plane as the ship. The British had invented a system of having the flight deck canted off, oh, fifteen or twenty degrees. The idea being when the plane comes in to land, if he misses the hook and goes straight he doesn't wipe out the whole thirty planes that were parked in the bow. He goes straight and maybe he can get speed up enough that he can come around again. At least he doesn't have to wipe out the whole carrier deck full of planes.

Well, an aircraft carrier was being converted. You could see that the flight deck canted. A newspaperman asked the question up there, "What is this?"

So, the question came down to our office and you should have seen me scurrying around the front corridors of the Pentagon trying to get approval for some kind of an answer on what it is. I was told that this is classified.

I said, "It can't be classified with the aircraft carrier up there with thousands of people looking at it every day. It must be, if you can't tell what it is you must have a cover story. There must be something."

It was silly. They might as well go ahead and explain what it was. That's what was done.

Q: It was in operation in the Royal Navy?

Adm. B.: Yes, it was already operating there. So, it was silly.

I had a difficult time with several other matters. I got a lot of calls for Navy speakers at various places. They needed a speaker here, and they needed a speaker there. There was no system set up. I wanted to set up a system in which, especially if they were asking for a flag officer to speak. We really ought to have a watch-list of who's the next one. We accomplished that when I was Assistant Vice Chief of Naval Operations. We set up a watch list of flag officers. Then, of course, it did not work as well as hoped.

Q: That only makes sense.

Adm. B.: Anyhow, at my level, I never found out how to do it. I went up and talked to Admiral Hickey about it one day. He laughed and he said in effect, "This is a hell of a problem for somebody." Yes! For me!

The Rotary Club asked for a speaker. They wanted a Rear Admiral to come and talk to them, or any kind of an Admiral. I couldn't get one to say yes. So, I went and talked to the Rotary Club.

A couple of weeks later there was going to be a world premiere of a movie about our naval operations in World War II and they wanted a flag officer to say a few words before the movie in front of the footlights. I couldn't get one to say yes so, obviously, I put on my blues and combed my hair a little bit and went down and made a speech. The whole front of the theater was full of admirals and generals. They all went to the movie, but they couldn't say a few words from the front of the stage. It was interesting though. By that time I was used to it. Those things never really bothered me.

Q: Would you say a few words more about that obstacle you ran into, the fellow who said the cantilevered deck is a classified matter? This is something that occurs in the Navy so often, isn't it?

Adm. B.: I don't think as much any more, but certainly it was in those days.

Q: Everything is classified.

Adm. B.: Yes, so easy to do.

The next item I'd like to mention bears on that; actually a unique solution to a problem of this kind. You recall the television series <u>Victory at Sea</u>?

Well, our friend Walter Karig was sort of our action officer for this one. He may have thought of it. With all of his contacts with the television stations and so forth, perhaps in the entire world, his contacts were tremendous. I would not be astonished by anything.

Anyhow, who invented the idea, I don't know, but certainly a sparkling one. Then when they started getting ready to do it they had a problem because in order to do it, really, they needed a lot of photographic footage that had already been taken. In other words, in order to make that we can't possibly get all those pictures by going out now with aircraft carriers and other ships.

Q: It had to be film that was made at the time?

Adm. B.: Yes. The Navy Photographic Center, over in Anacostia, was full of combat footage. They must have had, not millions of feet, they must have had billions of feet. They were all classified. They were all marked secret, maybe.

Now, what are we going to do? Obviously the television people had to have complete access to the footage, but it's all classified. Finally someone hit on a real good idea. There were a lot of people in the United States at that time who were reserve officers of one or the other of the armed forces. Lots of them worked for NBC, I think it was. So, maybe, they hired some extras. Anyhow, they sent down about a dozen, I think it was, about a dozen young fellows who were ex-officers of World War II. Perhaps they actually belonged to the Naval Reserve or the Army Reserve. Anyhow, they came down and were given a clearance suitable so they could look over the films. They looked over the film and chose the parts that they thought would be useful. Then those parts were viewed by the naval authorities as necessary to decide which could be unclassified. I imagine that second part didn't go very much. All they did was choose a lot of stock footage and away they went and turned out <u>Victory at Sea.</u>

Q: But they had gone through the motions?

Adm. B.: They had indeed gone through the motions. That took care of things very nicely.

A brand new submarine was coming to Washington. It was going to be at the downtown Washington Navy Yard and I got a call from someone in the office of the Secretary of Defense. A Mrs. Rosenberg was then Assistant Secretary of Defense for Personnel Matters.

Q: Anna Rosenberg.

Adm. B.: Apparently she had never been on board a submarine and would like to visit one. So, being a submarine officer, would I be willing to take her down to see the submarine?

Well, I was glad to go down and show her the submarine; away we went. We took her all through the submarine and she said, "This must be terrible living on board here."

I said, "Well, you know, if someone misbehaves, how we punish him?"

"Oh, you make them stay on here more?"

"No, we kick them off because we don't want anyone on our submarines who doesn't want to be here, who doesn't do a real good job." "The people who served on board a submarine requested that duty and, if chosen, are thoroughly trained."

We finished the visit and went back to the Pentagon and at the end of the working hours that day I went home to Arlington and when I came in the front door, approximately the same distance as we have here, my wife Vida was in the kitchen. I opened the front door and she said:

"Where did you go aboard the submarine?"

I said, "Down at the Navy Yard. How did you know?"

She said, "I could smell it when you opened the door."

There was a distinctive aroma, we'll say fragrance, to the inside of the submarine. It's a strange thing. I don't think it's true anymore with the nuclear-powered, we call nukes. But, there were so many noxious gases and so forth around the previous ones that it would get into your clothing that hung on board the submarine and when you wore them people could detect you.

Q: That's something that Anna observed when she went on.

Adm. B.: She probably did observe that. I considered the smell the attar of roses. It was great.

It reminds me of a story that ought to be told here. A submarine of the old diesel engine, storage battery variety was alongside of the pier and one night an enlisted man was coming back to the ship and he seemed to be holding some sort of a leash and when he came near the brow, that is the gangplank, to walk on board. When he came aboard the Petty Officer there at the top of the gangway said, "Say, what do you have there?"

He said, "I've got my pet skunk."

"A skunk? You know very well you can't bring that skunk on here!"

He said, "I don't know why I can't. Several of the crew

have a bird, or a cat, or a dog, and if they can have mascots so can I."

So, it immediately went up to the Chief Petty Officer and finally ended up with the executive officer of the submarine that was up there. They were having this discussion and the executive officer of the submarine said, "Jones, you know very well that you can't have that skunk on board this submarine. Think of the smell."

Well, he said, "I got used to it; so can the skunk."

Actually, it wasn't all that bad. The genesis of the fragrances of the submarine were of course diesel engines. Diesel engines do put out some fumes. Also, even more so, we have a tremendous number of storage batteries. Great big ones. They have acid in them and they do exude some fumes here and there. But, we submarine guys, we don't mind those at all. As a matter of fact, we spend the whole day submerged and come up and get fresh air and it smells funny. Anyhow, we thrived on it. Other people simply noticed it.

About that time Admiral Forrest Sherman, Chief of Naval Operations, was on a trip over to Europe. He had a stroke or a heart attack and died. He was relieved by Admiral W. M. Fechteler. He became the new Chief of Naval Operations.

Soon after he had become Chief of Naval Operations, I got calls from down in the Department of Defense press room as to "What is this business of two cruisers to be altered so they can fire guided missiles?" I hadn't heard any such thing. I said, "I'll try to find out."

So, I ran around in the front corridors of the Pentagon trying to find out and I found out, yes, that's true. The USS BOSTON and the USS ALBANY are going to get guided missiles. These are going to be antiaircraft guided missiles. But, this story is highly classified. The work hasn't started yet and we're holding it very closely.

Well, after two or three tries I couldn't get any data, but the story had gotten out somehow. So, I went up to whoever was then aide to the new Chief of Naval Operations. I asked him of this. He said, "Well, let's go in and see the boss."

So we went in to see Admiral Fechteler and he said, "Sure, I told so-and-so."

In other words, he had told a newspaper man this story and he didn't realize this was classified. Here they were jumping up and down and the person he had told--he didn't tell the rest of them where he had gotten the story but he was chuckling to himself. He had gotten an exclusive.

Q: From the CNO himself.

Adm. B.: From the CNO, and it's perfectly natural. Unless you've been in the PIO business it never occurs to you that you can't tell somebody something when it sounds like a good newsworthy item. There is really no reason for it to be classified except that you get those newspaper people absolutely nutty when you give someone an exclusive. You're not supposed to do that. The only time you give someone an exclusive is when he asked a question and you answered it. It's very hard to keep people happy.

Benson #7 -452-

New subject: One Sunday morning, I guess it was early in 1952, the aircraft carrier USS WASP, I'm sure, and an escort ship by the name of USS HOBSON were going across the Atlantic and just what kind of a maneuver they went through I'm not sure, but they had a collision. The HOBSON sank. She didn't sink very rapidly because they rescued most of the crew. There were lives lost in the collision. The story came into my office and I immediately went to the Pentagon. By the time I got to the Pentagon they had an inquiry from a newspaperman in Norfolk. This was the home port of the aircraft carrier. The home port of the smaller ship was Charleston, South Carolina. They had a question from a newspaperman, "Was the USS WASP in a collision?"

Now, where in the world that newspaperman got his question I have no idea, but we were frantically, at that time, of course, putting together a story ready to release whatever we could. I called up the Vice Chief of Naval Operations who at that time was Admiral Duncan, D. B. Duncan.

Q: Wu Duncan?

Adm. B.: Yes. I told him what was going on and that we were going to put out a bare-boned story of this collision. We were going to say, of course, that the names of the people who had lost their lives would be released as soon as we had had an opportunity to inform their next of kin. I don't like the expression "The names are withheld"; it's better to make a positive statement: "They will be released as soon as we've had a chance to tell their next of kin."

Well, we found out a very interesting thing that I had never dreamed of. When I was first in the submarine business, every time a submarine got under way, even for a day's operations you left behind what you called a sailing list. A list of the people on board. In other words, once every three months or so, whenever it was necessary, you mimeograph a list of everybody who belonged to the submarine. Then just before you got under way you crossed out the names of the people who were not going or were on leave or something. You added any extra passengers or anything. The last thing you did was to turn over your sailing list and you got under way.

Q: Isn't this true, as similar to the airlines and commercial passengers, that you have a passenger list?

Adm. B.: Sure. That's right. Now I was amazed. I had been shipmates with this procedure and had not given much more thought to it. But, I found on inquiry after this thing was all over, I found that when I was serving in destroyers we didn't have this procedure. But, I didn't know it. I never had to inquire about it, it hadn't come up. I just sort of assumed, I guess, well, you do that often. You assume that a logical procedure goes on, and if something comes up you find that that logical procedure was not going on. Apparently it was not the usual thing in the Navy and both the USS WASP and USS HOBSON had left that day on this cruise across the Atlantic; no sailing lists.

In this case we didn't know who had been on board that small ship, the USS HOBSON. Therefore, we don't know who's lost his life. Finally, someone hit upon the bright idea, and I think it was the newspaperman, I think it was the man covering the United Press. "Why don't we release the names of the known survivors?"

That leaves a question in a lot of people's minds, but less people will be uneasy if we release the list of the survivors than if we sit here and try to do what we can to figure out who must have been on board. So, that's what we did. People had come in on this Sunday to the Bureau of Naval Personnel to work on the records to try to figure this all out. Two or three newspapermen went over and offered their services. They were going to work for all the press, of course. They weren't going to get any exclusives. The first thing we needed to do was release who survived.

That was easy once the USS WASP sent us the message saying "Here's a list of survivors, and the names of their next of kin."

Of course, as soon as possible the next of kin of those who had lost their lives were informed.

About that time Captain H. Page Smith had been selected to become a flag officer and had been detached. A captain by the name of Lewis S. Parks, a submariner, arrived. He relieved Smith as Admiral Hickey's chief of staff.

Among many I had become acquainted with a gentleman by the name of Clay Blair. I had known Clay Blair for some time in this job because he worked for the Time-Life Corporation and was one of the Pentagon regulars. He had questions to ask now and then. But, when Page Smith was selected to be a flag officer, Clay Blair came to see me and said, "Now then, there is a Captain over in your Bureau of Ships and his name is Hyman G. Rickover and he is in the Defense Department telephone book as having something to do with nuclear power." He said, "I understand that this gentleman, Captain Rickover, was two years senior to Captain Page Smith. Page Smith was selected to be an Admiral, but Rickover was not and Rickover is two years senior to him. Why didn't he get selected?"

I said, "I can't give you the answer. I can tell you this though. That is that Smith and Rickover were not in competition."

He said, "What do you mean they weren't in competition?"

I said, "Well, when the selection board meets, they are supposed to select a certain number of unrestricted line officers. They are seagoing sailor men. They are committed to selecting that number of those. They are also to select "X" number of engineering duty officers. They are not competing against one another. In other words, the board has no choice. It is going to select, say, twenty seagoing sailor men and three engineering duty officers. They are not going to select two or nine or anything else. So, the engineering duty officers who are selected are competing only with other engineering duty officers."

And he said, "Well, it doesn't make sense, but it's all

right."

The following year out came the selection board results and Lewis S. Parks, who had relieved Page Smith as chief of staff to Admiral Hickey, was selected to be a flag officer. So, Clay Blair came in to me with fire in his eyes and he said, "How does this sound like a first sentence in *Time* magazine this week?"

I'm not sure of the exact wording, but the thought is there.

"As an indication of how the United States Navy looks to its future it has now, for the second year in succession, chosen its top propaganda officer, they call them public information officer, for flag officer rank. But, it has failed in its selection of its nuclear expert, Captain Hyman G. Rickover."

I said, "Clay, this is not fair. I told you last year that they are not in competition."

He said, "Yes, I remember exactly what you said. But, it doesn't make sense and Captain Rickover was not chosen again. I don't think this makes sense."

I said, "It's just that the Secretary of the Navy appoints a board and the board is sworn to do what in their judgment is the proper thing to do. Here are the results."

"Well," he said, "it doesn't make any sense at all."

Well, some time thereafter Blair came in to see me and he said, "You know, I haven't given up on that Captain Rickover." He said, "But I'm on the other side of the fence now. I'm trying to get to see him. He's over there in the old Main Navy Building and he's in the telephone book. He does something about nuclear power. I call up and he's not in. I call up and he's going to call me back. But, he never calls back. I think I'm entitled to go over and interview him." He said, "I've been interested in him for years and I think I ought to go over and talk with him."

I said, "Well, why don't you just call up."

I gave him the number of the Bureau of Ships PIO type.

He said, "Oh, I've talked to him many times. He says it's impossible."

I said, "Okay, I'll give it a try."

So I called up Captain Rickover. Naturally he immediately accused me of trying to give away all of the country's secrets. But, I had heard that before so that was no problem.

I explained to him that I think he should at least meet this news reporter.

He said, "What can I tell him?"

I said, "You know better than anybody what you can tell him. Maybe you can't tell him anything, but you can at least meet with him."

So, he said, "Okay."

Clay Blair went over to see him and I believe Clay Blair had a great influence on Admiral Rickover finally becoming a flag officer. He retired quite a few years ago and has been held on active duty since. He certainly must be in his eighties. He is a four-star admiral. He's doing fine.

I've had an association with him. He and I have gotten along pretty well. Of course, he is a hard man to shave. A newspaperman ought to be able to go in and talk to somebody. Regardless of how classified--you don't have to give away the country's secrets. This was quite an education in my two years in public information.

After this Captain Lewis Parks became flag officer--he relieved Admiral Hickey as the top man in the public information business, I relieved Parks as chief of staff. Commander Slade D. Cutter relieved me. He was a 1935 graduate of the Naval Academy. All-American football player and intercollegiate heavyweight boxing champion. My time in the public information business was just about over because about that time I got ordered to the National War College. Just to review the bidding of it, three years straight 1947, 1948, 1949 I had been chosen for the Naval War College. My boss would never let me go. Then we went through the Industrial College of the Armed Forces.

Q: On one day.

Adm. B.: In one day. No, from Friday to Monday. Three days. I heard the welcoming speech and drew my books.

The following year I was chosen for the same school. My boss wouldn't let me go. So, here we go. I was amazed. I actually did go to the National War College.

I reported there August of 1952 for a ten-month course in international studies. That's really what we do there.

We study the entire world. Particularly the political business. I'm not talking about partisan politics. I'm talking about international relationships. Naturally I was delighted. I had been trying to go to these higher schools in the service for years. Finally I got to go to one.

Q: If you persist eventually it works.

Adm. B.: Keep on and never quit. You keep requesting it all the time and you finally get there. That was a magnificent ten months! I enjoyed that thoroughly, not only because I was going to school, but the student body there. The student body was a hundred and twenty-five people, if I remember correctly. Maybe a hundred. They consisted of Army colonels, Air Force colonels, and Marine colonels; and captains of the Navy and Coast Guard; and people from the State Department and a few other U.S. government activities.

Q: This, I think, is a good place to stop.

Adm. B.: Fine.

Index to

Series of Taped Interviews with

Rear Admiral Roy S. Benson

U.S. Navy (Retired)

Volume I

Antisubmarine Warfare
  Planning and training in late 1940s for U.S. Navy to use its submarines against those of other nations, pp. 370-379.

Asiatic Fleet, U.S.
  Roles and responsibilities of in the early 1930s, pp. 60-61, 64-68; see also: Smith Thompson, USS (DD-212).

Athletics
  Gymkhana at Naval Academy in 1920s, pp. 38-39; boxing at Naval Academy, pp. 41-43; sports involving destroyer crews in early 1930s, pp. 106-109.

Atomic Bomb
  Benson questions validity of its use on Japan in 1945, pp. 316-317; Navy's top staff feels bombs unnecessary to compel Japanese surrender, p. 342.

Aviation.
  See: Naval Aviation.

Awards, Naval
  Procedures used in recommendations during World War II, pp. 228-229; Benson chided for lack of modesty in display of ribbons, pp. 261-263; Pacific Fleet Awards Board in 1944-1945, pp. 301-305.

Barents Sea
  U.S. submarines Cochino (SS-345) and Tusk (SS-426) sent there on reconnaissance mission in 1949; Cochino lost as result of battery fire and explosion, pp. 380-393.

Barnacles
  Effect on ships' bottoms, pp. 82-83.

Barracks, Robert A., Lieutenant Commander, USNR
  Helpful to Benson as head of press department in Navy's public information organization during the Korean War, pp. 431-433.

Batteries
  Storage batteries used in destroyer Hovey (DD-208) before World War II to activate magnetic mines, pp. 157-159; hydrogen fire in Cochino (SS-345) battery in 1949 leads to loss of the boat, pp. 384-389.

Benson, Roy S., Rear Admiral, USN (Ret.) (USNA, 1929)
  Boyhood, pp. 1-2, 7-13; family from Sweden, pp. 2-6; as musician, pp. 7-10, 35-38, 47-48; application for Naval Academy, pp. 14-20; as midshipman at Naval Academy, pp. 21-49; service in battleship New York, pp. 49-51; naval aviation training, pp. 52-56; duty in destroyer Smith Thompson, pp. 59-109; attached to submarine R-14 in 1934, pp. 114-118; student at submarine school, pp. 119-124; duty in submarine S-42, pp. 125-131; duty in submarine S-27, pp. 131-133; as navigation instructor at the Naval Academy, pp. 133-160; as executive officer of submarine Nautilus early in World War II, pp. 160-191; as commanding officer of the submarine

Trigger in 1942-1943, pp. 191-260; as commanding officer of PCO school for submarine skippers at New London, pp. 261-265, 275-284; as commanding officer of submarine Razorback, pp. 266-267, 286-295; as Commander Submarine Division 43 at Pearl Harbor at war's end, pp. 295-306; duties at Navy Department in Washington in 1945, 317-348; service as readiness and new developments officer on staff of Commander Submarine Force Atlantic, pp. 356-424; attends National War College in 1952-1953, pp. 425, 458-459; serves as Navy's Director of Public Information during Korean War, pp. 427-458.

Benson, Vida Connole
Widow of submariner David Connole has difficulty getting benefits after his loss on patrol, p. 337; marries Benson in 1948, pp. 362-363.

Blair, Clay
Journalist responsible for Hyman G. Rickover's selection for flag rank in the early 1950s, pp. 454-457.

Britain
See: Royal Navy.

Brockman, William H., Lieutenant Commander, USN (USNA, 1927)
Commanding officer of USS Nautilus (SS-168) in 1942, pp. 177-191; awarded Navy Cross for actions at Midway and against Japan while in command of the Nautilus, p. 191.

Bruton, Henry C., Captain, USN (USNA, 1926)
Gives Benson advice on antisubmarine warfare plan in late 1940s, stressing improvement in underwater sound equipment, pp. 372-374.

Chaplains
Fine performance by Asiatic Fleet destroyer force chaplains in early 1930s, pp. 104-106.

China
Warlords take over Chefoo in 1932, pp. 63-64; use of gunboats in 1930s, pp. 67-69; evacuation plans set up for U.S. nationals in early 1930s, pp. 69-70; extraterritoriality creates immunity for foreign governments from Chinese police in early 1930s, pp. 78-79; U.S. commissary procedures, pp. 93-95; use of Mexican-bought silver for currency during Chiang Kai-shek's rule, p. 96; venereal disease, p. 104.

Cholera
U.S. Navy loses man to epidemic in Chefoo, China, in early 1930s, p. 64.

Classified information
Declassification after World War II of wartime submarine patrol reports, pp. 348-351; folly of classifying story of first angled-deck aircraft carrier in 1950s, p. 444; declassification of World

War II combat film footage for NBC's "Victory at Sea" television series in early 1950s, pp. 446-447.

Coaling Ship
Refueling battleships and filling boilers with coal in 1920s, pp. 29-33.

Cochino, USS (SS-345)
Receives Guppy improvements in 1948, pp. 377-378; battery explosion in Barents Sea causes sinking while on reconnaissance mission in 1949, pp. 383-393; safety features introduced in other submarines as a result of her sinking, pp. 404, 407-408.

CominCh
Benson serves on Fleet Admiral E. J. King's staff right after World War II, pp. 317-328; Fleet Admiral Chester Nimitz relieves King as CNO in 1945 and CominCh organization is dissolved, pp. 342-344.

Commissary Procedures
On board Asiatic Fleet destroyer Smith Thompson (DD-212) in the early 1930s, pp. 89-95.

Communications
On board destroyer Smith Thompson (DD-212) in early 1930s, pp. 84-87; between submarine Trigger (SS-237) and shore bases during World War II patrols, pp. 226, 231-232; in submarine wolf packs, pp. 292-293; use of underwater telephones between U.S. submarines in 1949, pp. 382-384, 405-406.

Competitive Exercises
Used in training Asiatic Fleet ships in 1930s, pp. 84-89.

Connole, David R., Commander, USN (USNA, 1936)
Friend and former student of Benson's lost while in command of submarine Trigger (SS-237) in March 1945, pp. 305, 337; Benson marries Connole's widow, pp. 362-363.

Declassification
See: Classified Information.

Denebrink, Francis C., Vice Admiral, USN (USNA, 1916)
As navigation instructor at Naval Academy in 1937, pp. 134-135; aids officers preparing for navigation portion of promotion exams, pp. 141-142; consultant of reliability of magnetic compass, p. 151; warns Benson of pitfalls of being Navy public information director in 1950s, p. 437.

Dress Ship
Ships of various nations honor George Washington's birthday at Nanking, China, in 1932, pp. 73-75.

Fife, James, Jr., Vice Admiral, USN (USNA, 1918)
As Commander Submarine Force Atlantic Fleet in late 1940s, pp. 356, 360; description of personality, tough and thorough, pp. 364-

368, 370-371, 401; recommends Benson as Navy director of public information in early 1950s, pp. 427-428; defends Benson against charge of giving away nation's secrets, p. 437.

Fire
Battery explosion and fire on board submarine Cochino (SS-345) in 1949, pp. 384-389.

Food
See: Commissary Procedures.

Gallery, Daniel V., Captain, USN (USNA, 1921)
Approaches Benson after World War II with idea of moving captured German submarine to Chicago, pp. 346-348.

Gannon, Sinclair, Captain, USN (USNA, 1900)
Naval Academy commandant of midshipmen in late 1920s, then CO of battleship New York (BB-34), pp. 48-51.

Germany
Hitler youths travel with Benson on board liner Bremen in 1934, pp. 112-113; efforts to improve submarine speeds during World War II, p. 330.

Great Britain
See: Royal Navy.

Gunboats
Description of use of this type vessel in China during the 1930s, pp. 67-69.

Guppy Program
U.S. submarines given enhanced speed and streamlined topsides in modifications in the late 1940s, pp. 363, 377-378.

Hiyo
Japanese aircraft carrier damaged off Yokosuka by torpedo from USS Trigger (SS-237) in 1943, pp. 239-244, 254-255.

Hobson, USS (DMS-26)
Destroyer minesweeper sunk as result of collision with carrier Wasp (CV-18) in 1952, no list of crew available, pp. 452-454.

Holmes, Wilfred J. ("Jasper"), Lieutenant Commander, USNR (USNA, 1922)
Writes article concerning use of submarines to refuel aircraft, pp. 169-170; briefs Benson on assigned patrol area off Japan in fall of 1942, p. 194.

Hovey, USS (DD-208)
Four-pipe destroyer to which Benson assigned as executive officer in 1939, pp. 152-154; converted to high-speed minesweeper, pp. 154-159.

Hudson, Alec
   Pseudonym for Wilfred J. Holmes. See: Holmes.

Hydrogen Peroxide
   Used by Germans in submarines in World War II and considered by U.S. Navy after war, pp. 330, 354, 360, 377.

Intelligence
   U.S. submarines <u>Cochino</u> (SS-345) and <u>Tusk</u> (SS-426) sent on reconnaissance mission in Barents Sea in 1949 to collect Communist radar signatures, pp. 380-381.

Japan
   Takeover of Manchuria in 1931, p. 71; takeover of Shanghai in 1932, pp. 71-72; minelaying by U.S. Navy in Japanese waters in 1942, pp. 212-217; question of validity of use of atomic bomb to end World War II, pp. 316-317; Navy's feelings toward surrender and atomic bomb, p. 342.

Karig, Walter, Captain, USNR
   Public information officer helpful to Benson in Navy's press office in early 1950s, pp. 430, 446.

Kimball, Dan A.
   Secretary of the Navy capable in answering questions from the press in the early 1950s, pp. 442-443.

Korean War
   Begins in 1950s, p. 427; Navy's public information organization increases in size during, p. 430; need to increase number of airplanes for, p. 444.

Lockwood, Charles A., Vice Admiral, USN (USNA, 1912)
   Concern about torpedo magnetic exploders during World War II, pp. 244, 247, 254; inspiration to Benson and others as leader, pp. 256-257; head of Pacific Fleet awards board, pp. 301-302; unhappy at becoming Navy Inspector General in 1945, pp. 344, 356.

Lynch, Richard B. ("Ozzie"), Commander, USN (USNA, 1935)
   Valuable in antisubmarine warfare plan study in 1948 because of various talents, pp. 378-379, 422.

Magnetic Exploders
   Decision on inactivation made by Vice Admiral C. A. Lockwood during World War II, pp. 244-247; efforts by submarine commanding officers to use, pp. 247-254; Rear Admiral R. W. Christie adamant about keeping in use, pp. 249-250.

Mare Island Navy Yard
   Work on submarines in 1941, pp. 170-176.

Marshall, George C.
   As Secretary of Defense during Korean War, sets up procedure for

responding to derogatory material about armed services appearing in news media, pp. 439-440.

Midway, Battle of
USS Nautilus (SS-168) operates in the area during the battle in June 1942 and sinks carrier Soryu with torpedoes, pp. 184-190.

Midway Island
Site of "gooney bird lodge" built by Pan American airways and used during World War II, pp. 229-230.

Minelaying
Done more frequently than minesweeping in Pacific during World War II, p. 160; description of placement in Tokyo Bay in 1942, pp. 212-217; Japanese ships sunk by mine almost immediately after being laid by USS Trigger (SS-237) in 1942, pp. 218-220; use by U.S. Navy submarines stopped after fall of 1942, p. 311.

Mines
Storage batteries used in destroyer Hovey (DD-208) before World War II to activate magnetic mines, pp. 157-159; mines still in English Channel in 1949, p. 382.

Minesweeping
Shortage of minesweepers in U.S. Navy in 1939, pp. 154-155; technique used for exploding magnetic mines through use of batteries during pre-World War II period, pp. 155-160; problem of sweeping mines after they were no longer needed, p. 163.

Momsen Lung
Rescue breathing apparatus used in submarine training in 1930s, pp. 120-122.

Music
At the Naval Academy during the 1920s, pp. 35-40, 47-48.

Nautilus, USS (SS-168)
Large submarine in which Benson serves in 1941-1942, pp. 160-191; modernized in 1941, pp. 170-180; sinks Japanese carrier Soryu during participation in Battle of Midway in 1942, pp. 183-190; sinks Japanese destroyer in 1942 and photo makes Life magazine, p. 190.

Naval Academy, U.S.
Benson applies for, pp. 14-20; plebe year in 1925-1926, pp. 21-26; training cruises in late 1920s, pp. 27-35, 40-41; athletics, pp. 41-43; leave and liberty practices for midshipmen, pp. 43-46; Benson as instructor in navigation in late 1930s, pp. 133-151; midshipman training cruises in late 1930s, pp. 136-138, 143-151.

Naval Aviation
Flight training in 1920s and 1930s, pp. 52-53; branch dominates Chief of Naval Operations in post-World War II period, pp. 345-346, 351-352.

Navigation
  Use of submarine skippers as pilots at Pearl Harbor in 1930s, pp. 131-132; teaching of navigation at Naval Academy in late 1930s, pp. 136-137, 143-151; survey of water depth in New York's North River in 1938, pp. 143-148.

Navy Department, Washington, D.C.
  Organization of in 1945, pp. 317-328; role in developing post-World War II submarines, pp. 328-336; developments for new ships, pp. 334-346; unification plans, pp. 338-344; submarine patrol reports declassified for public use, pp. 349-351.

New York, USS (BB-34)
  Atlantic Fleet battleship commanded by Captain Sinclair Gannon around 1930, pp. 49-51.

Nimitz, Chester W., Fleet Admiral, USN (USNA, 1950)
  Presents awards to officers and crew of submarine Nautilus (SS-168) in 1942, p. 191; head of Pacific Fleet awards committee, pp. 228, 301-302; leadership qualities, pp. 257, 299, 306; moves part of staff to Guam in 1945, pp. 316-317, 327-328; becomes Chief of Naval Operations in December 1945, pp. 343-344; attempt to reorganize staff positions in Navy Department, pp. 352, 372.

Norway
  Local reaction when U.S. submarine Tusk (SS-426) goes into Hammerfest, Norway, in 1949 after rescuing survivors from lost submarine Cochino (SS-345), pp. 394-402.

Nuclear Power
  Recommended in 1946 for use in submarines, pp. 354-355.

O'Kane, Richard H., Commander, USN (USNA, 1934)
  Writes book on sinking of submarine Tang (SS-306) and his time in Japanese prison camp, pp. 272-273.

OpNav
  Organization and activities of the staff of the Chief of Naval Operations in the immediate post-World War II period, pp. 342-352.

Paravanes
  Use in countering moored mines, pp. 161-163.

Patrol Reports from Submarines
  Source of information for submarine division commanders in World War II, pp. 296, 301; declassified by former submarine commanding officers after the war, pp. 348-351.

Pay and Allowances
  Practices on board Asiatic Fleet destroyer Smith Thompson (DD-212) in early 1930s, pp. 95-98.

Pearl Harbor, Hawaii
　Dredging of harbor allows large ships to enter, p. 131; use of submarine skippers as harbor pilots to alleviate shortage in 1930s, pp. 131-132; success of 1941 Japanese bombing astounding, pp. 250-252; torpedo explodes by mistake at bottom of harbor in spring of 1943, p. 251; submarine division commanders based there at the end of World War II, pp. 295-303.

Periscopes
　Use of in submarine Trigger (SS-237) during World War II, pp. 236-237, 279-280.

Planning
　Plans drawn up in ComInCh staff in 1945 for post-World War II Navy, pp. 320-323, 340-342; war plans drawn up by ComSubLant staff in late 1940s, pp. 368-370.

Postwar U.S. Defense Plans
　See: Planning.

Prospective Commanding Officers' School
　See: Training.

Public Information Organization of the Armed Forces
　Armed services branches are consolidated into in late 1940s, p. 428; responsibilities during Korean War, pp. 429-458; relationship with the press, pp. 431-435, 450-458; problems with classified information, pp. 444-451; making of "Victory at Sea" television series in early 1950s, pp. 446-448.

R-14, USS (SS-91)
　Used for training of submarine school students at New London in mid-1930s, pp. 114-117.

Radford, Arthur W., Admiral, USN (USNA, 1916)
　Displays courtesy to Benson at meeting in late 1940s, pp. 327-328.

Razorback, USS (SS-394)
　Submarine which runs aground off New London in 1944, p. 266; heads through Panama Canal to Pearl Harbor, then participates in nine-boat scouting line against Japanese, pp. 286-294.

Repairs and Maintenance
　Refit period for submarines between patrols in World War II, pp. 258-259.

Rescue at Sea
　Submarines pick up downed pilots during strikes on Japan in World War II, pp. 307-308; men from stricken submarine Cochino (SS-345) taken aboard USS Tusk (SS-426) in 1949 in Barents Sea, pp. 388, 391-395, 404-405.

Research and Development
  See: Submarine Development Group Two.

Rest and Recreation
  For submariners in World War II at Royal Hawaiian Hotel, pp. 209-210.

Rickover, Hyman G., Rear Admiral, USN (USNA, 1922)
  Nuclear submarine proponent described as perfectionist, pp. 26-27; reluctant to be interviewed by news media, pp. 455-458.

Rose, Rufus E., Lieutenant Commander, USN (USNA, 1924)
  Capable commanding officer of destroyer Hovey (DD-208) shortly before World War II, pp. 153-154.

Royal Navy
  Description of Joint Antisubmarine Warfare School in post-World War II period, pp. 358-360; advances in underwater sound equipment, pp. 359-360; studies of German Type 26 submarine after confiscation in postwar period, p. 360; construction improvements made on aircraft carriers, p. 444.

S-27, USS (SS-132)
  Submarine operating from Pearl Harbor in mid-1930s, pp. 128-132.

S-42, USS (SS-153)
  Submarine operating from Pearl Harbor in mid-1930s, pp. 119-120, 125-126.

Safety, Naval
  Jammed rudders cause torpedoes to run in circles during World War II, pp. 268-275; lead acid storage abtteries in submarines, pp. 384-391; loss of seven men on board submarine Tusk (SS-426) in 1949, pp. 387-390; deck track for safety belts introduced as a result of 1949 Cochino (SS-345) incident in 1949, p. 404; wet suits, p. 405.

Sherman, Forrest P., Admiral, USN (USNA, 1918)
  As Chief of Naval Operations in 1950, leads to Benson's assignment as director of public information for Navy, pp. 427-429; described as bright, rarely laughing, pp. 440-442, 450.

Shevill, William
  Valuable contact at Woods Hole Oceanographic Institution for research in underwater sound equipment in late 1940s, p. 412; takes four submarines to Bermuda to test geophone, pp. 414-420.

Ship Characteristics Board
  Considers designs for post-World War II submarines, pp. 328-336.

Shore Patrol
  Use in China in early 1930s, pp. 103-104.

Smith Thompson, USS (DD-212)
　　Four-pipe destroyer in Asiatic Fleet in early 1930s, pp. 59-109; characteristics, pp. 59-60; pattern of operating in China area, pp. 61-83; communications and signaling, pp. 84-87; competitive exercises, pp. 84-89; commissary and pay practices, pp. 89-98; training of personnel, pp. 100-102; sightseeing and recreation, pp. 77-84, 103-109.

Snorkels
　　Used by German submarines at end of World War II, pp. 328-329; recommended by Naval Research Laboratory in 1946 for new U.S. submarines, p. 354; Benson rides first snorkel-equipped U.S. submarine in 1948, p. 363.

Sonar
　　See: Sound--Underwater.

Sound--Underwater
　　Mine-detecting sonar effective in saving submarines in World War II, pp. 311-313; need for special submarine type sonar evident during World War II, pp. 313-315; extensive research at Navy's Underwater Sound Laboratory in 1947, p. 355, 357; British more advances in listening aspect in post-World War II period, pp. 359-360; equipment inadequate at New London submarine base, pp. 374-377; importance of underwater telephones, pp. 382-384, 405-408; improvements in sound equipment after World War II, pp. 409-424; National Defense Reserach Committee's involvement in postwar sound research, p. 411; National Academy of Science's postwar contribution, pp. 411-412; Woods Hole's involvement in, p. 412; dunking sonar experiments, p. 414; geophone tests off Bermuda, pp. 415-426.

Sports
　　See: Athletics.

SubLant (Submarine Force Atlantic Fleet)
　　Benson's service on Vice Admiral James Fife's staff in the late 1940s, concentrating on new developments in submarine warfare and underwater sound, pp. 356-376.

Submarine Development Group Two
　　Organization set up in late 1940s to investigate use of submarines in antisubmarine warfare and conduct experiments in underwater sound, pp. 370-379, 409-426.

Submarines, U.S.
　　R-boats, pp. 115-117; S-boats, pp. 119-120; flood valves done away with in World War II, pp. 179-180; U.S. increases submarine production in 1943-1944, p. 231; periscope techniques, pp. 236-237; visibility of submarines from aircraft, pp. 279-281; rescue operations in Pacific in World War II, pp. 307-310; submarine design conference in 1930s, pp. 324-325; effectiveness against Japan in World War II, pp. 348-349; nuclear power recommended for submarines

in 1946, pp. 354-355; postwar conversions incorporating improvements, pp. 360, 377-378; deck track for safety belts introduced, p. 404; lead acid battery causes explosion in USS Cochino (SS-345) in 1949, pp. 384-391; description of odor inside submarines, pp. 449-450. See also: Cochino, USS (SS-345); communications; Guppy Program; magnetic exploders; minelaying, Nautilus, USS (SS-168); periscopes; Razorback, USS (SS-394); rescue at sea; safety, naval; Tang, USS (SS-306); Tang (USS (SS-563); torpedoes; Trigger, USS (SS-564); Tusk, USS (SS-426); wolf packs.

Submarines, German
 Analyzed by U.S. Navy after World War II as a source of possible design improvements, pp. 328-331, 354, 360, 377.

Submarine School
 Curriculum covered at New London in mid-1930s, pp. 117-118, 120-122; Benson heads submarine prospective commanding officer school during World War II, pp. 263-265, 275-284, 409.

Submarine Scouting Lines
 Uneventful when used by U.S. Navy in Pacific between Philippines and Palau in 1943, pp. 289-292.

Submarine Tactics
 Down-the-throat torpedo shot, pp. 202-207; end-around, p. 234; use of sonar when periscope impractical, pp. 280-281.

Sweden
 Swedish immigrants in the United States in the early years of the 20th century, pp. 2-6.

Tactics
 See: Submarine Tactics.

Tang, USS (SS-306)
 Submarine sunk in October 1944 by circular run of one of her own torpedoes, pp. 270-273.

Tang, USS (SS-563)
 One of first U.S. submarines built to post-World War II design, pp. 331-333.

Television
 Navy declassifies World War II combat film for making of NBC "Victory at Sea" series in early 1950s, pp. 446-447.

Texas, USS (BB-35)
 Makes Naval Academy midshipman cruise to New York and Europe in 1938, pp. 143-151.

Thew, Joseph P., Lieutenant Commander, USN (USNA, 1924)
 Becomes commanding officer of submarine Nautilus (SS-168) in 1941, then relieved while off the boat for medical treatment, pp. 167, 177-178.

Torpedoes
   Defects in magnetic exploders cause poor results, pp. 244-254; circular torpedo runs as a result of torpedo rudder jamming, pp. 268-275.

Training
   For officers and enlisted on board destroyer Smith Thompson (DD-212) in early 1930s, pp. 100-102; at prospective commanding officers' school for submariners at New London in World War II, pp. 263-265, 275-286.

Treaty Ports
   Extraterritoriality creates immunity for foreign governments from Chinese police in early 1930s, pp. 78-79.

Trigger, USS (SS-237)
   Launched at Mare Island in 1941, p. 171; runs aground at Midway in 1942, p. 184; Benson becomes commanding officer in August 1942, pp. 191-193; war patrol to Japanese home islands, pp. 193-208; gun duel with Japanese surface ship, p. 195; sinking of cargo ship off Japanese coast, pp. 199-201; sinking of Japanese destroyer, p. 208; minelaying in Japanese waters, pp. 211-220; completion of patrol and return to Midway, pp. 220-227; reconnaissance patrol in early 1943, pp. 230-235; patrol in mid-1943 which included torpedoing of Japanese carrier Hiyo, pp. 236-244, 254-255; refit at Pearl Harbor, pp. 257-260; circular torpedo runs occur twice during patrols in 1942 and 1943, pp. 271-272; lost with all hands in spring of 1945, p. 305.

Trigger, USS (SS-564)
   One of first two U.S. submarines built to post-World War II designs, pp. 331-333.

Tusk, USS (SS-426)
   Submarine used for efforts to improve underwater sound capability in late 1940s, pp. 377-378; sent with USS Cochino (SS-345) on intelligence mission to Barents Sea in 1949, pp. 380-381; rescues crew from damaged Cochino and loses her own men overboard, pp. 383-390, 407.

Underwater Sound
   See: Sound--Underwater.

Underwater Sound Laboratory
   Navy laboratory at New London, Connecticut, doing research in late 1940s, pp. 357, 410-411.

Unification
   Desire on part of Army for new Department of Defense after World War II, pp. 339-344.

Utah, USS (BB-31)
  Descriptions of coaling ship and firing boilers on board this battleship during Naval Academy midshipman training cruise of 1926, pp. 27-33.

Veneral Disease
  In China during the 1930s, p. 104.

"Victory at Sea"
  See: Television.

Vine, Allyn
  Valuable contact for Benson while at Woods Hole Oceanographic Institution while doing research on underwater sound in late 1940s, p. 412; takes four submarines to Bermuda to test geophone, pp. 414-420.

Wasp, USS (CV-18)
  Aircraft carrier which collided with destroyer minesweeper Hobson (DMS-26) in spring of 1952, pp. 452-454.

White, David C., Captain, USN (USNA, 1927)
  In charge of undersea warfare at Navy Department in the late 1940s, pp. 319, 321, 326.

Wilkins, Charles W. ("Weary"), Captain, USN (USNA, 1924)
  As commanding officer of submarine S-27 in mid-1930s, pp. 128-129; in command of U.S. submarine scouting line between Palau and Philippines in 1943, pp. 289-290.

Wolf Packs
  Groups of submarines used by U.S. and German navies during World War II, pp. 292-294.

www.ingramcontent.com/pod-product-compliance
Lightning Source LLC
Chambersburg PA
CBHW080626170426
43209CB00007B/1521